ROADS to BERLIN

Also by Cees Nooteboom in English translation

Roads to Berlin
Cees Nooteboom

Detours & riddles in the lands & history of Germany

*Translated from the Dutch
by Laura Watkinson*

*With photographs
by Simone Sassen*

MacLehose Press
New York • London

MacLehose Press
An imprint of Quercus
New York • London

First published in the Netherlands as *Berlijnse Notities* by
Uitgeverij De Arbeiderspers, Amsterdam, 1990
Later published with additional material as *Berlijn 1989-2009*
by De Bezige Bij, Amsterdam, 2009
This book was published with the support of the Foundation
for the Production and Translation of Dutch Literature.

ISBN 978-1-62365-844-1

Library of Congress Control Number: 2013937915

Distributed in the United States and Canada by
Hachette Book Group
237 Park Avenue
New York, NY 10017

Manufactured in the United States

10 9 8 7 6 5 4 3 2 1

www.quercus.com

For Willem Leonard Brugsma

CONTENTS

LIST OF ILLUSTRATIONS

All photographs © Simone Sassen unless otherwise indicated

PART I

Prologue: Crossing the Border

January 23, 1963. On either side of the Auto-
bahn, white landscapes open out towards other parts of Germany.
We have been driving down this road all day, the most unreal road
in Europe, a road that does not pass through any country. No cities, no villages, just traffic signs, *Tankstellen* and *Rasthäuser*. This is
driving across the face of the earth, not through a nation. It is only
when we reach Helmstedt that past and politics finally make an
appearance, in the guise of their symbols: guards and guard posts,
flags, barriers, signs. Slowly, they draw closer: the small buildings,
the flags of America, England and France flapping in the frozen air.
How could anyone have explained this future to a German thirty
years ago?

The checkpoint procedure here is straightforward. Yet another
sign clearly states (to avoid any misapprehension) that we are leaving the West and entering the East. The German uniforms are the
same, but different. We have to get out of the car and they send
us over to a hut. A childish thought: *So this is it*—I look around

with eager eyes, but what is there to see? I join a short queue at a low counter with a man and a woman sitting behind it. The man, booted, in uniform, is puffing out clouds of smoke. He looks cold. It is chilly in there. The woman, who is closer to the heating stove, flicks through my passport. She looks at my photo, up at me, and then back down again. Yes, it's me. How much money am I carrying? She notes the amount on a small piece of grey paper, with a carbon copy. Do I have a camera? A radio? Foreign currency? Any coins? Everything goes down on the piece of paper, which I have to sign. Passport and paper disappear to another department. The copy goes into a drawer. I am filed away forever, with my 450 Marks, my 18 guilders, my 20 Belgian francs. Through the frosty window, I see snow-covered trees, a barrier, also covered in snow, a tall watchtower built from large tree trunks. No one is up there watching. They hand me a pink form to fill out in a different room. There are some metal chairs, but it is too cold to sit down. Later they return my passport and I have to pay some money. I notice the woman's big black boots under the small wooden table; she is scuffing the soles across the floor. What else is there to see in this place? Not much, just a surreally thorough check that takes as much time for them as it does for us—and that is a long time.

I pick up a newspaper from a pile. The layout is designed to mock the garish sensationalism of the West German *Bild-Zeitung*, and the paper has the fitting name of *Neue Bild-Zeitung*. The D.D.R.'s agricultural show in Tamale, northern Ghana, is attracting lots of African visitors every day. And, in Dar es Salaam, the vice-president of Tanganyika has declared that the issue of German reunification must be solved through peaceful means. Inside the newspaper, a modern West German sculpture stands alongside one from East Germany. Question: Which country is most effectively preserving the legacy of the German *Nationalkultur*? I think about those people in their uniforms and wonder how interested they are in their

Nationalkultur. On the walls are quotes from Ulbricht and others, about peace, productivity, democracy. A biting wind is blowing on the other side of the door; this border territory lies there, naked, exposed. Cars are inspected; people show their papers; a Russian soldier walks through the snow; different flags, redder ones, are waving here; an officer in a guardhouse talks on the telephone; barriers go up and down, up and down. I read the signs: *Laßt euch nicht zur Provokation gegen die D.D.R. mißbrauchen. Die D.D.R. hat den Frieden in Deutschland gerettet.**

Big photographs of workers beside a steel furnace. Big photographs of workers in a car factory. Big photographs of Ulbricht. That is what it looks like here: drab, frozen and incredibly German.

We are permitted to drive on. Show the passport, barrier rises, show the passport again, another barrier rises. And suddenly we are out on the other side. The same snowy landscape rolls on into the distant fog. In the woods to our right, more fences and watchtowers. And then, as we drive over a bridge, we see the shocking image of two men in white hooded suits, men made of snow, with a black dog, panting, tugging, tongue lolling. Long rifles on their shoulders, they vanish into the woods, hunting for humans. We are still driving along the same Autobahn. Sometimes, in the distance, there is the shadow of a village, a cluster of farmhouses with a small church. What are the people there doing right at this moment? Only once do we see movement: a group of whooping children, a painterly addition to the scene. And, at regular intervals, signs welcoming delegates to the party congress: *Wir begrüßen die Delegierten des VI. Parteitages der S.E.D.!** Here you can actually feel that the road is still the old Autobahn, Hitler's highway. A small jolt after

---

* Do not agitate against the D.D.R. The D.D.R. has safeguarded peace in Germany.
* Sozialistische Einheitspartei Deutschlands (S.E.D.)—Socialist Unity Party of Germany. See also Glossary.

every slab of concrete: an asphalt strip. Or could it be the hatching that you see on maps in history books, those thin lines indicating conquests, decline, transformation? Roman Empires that were once Holy, principalities, republics, Third Reichs, zones? Battling against the wild, insane flurries of snow, we press on, creatures possessed by micromania, beetles scuttling across this space that history has written all over, yet where there is nothing to see.

January 15, 1963. West Berlin. You drive down Kurfürstendamm, which is bedecked with high, white lights, to the corroded, mutilated Gedächtniskirche, and then onwards. To your surprise, you see that the West has its own ruins: magnificent, hollowed-out monuments and empty windows with no rooms behind them, chunks of fossilised war, bricked-up doors that no smiling father will ever pass through again, off for a walk with Werner the dog. The only crossing point for non-German, non-military personnel is in Friedrichstraße, but we end up at the Brandenburger Tor by mistake. Snow and moonlight. Nothing on the frozen square in front of the gate: no people, no cars. Along the edge of that space, the black columns topped by the quadriga, the triumphal chariot. Four horses race along, pulling a winged figure that holds aloft a wreath, towards the east. Beneath, a quarter of the height of the columns, the blunt teeth of the Wall. A West German policeman signals that we are not allowed to drive on. So we stay where we are and watch things not happening. Two Russian tanks stand up high on huge pedestals, a reminder of 1945. We see two Russian sentries, shadows amidst the marble.

Friedrichstraße is not far from here. The same checks as at Helmstedt: documents, pieces of paper, money being counted, barriers, a classic copperplate engraving through which we move, remaining as human as possible. Two low walls have been erected across the road so that a driver would have to perform a dramatic swerve if he wanted to get through quickly. When all of the German boxes have been ticked, we are allowed through, and the city continues, the way cities do after walls: the same, yet different. It is probably just me being oversensitive, but it smells different here, and everything looks browner. We drive around for a while: Wilhelmstraße, Unter den Linden, names with which I have never had any personal connection, but which, simply because of the way other people say them, have gained a certain flavor, often a rather melancholy one. It makes sense that I had always imagined something very pale green when I heard the name of the street: Unter den Linden, under the lime trees. What makes less sense is assuming that the lack of green is not simply because it is winter. Buildings, more ruins, streets, Karl-Marx-Allee flanked by tall edifices. Not much traffic. Lots of neon signs. Is it a disappointment? Would I have liked it to be more dramatic? And why do I think I have any right to expect something? Two motionless soldiers stand guard in front of a monument. At Alexanderplatz, a steam train passes over a viaduct, but otherwise there is nothing to report—the occasional sign with words that look rather unread, slogans talking to themselves.

We visit a nightclub. All of the big clubs and restaurants here are named after the capital cities of the Warsaw Pact. This one is called Budapest. It is packed. A two-man band, not Germans, plays cheerful tunes. People are doing the twist. The atmosphere is provincial, joyless. Lots of lonely girls. Three young *Volksarmee* officers are sitting at a table behind us, drinking a bottle of Bulgarian red. One of them stands up, raises his glass and says, "*Meine Herren, zum Wohl!*" A waiter in an airforce-colored jacket . . . and so on. There really is nothing to report. People look at us, just as they would in Limoges or Nyköping, but you keep asking yourself the same, inevitable questions: How many people here have families in the West? How many would like to leave? How many would like to stop others from leaving? These may be rhetorical questions but, half an hour later, when we go back through the same checkpoint, I receive a written response from the East: a small orange pamphlet with a title that sounds like a children's book: "Everything You Need to Know about the Wall." It has ten short sections: 1. Where is Berlin? 2. Did the Wall just fall from the sky? 3. Was the Wall necessary? 4. What has the Wall prevented? 5. Was peace truly under threat? 6. Who lives on the other side of the Wall? 7. What is really keeping families and friends apart? 8. Does the Wall threaten anyone in any way whatsoever? 9. Who is making the situation worse? 10. Is the Wall a piece of gym equipment?

The answer to the last question is abrupt: "Let us state this most clearly: No. This protective wall is the state border of the D.D.R. The border of a sovereign state must be respected. This is the case all over the world. Anyone who ignores this has no cause for complaint *if he should come to harm.*"

A few other thoughts: How welcome is the Wall in Bonn? If everyone had left East Germany—which is how the situation was starting to look—all of that empty hinterland would be populated by Slavs. That is not an appealing thought for Germans who are still dreaming of reunification. 2. How welcome is the Wall in Moscow? Is Ulbricht a more attractive ally for them than, say, Salazar is for us? 3. How terribly German the Wall is. As a taxi driver in West Berlin put it, this could not have happened to any other people.

January 17, 1963. Three o'clock in the afternoon. Lashed by long whips of snow, we make our way across the square in front of the station. The bare, concrete-colored concourse, which smells of East Germany, is still empty. A few English, Italian and American reporters stand around shivering in the emptiness, sustained by the rumour that Nikita Sergeyevich Khrushchev is going to arrive here at three o'clock or four, five, six, maybe seven . . . The cold is unbelievable.

We walk up and down, constantly followed by the curious gazes (some shy, some aggressive) of the East Germans who are in attendance. The station is magnificent. Flags hang from long, gold-painted lances, black, red, gold, blood-red, the same flags you can see from West Berlin, on the other side of the Wall, fluttering on tall buildings and factories, flags of the moon, beyond our reach. The lances stand at an angle and look rather medieval, as if waiting for a tournament to begin. A man is busily carrying little flowerpots to decorate the stage. Khrushchev is sure to be delighted. It certainly looks impressive, like a set for a school play in Utrecht: walls hung with colored cloths, the pots with their neat little plants and, in the center, a plywood rostrum where someone will soon stand and say things that are not normally heard at school plays.

An old man climbs up to the microphones and declaims, "*Eins, zwei, drei!*" The sound booms around the empty space. High up on the grey gantries behind me, camera crews from East German television are working away, grey-looking men in fur hats. They have been up there since six this morning. The cold is all-pervasive. The Italians are really feeling it and they are not suffering in silence. I carry on doing circuits and reading the slogans, welcoming, cheerful and inspirational, that are plastered all over the station just as they are throughout the city: *Ganz zu Ehren des VI. Parteitages. Der wissenschaftlich-technische Höchststand.*

Words cannot quite capture the stiffness, the wooden reality that reigns in this place. It is a backward, infantile, old-fashioned world, but it is a world that exists, and not without reason. And it is this reality, this desiccated, fervent past which claims to be a vision of the future, that creates such a sense of alienation. Surrounded by fragments of a doctrine of salvation that has taken

---

* In honor of the sixth party conference. The pinnacle of science and technology.

physical form and so become dangerous, I stand in that future, a perfect stranger; it is as though I have been standing here for a month, or a year.

Occasionally, I see signs that something is about to happen. German officers give German orders to German soldiers; a phalanx of men takes up position on the steps, sending small eddies swirling through the crowd. But then the men disappear into a hole plastered with more slogans and leave us to our waiting. A West German journalist starts up a melancholy conversation with an East German. I stand about a meter away, watching them. Their discussion is pointless. A wall runs between these two compatriots that nothing can penetrate, except maybe bullets. Every thought, every argument, ricochets off it and falls to the ground at our feet, there for the taking: Globkes and walls, Adenauers and fugitives shot dead in the water, constant atonement for the past. The foreigners stand around, watching in silence. It is five o'clock, then six. Suddenly, the concourse fills. Television lights go on and start gleaming: white faces above leather, German jackets. Groups of women with terribly red flags. The journalists, with no specific position allocated to them, are scattered and outnumbered. A long line of military cadets enters in single file. They receive an order and begin to knead away at the crowd. First one way, then the other. I am half-crushed against a camera gantry, where a soldier grabs me and pushes me even further back. When it is all over, I find myself standing quite a long way from the stage, surrounded by large, hefty men, whose huge fingers are holding on tightly to their ridiculously tiny flags. Military music whines out of loudspeakers high up on the walls, one record after another. There is some shouting and then little Ulbricht with his unmistakable features makes his entrance, striding past the people with rapid steps. The others follow—Bulgarians and Mongols, Czechs and Germans—a tight cordon of sturdy men climbing the stairs, which two old ladies have just swept clean for the tenth time. A red carpet to fend off the cold, a line of cadets to protect lives, Germans behind me shouting at others to take off their hats: "*Hut ab! Hut ab!*" Then, a sudden silence as the music vanishes and the little Russian man comes down the stairs, surrounded by the faithful, governors of a world that begins at Helmstedt and ends at Shanghai. The little man, his fat face very white under the scrutiny of the television lights, waves in response to the cries of the crowd: "*Druzhba, druzhba, druzhba!*" Paper flags ripple in the air like a blast of heat; a group of Algerians shout their own welcome, before the silence of anticipation descends once again and the ceremonial greeting of first secretaries of central committees begins—old, long-winded titles replaced by new, long-lasting titles, and not a single one is omitted.

Every name brings applause in its wake. I stand on tiptoe to look at the assembled officials on their illuminated podium. Little Ulbricht comes forward, receives a kiss and, in his prissy Saxon voice, he begins to tell a story. The crowd pays attention. Then Khrushchev speaks. There is no doubt about his popularity with the party faithful on the concourse. It is hard not to be impressed by that voice. It is weighty and archaic; it flows, argues, persuades, ridicules, recounts, threatens. The pitiful, high-pitched voice of the interpreter follows, drawing red, German lines beneath his speech. Looking at myself in this crowd, where the only thing distinguishing me from the others is the cut of my clothes, it occurs to me that I could just as easily be standing there shouting and singing a German song, being a Party stalwart—and I see myself as part of a crowd in a way that they can no longer see themselves, because I am here and helping to fill a hall in the same way as they are filling it, but merely looking at them and listening to that emotionally charged German shouting creates a sense of ludicrous isolation and fear of a world that is so full of its own reality that it has no place for outsiders. It is still snowing when I go back outside. A long line of officers stands in silhouette against the whiteness of the snow on the empty square. Taking a detour through dark, silent streets now hung about with black flags, I return to my car. Half an hour later, I am back in the West. That is how simple it is.

January 19, 1963. "Comrades, there now follows the closing speech of Walter Ulbricht, the first secretary of the Central Committee of the Sozialistische Einheitspartei Deutschlands." The journalists in West Berlin's luxurious press center lean back in their chairs and look again at the same scene they have viewed so often this week: the immense hall, packed with four and a half thousand delegates of Communist parties from seventy countries. Walter Ulbricht strides through serried ranks of human bodies, his own head gliding past the white marble head of Lenin. He starts to speak. There is a slight sheen on his forehead; the light is shining on his glasses. By his standards, it is a good speech. Relaxed, gently amusing, almost chatty at times, he quotes the familiar articles of faith.

The atmosphere is extremely friendly, even a little touching. Ulbricht's Russian friend sits behind him, a cord dangling from his ears, with a translator's Russian voice travelling along its length. The camera occasionally pans across the delegates. I recognize some of them, but most are unfamiliar. The Chinese do not appear on the screen—even though, only that morning, so many friendly Chinese men shouted and whistled when, in spite of Khrushchev's friendly request for détente, the Chinese delegate once again attacked Russia, this time citing the revisionism of the South Slavs. Ulbricht does not enter into a discussion. He thinks everything is going to work out, yes, it is all going to be perfectly fine—and there is disagreement in the West too; you only have to look at de Gaulle.

Ulbricht's mirth is matched only by the mournfulness of his republic. No, Germany is no longer the most westerly socialist country in the world. That is Cuba now, which is a great advantage, because it means that Germany is much closer to America. Why is that? Because of our ambassador in Havana! Laughter. He becomes more serious when he talks about his party manifesto. Once again, it is clear that we will never be able to dismiss this world by damning it, just as any half-hearted sympathy will not make us part of it. In that hall, a sense of being in the right reigns supreme. We sit in our seats, watching it all happen, no more than a couple of kilometers away. Through the screen, the power of the proletariat flows over us, the advancement of socialism, the transition to Communism, the articles of faith.

Between them and us lies the Wall, that document in stone. But it is a document that means nothing there, except perhaps to underscore just how right they are. They go to look at it themselves, just as Western journalists go to look at it, and they shake French tourists by the hand, wave at the people. They are sure of their cause.

The parallel with religious sects keeps coming to mind. This is a faith that became a state, then many states. And so the faith had to change. Schisms and rifts divide this hall, and that is something else that we are watching: the practice of being right, a book by Marx, by Engels, by Lenin, which turned into Cuba, East Germany, North Korea, which turned into this hall, where the little man, occasionally, when he leans forward in a certain way, suddenly looks like a black man, as he tells his stories about engineers and workers in that slow German voice, becoming emotional as he speaks about the pure happiness of labor and the joy that factory construction can bring, then finding himself at a loss for words and declaring that this is the sort of thing writers should describe: real life, the delight of work.

New stories from this new folklore are presented too: the professor who spoke to the young agronomists, the writer who received a reprimand because he was too far removed from real life and had not learned a proper trade. The crowd laughs and claps; now and then a camera catches a single face, serious, joyful, elated, indifferent, its expression setting it apart from the others. I watch and I think: That man up there comes from what might be the most horrific country in the world. He is just standing there, talking to the West Germans, repeatedly inviting them to come and visit the East and talk to workers and farmers, but what does he think they will see, those people who come from the West to look at the East?

A country, he says, where everything is collective property, and he elaborates on this theme, not neglecting to mention the exploiters and the militarists. As his voice goes on and the camera scans the delegates, over in the press room we experience that familiar emotion yet again, that feeling of complete alienation, a fashionable word that signifies fear as much as repulsion and complete incomprehension. A third of humanity is ruled by these men, following an ideology that is riddled with ossification, an ideology that can no longer flourish and sometimes does not even appear vibrant enough to live up to the ideals of its own handbook. The only response to the dangerous ossification on the other side of that Wall is not to become paralyzed by even greater ossification. Attending a conference like this can be a valuable experience.

So much is written about Communism that many people have probably forgotten that it actually exists, that it is a reality. And right now, that reality has taken the form of a thorough self-examination, accompanied by the necessary détente.

Within the Communist camp, opinions differ on every important point: capitalism, war, revolution, schism. When Khrushchev says that the aim of the working class is not a spectacular death, but the construction of a happy life, Mao responds that a war would inevitably result in the destruction of imperialism (us) and the victory of socialism (them).

Complacent indifference to this ur-dialogue has been one of the main reactions from the West. And that is also why so many journalists were quick to leave this tedious congress, whose lack of drama was something of an anticlimax.

I

ONCE UPON A TIME, THE FIRST TIME. I HAD DRIVEN
to Berlin with Eddy Hoornik and W. L. Brugsma. A visit from
Khrushchev, a congress of the East German Communist Party. It
was my first visit to an Eastern Bloc country since Budapest in 1956,
seven years before. Budapest had been a watershed in my political thinking, which back then was still closely linked to emotion.
It had brought back the scent of war. I had left before the Russian
troops closed their pincer movement towards the border, and I felt
as though we, and therefore I, had betrayed people, that I was leaving behind something that would be locked away forever.

Now it was 1963. I was driving in the opposite direction, and
that also came with a feeling attached: fear. This was the forbidden
kingdom, protected by guards, dogs, towers, barbed wire, barriers.
It was cold, winter. There was snow on the ground, and the searching, panting dogs you could see from the car looked sinister against
that whiteness.

In another present, 1989, there are still guards, still dogs, still
barriers. But the weather is spring, the border crossing is wider than
it was back then, and there is more traffic, and yet still it refuses

to become normal. The feeling of fear is no longer there, but the Cold War and the memories of back then are still deep in my bones. Service here is prompt. I am missing some document or other, a *Genehmigung*, and at first I cannot understand what the representative of the People's Police is yelling at me from his hut. He tells me to move my car out of the line and park up and then walk over to another wooden hut to pay. No big deal, but all of this has happened before: the shouting, the German, the uniform. I am never going to escape that war.

I drive through that piece of East Germany at a hundred kilometers an hour, with one eye on the speedometer. Two kilometers more, my friends have told me, and "they" will leap out from behind a bridge, a tree, a house, and present you with a fine. It is not the fine that bothers me, but I want to avoid the confrontation. Everyone else must feel the same way, as the cars whine along the wide Autobahn, thick as treacle.

When I reach the door of my new house, I receive a sharp reminder. I have not even parked the car to unload my luggage and my books for the next six months when a window flies open and an old man starts screaming down at me, calling my behavior *unverschämt*: shameless, outrageous. I am home.

Home is an apartment in a large, dark building in Goethestraße. Enormous rooms with huge, obsolete heating stoves that are taller than me, like great square idols. Before me, a Chilean writer lived here for many years, but he has returned to his own distant country for now. *Tempora mutantur.* Some of his books are still here. You're acting like a dog, Simone says. She is right: it is canine behavior. I sniff at the books. Sniff sniff, Neruda. Sniff sniff sniff, Heine, Kleist. A *Philosophisches Wörterbuch* with a Marxist bent, Günter Grass in English, *Third World Affairs 1987*, plenty of Spanish, plenty of authors I do not know, a *Diccionario del habla chilena* and, thank goodness, plenty of poetry. The furniture stares at me and I stare back. This is the furniture of chance; you can push and pull it around and it will not put up a fight. It has not chosen you and you have not chosen it. This furniture bears witness to the life of exiles, and that suits me fine. I spend half of my life in hotels; it is becoming my natural state, always the cuckoo in some-one else's nest. A painting-cum-sculpture featuring a rather terrifying hammer, which refuses to budge, a Dufy reproduction, two Hoppers, a gloomy painting of prisoners and missing persons, a Matisse poster, a playbill for a drama by the absent Chilean author, featuring a quill that appears to have been dipped in blood, in which it has just written the word "Freedom." Now the sorting out and settling in can begin. Out in the courtyard there is a chestnut tree that will soon be green.

Conquering a city. Just as with a real war, it begins with topographic maps, reconnaissance. Friends provide covert intelligence. The house serves as the base of operations and always offers the option of strategic retreat. The lines of communication: tram, underground train, bus, feet. Provisions: where is the market? Gradually, the surrounding city begins to take shape: flickers of recognition, the shortest route, *points de repère*, library, department store, museum, park, Wall. Negotiation, capitulation—the house starts to behave like a house, we begin to act like residents. The building's main hallway is dark; there is a lion's head on the stair rail. I stroke it every day and the lion starts to greet me, while the other residents still do not. The postman has come to have a sniff. He is tall, a grey man in a uniform with a cap, and the dialect he speaks is almost incomprehensible. The letterbox has been hacked into the door of the apartment, a hand's breadth and only two centimeters high; almost nothing can get through it. It is a faulty connection to my home country. I read the *Frankfurter Allgemeine* now, a serious business. This country does not treat itself frivolously. There is none of the casual irreverence I am used to at home. A stern front page, usually without a picture; I probably even look different when I am reading it.

I saw a poster on the U-Bahn for a *Gesprächskonzert* with Mauricio Kagel, an Argentinean composer who has lived in Germany for a long time. I love his music and have been commissioned, together with Hugo Claus, to translate the words of his oratorio *La Trahison orale* for the Holland Festival. The concert is in the auditorium of the Sender Freies Berlin. Anyone from Amsterdam could not fail to be struck by the sheer scale of things in this city. You are constantly dwarfed by vast empty squares, wide avenues. In the U-Bahn, I spot the other people who are heading to the concert, and I am right; all I have to do is follow them, a small, scattered shoal with a Japanese man as pilot fish. There is someone from Japan in the orchestra too, of course. It is a secret Japanese agreement: there has to be one Japanese person in every aeroplane, restaurant, orchestra. They are employed specially. The Japanese person in this orchestra is a cellist, and he plays magnificently (as I hear when he has his solo), but then the whole orchestra plays magnificently and it is a wonderful evening. The composer is sitting beside the conductor on the stage. Tall, balding, large horn-rimmed glasses. It is as though Harold Pinter were up on stage, watching one of his plays being performed. There is only one piece on the program this evening: "Quodlibet," but this is not just the title (literally, "what pleases"), but also the name of the genre. A quodlibet is a form that dates from the sixteenth and seventeenth centuries, mainly French, which parodies and comments upon a large number of songs in counterpoint. It is a piece for several voices. The singer this evening, Martine Viard, is able to sing all kinds of different voices and she does so with verve. She looks serious in her long blue gown and glasses, but those sustained high notes and displays of masculinity undermine her seriousness. The conductor is Gerd Albrecht, white-haired, *bell'uomo*, exactly what a conductor must look like in every

young girl's dreams, and what is more, his deconstruction of the
piece is exceptionally deft; he interrupts, disassembles, dissects,
regroups. The composer has compiled the lyrics from Old French
texts. The piece, about an unhappy and dramatic love affair, begins
with the singer in a state of utter confusion:

Ma . . . ma fantazie . . . est . . .
Est tant . . . troublée
De quoy faictes si long séjour
Sans venir . . . sans venir vers moy . . .
De retour . . .
J'ay paour que ne soyez changée . . .

After only a few bars, the conductor stops, the singer's voice
trails off, and then the process of dismantling begins. He shows how
the layers of music are constructed by peeling them away. There is
something fiendish about the whole process, as though I am being
made to feel stupid and clever at the same time, stupid because of
what I did not hear before, clever because of what I now know I
am hearing. What was previously just a fine, complex sound is now
lying on the analyst's couch. The alto flute . . . (*"ein schwebender,
irisierender Klang,"* a floating, iridescent sound—the flautist plays
and the lonely notes shiver through the room) . . . now he adds the
horn over the top . . . (*"klingt unheimlich sinnlich,"* sounds incredibly sensual) . . . and then the piccolo . . . (*"klingt nicht ganz so sinnlich,"* does not sound quite so sensual) . . . then the "ragged" playing
of the cellos . . . *"und jetzt lege ich das noch einmal zusammen"*—and
indeed, he does put it all back together again and you can hear it,
"eine ganz kleine Geste" (a very small gesture, which soon vanishes,
as in Puccini)—does Herr Kagel agree? Yes, Herr Kagel agrees:
important things should be brief, as they should in literature, too.
He once wanted to be a writer himself, when he was still young, in

Argentina. Jorge Luis Borges was once his English literature tutor—
that should be enough to keep him going for a lifetime.

Now another deconstruction, two-four time on top of three-four
time, an extremely short passage lasting only two bars, brass and
piano as the *Zweier*, overlaid with the *Dreier* of the horns, and over
that the *Schlagzeug und die Klarinetten*, forever drumming into me
what I do not hear in everything I hear and, worse than that, everything other people hear and I do not. This is a gap in my education,
but it is too late for me now. Kagel talks about his teaching methods:
how he forces his students to describe the plot of an opera chosen at
random, even though they might find it absurd: "The absurdity of
opera is a given; the composer must be his own dramatist. They need
to learn that." He also gives them four hours to extend three bars of
Haydn to eight, which teaches them to "discover" rhythms.

We return to the music: an erotic passage for the singer, ranging
from sexy mewling to a short, insane section involving sustained
orgiastic notes, is now reduced from "vaginal to virginal." The same
passages, with the same notes, are sung again, but this time in the
style of an eight-year-old. Which, in my opinion, does not work as
the previous version lends this childish voice perverted connotations, if only because the *molto vibrato* of the deeper woodwinds
and the tuba are accompanying the virginal shrieking, and the
innocence jars against that background of masculine panting.

So how does Kagel like being in Germany? Kagel likes being in
Germany, but even so he quotes a letter from Max Ernst to Tristan
Tzara: "German intellectuals can't even shit or piss (*faire caca et
pipi*) without ideology." The audience laughs politely, even when he
adds that Adorno said that Germans confuse ponderousness with
profundity, "*Schwerfälligkeit mit Tiefsinn verwechseln*"—and why
shouldn't they laugh? It is always about other Germans; personally,
they have no problems going to the loo without ideology. The music
begins again, and the entire piece is played once more, sparkling,

moving, stirring, and suddenly I wish it was a century later, two centuries, and that I could hear with the ears of the future, but that thought is too farfetched. Countless people would have to procreate to produce the future trumpet players who would place their inconceivable lips on their trumpets and play those same notes, and anyway, why those nonsensical two centuries? I am hearing it *now*, I have heard it, dined on it, eaten it all up: a long time ago in Spain the quodlibet was known as an *ensalada*, while in France it was sometimes called a *fricassée*. These culinary metaphors are not wasted on me as I drift, full of music, out into the wintery night in Berlin, on my way to find sausages and bacon.

Sunday here starts on Saturday. Everything is closed, the streets are empty; on the day of rest itself the bells ring out as though all the dead from Charlemagne onwards need to be summoned. No one responds. An awful silence fills the wide streets; the hours stretch out, following some mysterious law: it is time to think about time. There are plenty of opportunities for meditation and reflection, including three photographic exhibitions extracting their black honey from the past. *Revolution und Fotografie, Berlin 1918–19* is the first one I visit. During the week, I go everywhere on public transport, but now, because the city is so empty, I take the car. Other people probably do the opposite, or maybe they just stay at home and ponder. Berlin 1919, seventy years ago; seventy years from now, the photographs of 1989 will wear the same masks, the masks of distance, of past time, of hindsight. Power and impotence: we have power over the dead people in photographs because we know what happened. Language does not permit us to have "impotence over" something, and yet it happens. We are powerless; even with our superior knowledge we have no way to get inside those photographs. They are closed and the people inside them cannot hear us. A group of men stands on the cover of the exhibition catalogue. "Stands" is not the right word, though. Two of them definitely are not standing; they are kneeling beside a machine gun. One of them is in civvies. He is wearing a hat, his shoes are polished and gleaming; he could be kneeling beside anything, anything but a machine gun. But there it is, black, gleaming, antiquated, menacing. Most of the other men are in uniform. They are looking at the photographer and pointing; one of them is about to run over to him. They are shouting something, but I cannot hear them. What I hear is the empty street, the bare wintery trees, the big Berlin houses, the same houses I always see. Not everything is gone. Of course, there is no prescribed clothing for revolutions, or for workers, but it is still strange, those men in their ties and hats, guns clutched under their arms, vulnerable figures at empty street crossings, silhouettes against the stark light, the grim sheen of the pavement. The past inevitably assumes the appearance of the available technology. No one can imagine the First World War in color, and it is inconceivable that the people we cannot see in color were in fact able to see colors themselves. The alchemy of inadequacy: the black patch beside that body was red.

The exhibition is at the Neue Gesellschaft für Bildende Kunst. The visitors are young, quiet, serious; they wear the uniforms of the newly disinherited, the student proletariat of the extravagant West. It is the stillness here that really strikes me, as it reflects the stillness suffusing the photographs. No colors, no sounds, only past time, which since the time portrayed in the photographs has traveled on in a straight line and into these young people's lives. If there is one place in the world where the past feels at home, it must be Berlin. What these visitors read in the photographs and accompanying captions is a boisterous "what if?"

What if the bankrupt empire of Wilhelm II had collapsed more definitively? What if so many of the old economic and hierarchical remnants had not remained intact? What if Social Democrats like Noske had not betrayed the revolution, had not allowed the army to

shoot at their own people, not allowed the murderers of Karl Liebknecht and Rosa Luxemburg to go free? The "what if?" of history is
closed, sealed with the photographs hanging here, but at the same
time it embarks upon another life: what has not happened becomes
the cause of what did in fact come to pass—a failed democracy, a
dictatorship, genocide, a new war, another peace—until we finally
reach the point where we are now. Then history is suddenly called
politics and that, in turn, is no more than future history.

The display cases contain the silent witnesses: reports of post-
mortem examinations; a hospital bill for a murdered revolutionary;
the large, old-fashioned cameras that captured all of these pictures;
the technical equipment used to develop the photographs, neutral,
impartial machines, mindless hulks, serving the newspapers of Left
and Right; then the newspapers themselves, full of hope and rhetoric, full of unimaginable anti-Semitism (*Zwei Rassenfremde: Karl
Liebknecht und Rosa Luxemburg hetzen zum Brudermord*—Two
Racial Aliens: Karl Liebknecht and Rosa Luxemburg agitate for
fratricide) and revolutionary pathos (*Bewaffnete Arbeiter und Soldaten hinter Barrikaden aus Zeitungspapierrollen*—Armed workers
and soldiers barricaded behind rolls of newspaper). Starting as an
uprising of mutinous sailors and widespread strikes at Siemens and
Daimler, with vast crowds and speakers without microphones, this
should have been the first revolution in a highly developed indus-
trial society. The Kaiser abdicated and disappeared; the power was
on the streets. The Social Democrat Philipp Scheidemann proclaimed the German republic; two hours later, Liebknecht did the
same for the socialist republic. A day later (10 November), a joint
meeting of the Berlin Workers' and Soldiers' Councils authorized
a provisional government combining both movements. Friedrich Ebert, another Social Democrat, did a deal with the army
commanders, and, four days later, "*das Kapital*" (which is what
it was called back then—that sounds a little more magical than

"employers") recognized the unions as negotiation partners. There followed a putsch by the right-wing military, which was foiled by the people's navy, which viewed itself as the protector of the revolution. Then everything went wrong. The Sozialdemokratische Partei Deutschlands,* led by Noske, governed alone from then on and, with the help of the former government troops and a newly formed *Freikorps* paramilitary organization, occupied parts of the city and carried out raids. Liebknecht and Luxemburg were murdered (photographs of Liebknecht's corpse, of the murderers celebrating at Hotel Eden, an account of Luxemburg's murder: ". . . *die alte Sau schwimmtschon*," the old sow is already swimming), and the S.P.D. won the elections on 19 January. Das Theater des Westens staged a production of Franz Lehár's *Die lustige Witwe*. On 3 March, a major strike broke out. The strikers called for political prisoners to be released and the *Freikorps* to be disbanded. The socialist government declared a state of emergency; the fighting continued for five days. Noske imposed martial law. The result: 1,200 deaths, 113 of them on the government side. The revolution was over. Germany was on its way to Weimar and what was to follow.

And what is still to follow. My mother always used to quote an old Dutch expression that says when the sun is shining and it is raining at the same time, it means there is a funfair on in hell. That is the state of the weather when I step back outside, out of the past. Fat drops of rain beat away at the leaden water of the Spree, and the fake, brassy sunlight lends a strange glow to the bewitched buildings. Nonsense. Nothing is bewitched here; I am in a major European city. I get into my car and drive past the places I just saw in black and white, allowing them to fill with color and the absent dead. The rain stops. My car can choose where it wants to go, and

---

* Sozialdemokratische Partei Deutschlands (S.P.D.)—Social Democratic Party. See also Glossary.

it wants to go to the East, to neighborhoods I have never visited before. I drive down a side street, a dead end that finishes at a wall. But it is not *the* Wall, because there is a hole in it. I park the car beside a couple of Turkish men who are washing their own vehicles, and I walk over to the hole. *Trompe l'œil*? No, because I can see the river through the hole, an East German patrol boat, the opposite bank with the actual Wall and barbed wire, two guards walking along and having a chat. Boat, Wall, guards. No other signs of life. I know very well that there is life over there because I have been there, but there is no life to be seen right now. The city of silence, empty and mythical. Like a painting by de Chirico: an open space, large buildings, a tower, shadows that have suddenly fallen and are pinned to the ground. There is something very still about those paintings. Sometimes they have a horse in them, which has wandered in from some myth or other, large and white. Or a man like a marionette with no face, just a wooden oval with no mouth or eyes.

The banks of the Spree near Oberbaumbrücke, West Berlin, March 1989

Life imitates art, and it is not long before I see that man for real. I drive back out of my cul-de-sac (Brommystraße), and head down Köpenicker Straße to Oberbaumbrücke. Signs in German and Turkish advise me that the riverbank is dangerous. It may be dangerous in duplicate, but people are still fishing there. I walk to the bridge and climb up to the viewing platform. Everything here is dilapidated; this is a world of demolition. Still the same riverbank opposite, but people are walking across the bridge. An old woman with a cane moves very slowly; she has a view of two countries. On my side of the bridge, an old Mercedes stops and a man with a bag gets out, followed by a young man and woman. They talk, walk down the left side of the bridge, disappear from sight. The woman says something about an *Ausweis*, but no one stops them to ask for I.D. They return a few minutes later, but without the older man. They look back one more time, without waving, and then drive away. I suddenly notice a movement in that dead hut directly opposite: a faceless man behind narrow bars. He is looking in my direction, towards what we call the West. Even though he is facing me, I cannot see his features. I can see his epaulettes, however, and I remember how I once started a story about two epaulettes that did not have a body to go with them. The body did not come along until later. That is not the case now, though: I can see the light falling through the bars onto the two epaulettes and I spot occasional movement. Then I see some other men, in a tower further along. I cannot make out their faces either; they are too far away. One of them is looking through binoculars. A few black Americans have come to stand beside me. They wave at the man with the binoculars; he does not wave back. In the distance, two more men stand on the roof of a tall building. They have shotguns. They are talking to each other. What about? Girls? What is the man with the binoculars looking at? Is he bored? What sort of conclusions should I draw? None at all; I am not the judge of the world. People are simply walking across this bridge, even though one of them was shot dead this week. Simone returns to the bridge the next day, hoping for better light. There were lots more people walking across the bridge, she said, and no guards in sight, not a single one.

When I get home, I take another look at the photographs in the book. What was Noske's motive for quelling an uprising of his own people? It did the Social Democrats in Germany no good at all; they had been used to exorcise the danger, to sanction the murder of the people who seemed most dangerous. Dangerous for whom? His motive was the fear of chaos, but what does that mean? Chaos is when one person can no longer see his place in the order of things, because another person wishes to abandon his own position. Whoever holds the power at that point is the winner. In this case, the new order looked so well ordered that no one could imagine the chaos it would bring. The consequences came in the form of death, war, defeat, occupation, division, and the orderly structure of a wall, that binary factotum designed to divide the visible world into two sides: front and back, right and wrong. One side is viewed from a platform, and the other through binoculars. Or the other way round. I have seen it for myself. The people who built that wall legitimized it with the fear of chaos. And what should the person behind the wall, the person who would like to tear it down, be most afraid of? The others: the people on his own side of the wall who are afraid of chaos or what looks like chaos.

In the *Frankfurter Allgemeine*, there is a photograph of Stephen Spender looking far too young. He is turning eighty, but in the picture he is no more than fifty. His hair, which I have known as white for years now, is still black. The first time I met him was in 1962, at a writers' conference in Edinburgh, where Gerard Reve (or whatever he was calling himself at the time) described me as "N, the moribund little monkey." He had a point: it was a perfect diagnosis of my state of mind at the time. Spender stood on a landing, talking to a few people, and I was fascinated by his tie, a long, silver-white goose quill on an ice-blue background. "What a beautiful tie," I declared, with feeling. Without a word, he undid the tie and gave it to me: "If you like it, you can have it." It was only then that I noticed the two letters at the bottom of the quill, a J and a C. Jean Cocteau had painted the tie. I still have it, and I wear it whenever I win a prize. That is why I never turn anything down.

The second time I saw Spender taking off a tie was in Paris, in '68. He had just told me that Louis Aragon had told him he had dined with the Central Committee of the French Communist Party and had heard that the Communists would not support the student uprising, as it was too Trotskyite. Aragon had then passed on this news to Rothschild, for whom it was not without significance, and Rothschild had in turn told Spender, and so now I knew about it as well. A day later, de Gaulle flew to meet General Massu in Baden-Baden. The world as a conspiracy—that corresponded to my most childish fantasies. As Spender was telling me this story, a group of demonstrators with red flags walked past the Odéon. The poet, already white-haired, removed his tie, opened up his collar as Ben-Gurion and Begin always did, and posed with me for the photographer Eddy Posthuma de Boer. I look a little rotund and foolish in the picture, but already considerably less moribund than I had been.

The next time was also in Paris, many years later. Spender told me a story on that occasion, too. He had been sitting with W. H. Auden and Auden's friend Chester Kallman at a table outside Caffè Florian in Venice when Kallman suddenly stood up and set off across Piazza San Marco, saying that he was going to pick up a sailor. Auden, said Spender, sat there in silence, large tears rolling down the many folds of his face. I thought this story was worse than the one about Aragon.

The last time was in New York, dining with a mutual friend, the poet William Jay Smith. "The poet nearing eighty," but still smoking a strong cigarette and holding a vat of whisky. Big hands, thick wrists. He was on a tour of America ("the poet earns his money") and told me he had just received a telegram from Beaumont College in Texas that said, "Dear Mr. Spender, May we remind you that the attention span of our students is about fifteen minutes." "The last survivor," the *Frankfurter Allgemeine* calls him, and that was exactly what he looked like as he walked away down York Avenue, a white-haired oak, on a journey with his poems. The newspaper also refers to him as the "last *Statthalter*," assigning him "the role of the last steward (*Statthalter*) of the legend of the 1930s." Some words never come alone; they always travel in packs. That same day I read in the *Encyclopaedia Britannica* (1911 edition): "Goethe, Novalis declared, was the '*Statthalter* of poetry on earth.'" Poet, steward— both words sound better than emperor or prince.

March 18, 1989

II

LIVING SOMEWHERE ELSE IS DIFFERENT FROM travelling—I can tell by the way I look at things. My gaze does not constantly have to be focused. I still have enough time; I am staying in Berlin until the summer, and returning in the autumn. Just last week, I realized that I had actually forgotten to look at the exterior of my building. Some inner authority must have assumed that it would trickle into my consciousness of its own accord. When someone from the Netherlands asked me what sort of house I was living in, I realized that the Dutch concept of *huis* did not cover it, because my house here was inside another house, and it is that other house, the big one, that they call a *Haus* here in Germany. *Haus* is the name for these huge residential blocks with various layers of homes stacked up around square courtyards. They used to refer to such tenement buildings as *Mietskasernen*, rental barracks, but that does not feel right, if only because I hardly ever hear my neighbors. There is no caretaker, but there is a board on the street outside with our strange mix of names on it. The common areas are not kept particularly clean. There is a fine layer of dust on the balustrades that could possibly date back to before the war, because an ancient neighbor has told us that the house was already here back then. Everyone takes their own rubbish down to the courtyard, where the large plastic containers line up in silence: one for bottles, one for paper, the others for general rubbish. The system works perfectly. Twice a week, at half past seven in the morning, the bin men press all of our doorbells at the same time and there is always someone at home to open the main front door for them. The only neighbor I know is the old woman who lives downstairs. The others, most of them young people, say hello, and I say hello back. Out in the hallway there is a pram and there are two bikes in the courtyard, but I do not know who they belong to. Our homes all look out onto the central courtyard. When I arrived, the big chestnut tree out there was bare, but now it is growing fuller by the day, almost as if it wants to reach out and touch all of our windows. I am very fond of him, the tree, and I marvel at his vitality, at the power he must have deep within his wood. You cannot have a conversation with him, but I still speak to him now and then. I think he likes it. And he has towers too—that is what I call his flowers—those upright, white towers that always give me a good start to the morning.

The doorbell rang at quarter to seven this morning, one of those fateful shrieks that penetrate into the very marrow of your dreams, merging with them, until stopped by a second jolt of electricity. In your other life, in the "real" world, you stand dazed at your own front door, faced with someone who has been awake for hours, who is uncontaminated by sleep and night-time visions. "*Eilbote!*" Whistling, the courier clatters back down the stairs. When have I ever received an express letter in the Netherlands at that time in the morning?

The day has started for me as well now, and I realize that it is a good time to take a look at my house from the outside. I live in Goethestraße, which suits me well. Lime trees, a birch, around the corner a pedestrian area with lots of shops, Wilmersdorfer

Straße, with Sesenheimer Straße around the other corner—not a bad location. This is my home now. A square nearby, with a church, and a market on Wednesdays and Saturdays, which is very good. I walk to Wilmersdorfer Straße and look up at the house of many houses. To identify my own part of it, I have to count from the ground up. What I notice now is the color. Solidified mud, desert sand, at any rate something involving earth; dry and jagged, it would hurt your hand if you rubbed it. I stand beside the kiosk where they sell *frische Putenteile* during the day, right across from Nana Nanu, with its artificial flowers and electric-blue nylon animals in the window. Yellow ones too, the color of egg yolks gone bad. These are not real animals; they do not occur in nature, but were dreamed up by an angry blind man. Then there is the Goethe-Apotheke, which has been here since 1900. Next comes Zum Wirtenbub, a gloomy bar I have never been inside. People play dice in there; I can hear them whenever the door is open. Across the way is the Video Galerie, which I have also never visited. Large helpings of Eros and Thanatos, breasts and machine guns. Lust and blood—it washes through me as I walk past. I read the titles and reassemble them into a *cadavre exquis*. Surrealism is never very far away, and that is certainly true in this place.

"So, what is it like now?" my friends ask me on the phone. That is a good question, but I do not have an answer. "It is," I would like to answer. "It is. I am here." I live in Berlin. It is not only different from the Netherlands; it is different from anywhere else. But I cannot quite express that difference, that *otherness*, in words yet. It has something to do with the people: they are much more my other people than Americans or Spaniards. I am still not sure how to act around them, and I cannot speak their language with confidence. I prefer just to walk in between them; after all, you do not really need to say very much. I sit on the U-Bahn and observe them. They are often Greeks, Turks, Yugoslavians, Colombians, Moroccans. I am more at ease with them, because they are not as powerful. Or maybe they simply feel closer.

At times it feels claustrophobic. I never felt that way when I was just a visitor. The Wall, the border—you know you can just go over, get out. So it can't be that. Yet even so. I notice it on Sundays. That is when I want to get out. There is plenty of green on the map, lots of *Wald*. So that is where you go, and you can get there in no time. You find that everyone else is there too. Anyone who is not driving or flying to West Germany remains inside the fence. I do not know if they feel the same way about it as I do. The city is not even that small in terms of square kilometers, but still.

I often go to Lübars, which is like a real village. But it is an illusion, as if there were lots of countryside stretching out all around. Two village pubs, a water pump, a small church, a few graves. I walk out of the village along a path I have discovered. The first time, I came to a small river. I stood looking into the water,

The Wall at Lübars, West Berlin, April 1989

dark-colored, fast-flowing, swaying water plants, the thought of fish. That was when I noticed the sign. It said that the border ran down the middle of the stretch of water. The Wall might have been some distance away, but the other side, those dry reeds, that scattering of trees, that was the land of the Others. Now I saw the water differently. It was no more than a couple of meters wide, but in the middle of that moving, transparent element was the border. It is not something you should spend too much time thinking about, but I still did. East water, West water. Absolute nonsense, and yet that border is real. It is there. I carried on walking, up a hill. I had a good view of the Wall from up there. There were in fact two walls, with between them a kind of anti-tank ditch, loose sand, earth, soil. The strip of land rolled away into the distance. I walked on to where I would encounter the Wall itself; it was not made of bricks or concrete at that point, but of transparent steel mesh. A hundred meters beyond, in front of the other Wall, was a tower. A small car stood beside it. Then a window opened in the tower. I could see the silhouettes of two men. One of them pointed his binoculars at me and took a good look. A one-way process. He could see me perfectly, but I could not see him. What did he think he was going to see? Why was he looking? I stood there for a while, experiencing the strange sensation of allowing myself to be looked at. I wanted to know what the man was thinking, but I never would. I did not want to know what he thought about me, but what he thought about himself. There was no way of knowing. Was he looking out of a sense of duty, conviction, boredom? Did he believe in what he was doing? There was, as far as I could tell, no way that anything could ever occur between those two walls, not in that place, certainly nothing initiated by me. So what was the point of watching? Did he spend hours of unutterable boredom in the tower? Or was it pure conviction? Did heading off to that tower every morning give him a sense of job satisfaction? What I really wanted to do was go up into the tower and have a chat with him, but there was no chance of that happening.

Maybe I even had a proper look at him yesterday, without realizing that it was him.

Yesterday was May Day, and I watched East German television in the evening, as I often do. This is a useful exercise in many things, but particularly semantics: how the same news is expressed in different words and therefore becomes different news. This was particularly obvious after the Russian elections. If twenty out of the one hundred party candidates are not elected, you can of course mention that fact, and if it is for the first time in history, then you can really make a point of it. That is what happened on the television on my side of the Wall. On the other side, they said that eighty party candidates, the vast majority, had been re-elected. The duality of the same factuality, the Janus face of one and the same fact, as one person keeps quiet about something while another person emphasizes something else, and does so in the same language, which can be understood and also heard on both sides of the Wall. That forces you to train your ear. The eye is a much more deceptive organ.

On that first of May, there were all kinds of things to see on both sides of the Wall. On my side, there was the violence of the *Chaoten*, as they call the anarchists here. Perhaps the situation they created was chaotic, but the *Chaoten* themselves are not. They make straight for their goal, which is violence. Lots of violence, intended as violence, put into practice as violence. Against the police, against shops, against cars. Waves of attacks, people in disguise, invisible and therefore non-existent, faces behind black cloth. Hate. Leather, boots, smoke, fire, injuries.

On the other side, there was peace. What I saw were the edited highlights of a procession that had gone on for over five hours.

Honecker on a podium, for five hours. Sometimes with a sunhat, sometimes without. Around him, the government, the military. In front of him, children, artists, workers, a black dance troupe, firemen, Vietnamese, Cubans, factory delegations. Could I really believe my eyes? Happiness, singing, children in their parents' arms, proud fathers, a beaming head of state.

In themselves, images cannot be semantic; it is only when you start to say something about them, when you attach meanings to those images, that the semantics commence. But then you have to address the issue of the images that are *not* seen. What kind of images might they be? A meeting of the Central Committee where the theme for discussion is how to handle the democratizing tendencies that are making gradual inroads in the D.D.R.? What attitude to take to the memoir written by Markus Wolf, the former head of the secret service? Or how to handle something as innocent as five demonstrators, each holding a candle, who are demanding the right to be allowed to travel to the West?

More images followed later that evening, from other, identical processions in all parts of the Democratic Republic. Stages, leaders, rosettes, marches. Within five hours the Wall will be gone, say some people on my side of the Wall, pointing at the images of Hungarians using shears to cut through their own iron fences. But what will happen if that happens? Suddenly there would be a very large and powerful country in the middle of Europe, where many people thought it would never be seen again, and no one knows what kind of country it might be.

The Wall is a cliché, I am well aware of that. But it is a cliché made of concrete. I can see it from the air when I manage to get away for a few days: a caesura in the landscape, foolish and unreal when seen from above. A scar, as so many must have said before me, but that is what it looks like. And what does it look like inside the people? I ask a German friend whether the people in the two countries feel some sort of *Heimweh*, homesickness, nostalgia, for one another. What is reunion? An illusion, a desire, a possibility? Not a possibility, he says, because there is no desire and no nostalgia. It is just an illusion for the other Europeans, who are afraid of a united Germany. Things will not come to that. People want it in the East, but the people in the West will never want it. The hostile attitude to the Polish and Russian Germans who are now coming to the West in large numbers only goes to prove that. The Germans in the West do not like them; they do not even see most of them as Germans. They are poor and backward and they do not fit in with this modern, Western, rich Germany. The Germany you are talking about, he says, existed for less than a hundred years, only after Bismarck. We do not have the slightest sense of nostalgia for it. And we do not want to pay for it either.

But, says our Hungarian friend, the Germany we're talking about existed for a long time before it actually became a state, didn't it? It existed as a language, as a community. What you're saying now implies that you as West Germans are making the East Germans the actual losers of the war. They still have to do penance, while you're wallowing in prosperity. And besides, can you really imagine the Wall still standing in ten years' time?

But the German has his answer ready: "If the Wall comes down, we'll have twelve million Germans heading this way. We'll be begging Honecker to keep it standing."

The Dutchman and the Hungarian pause for a moment. Then one of them asks, "And what about the shared European homeland? Is the D.D.R. just supposed to lie there in the middle of it like a locked room? If the D.D.R. opens up, isn't that a huge opportunity for West Germany too? You could help out the East with some kind of Marshall Plan, couldn't you? Bring their antiquated industry up to date? Supply machinery? Just think of the market that would open up for you . . ."

The German has an answer to that too: the West German tax-payer has no intention of spending a single Pfennig on his long-lost brothers. I am not quoting this conversation because I found it so illuminating or even politically astute. If this discussion—and thousands of conversations like this are taking place—has any value, it lies in the fact that it is taking place in the shadow of the Wall. That concrete construction is not merely a thing; it is also a metaphor for a refusal whose reciprocal nature we have perhaps not always adequately grasped. Behind the Wall live the Others, and they are very different, so different that they had best stay where they are, if only because undoing that separation places such outrageous demands on the imagination. Berlin one city again? The capital city of whatever construct might result? A peculiar alliance, a contrived federation, a dream union? How would that work? Then it does indeed become inconceivable, as unfeasible as an eternal status quo, synthesis as chimaera, a nightmare vision for both those within and those without.

I am going to the other side. I say "other side" without thinking about it, but then I hear the phrase myself and it sets me thinking. "Other side." As if the Wall is a river. A natural phenomenon, not a human creation. Going to the other side is usually easy. Not this time. I take the S-Bahn from Bahnhof Zoo to Friedrichstraße, where the checkpoint is. Canopy, iron, long trains, subdued lighting and—I cannot help myself—always a touch of Graham Greene and John le Carré. Down the stairs, the shuffling and shambling of my contemporaries. Then you enter the concourse. I know my way; I have to turn right towards *Andere Staaten*, other states. There are five channels today, narrow passages, and we are pushed through them as if through a sieve. It is not modern, but awkward, clumsy, makeshift, as though no one had reckoned on it lasting this long. The crowd I am in: Poles, lots of old people. I am not tall, but they do not even come up to my shoulders. They are old and small and lugging large suitcases and boxes. It all happens infinitely slowly; we have to go around a corner and filter into the channel. I am on the inside of the curve; the outside is moving more quickly. Even the queue jumpers, the old hands, the obvious Westerners are now stuck. At the point I have reached, where the procession turns ninety degrees, everything appears to have come to a standstill. I still cannot see the way through, but I know what it looks like. The lonely official sitting in his wooden box. The color is beige, a very pale beige. He sits up above; you have to hand over your documents at neck height; the old people reach up over their heads. He sits there, looks at your picture, looks at you. His cap hangs behind him on a hook, a strange round thing, a green decoration on the wall. You hand over five Marks for your one-day visa and receive a piece of paper. After that, it all goes very quickly. You shoot out of the channel on the other side, change the obligatory amount (25 DM), and suddenly you are outside. You are there. There. And you find that the world is there too. Trams, cars, Trabants. They roar and let out a stink. I stroll to Unter den Linden. Nothing special. People, shops, footsteps. Not much traffic; work is over for the day. I am on my way to the theater; all is right with the world. The Branden-burger Tor, which I usually see from the other side, shimmers in the distance. I know that the statue on the top has turned around, even though I cannot see it. All I can see are the open spaces between the columns, and they look the same from here or from there. It is just that "there" has become "here" because it is where I am now.

The play, by Thomas Bernhard, is called *Der Theatermacher*. I have already read it. The showman Bruscon and his browbeaten family have recently arrived in some provincial dump, a place so unimag-inably mortifying for a man of his stature that he refuses to remem-ber the name: Butzbach, Utzbach, something like that. A dirty, run-down room in the local inn; outside, the squealing of hungry pigs. His play *The Wheel of History* is to be performed there, with himself in the leading role. His coughing wife and his unsightly, talentless children will play the other parts. Thomas Bernhard is all about destiny, submission, humiliation, cursing, megalomania, hideous sycophancy, endlessly harping on details, in this case the emergency exit sign, which the actor insists must not be illuminated during the final minutes of the play. All of this comes in waves of rhetoric, repetitions that wash ashore again and again, until the melancholy, agonising tedium presses into your very bones and the inescapable destiny of everyday life twists into your brain like a screw, as in the work of Willem Frederik Hermans. Only then are you allowed to leave, defeated. The inn is on fire, the play does not go ahead, but you have just seen your play. Outside, there is the squealing of people and pigs, the statue of Stalin has fallen from the wheel of history and is lying on the boards, stiff and foolish, and the theatrical family can travel on to another place of horror. No catharsis, no on-stage purification, no form of solution whatsoever, and yet still there is that strange effect on the viewer: all the filth that has flushed through you somehow feels cleansing.

A play by Bernhard is a straitjacket that you allow yourself to be strapped into, knowing that, if it is a good performance, the straps will become tighter and tighter and you will feel them for some time to come. In this play, the author—at least in the version I read—hits out at Austria again, ritually jeering, mocking, hating, as in all of his work. But for this performance, the director has come up with another idea: the criticism of Austria has become criticism of his own regime, a subtle but effective shift of complaints and allusions to the place where we are now. This transforms the pathos of Bernhard, his Austrian self-hatred, into something more like political cabaret with comments on proletarian culture, on state actors, on Nazis, on the system. It is no coincidence that it is Stalin who is left lying on the ground at the end. I had read about this, about how extraordinary it was that this could happen in the D.D.R., and of course that is true, but you cannot tell by the sound of the laughter whether it is coming from East German throats or West German ones. A peculiar duplication: in the Western laughter there is astonishment, and also a kind of joy about the Eastern laughter, the fact that it is allowed, but that lends the laughter a certain ambiguity, even if only because of the awareness of the piquancy of the situation. The acting is marvelous. The leading man, Kurt Böwe, draws the audience into his dreadful megalomania, his sadism, his failure. Because my points of reference are in the past, I cannot help but think of the Dutch actor Ko van Dijk, and how wonderfully, wildly, wretchedly he too would have played this part.

The theater itself is a restored chocolate box: statues, paintings, cream-colored, elegant. Who is from the East and who from the West? You only have to look at the shoes, says my Hungarian friend. But West Germans sometimes wear those ghastly grey or beige shoes too. No, you have to look at the seams of the clothes, an expert on Germany from West Berlin once explained to me, but I think that is taking things too far. It is enough for me that I can sometimes see the difference and sometimes not, and that maybe I do not want to see it at all. That is their game—let them enjoy it. During the interval, powerful cocktails are poured at the bar; mine comes with such a large splash of Cuban rum that I float back into the auditorium.

I know that I need to be out of the country before midnight, so I eat at a restaurant next to the station. Waiters with white bow ties, practically attired in evening dress, candles, Hungarian, Romanian, Bulgarian wine, no beer, an extensive menu, once again very elegant. Outside, the dark canopy of the station, the channels, the uniform, the penetrating gaze that moves from photograph to face, the near-empty S-Bahn, that tiny distance that is so very huge.

I go to see a play in West Berlin, too: *Die Zeit und das Zimmer* by
Botho Strauss: Time and the Room. As usual, the time itself cannot be seen, at least not at first, and in the semi-darkness before
the performance the room appears to be just a room. Fairly empty,
pretty bare: the room as space. Three windows. In front of one of
the windows, two chairs placed at angles to each other. In those
chairs, two men sit smoking. They cannot see each other unless
they turn their heads ninety degrees. In the dim light, the audience
peers at the small program with its small font, and because I, as my
own audience of one, have a particular way of looking at things, I
find lots to like in it, as well as some things I already know. Borges
on time, Augustine on time. Time then, that is what this is about.
Bergson, Plotinus, Karl Jung, Lewis Carroll, Ballard, God and the
whole world are quoted to make it clear that this is all about time.
That initial lower-case letter is insufficient. I feel that Time here
calls for a capital letter, as in German. It needs to be big, to indicate
a concept, not just any old, random, tiny time, but Time, the enigmatic element in which all times reside, time of once, time of then—
worn out, mouldering, forgotten—and time of one fine day, time
of later—empty, new, elusive. Time measured and immeasurable,
the sorry minutes and seconds of our measuring scale and the vast,
expansive light years of the Milky Way, the quasars and the velvet
eternity beyond. In that context, the anecdotal essence of every play
is crushed. I know now that someone wants me to see something in
the sacred aura of his higher purpose, but I do not see it and I do
not need to see it. What I see is already strange, captivating, exciting enough. Preposterous scenes, arias of insanity, operas, fights,
riddles, despair. Libgart Schwarz as Marie Steuber, the woman
the two seated men were discussing as though she were a casual
passer-by observed from a window, has now come into their lives.
She is followed by a suite of other sudden, equally random figures
who enter into short-lived chemical affinities, a pandemonium of

relationships, woven together and then fraying apart, furious and passionate scenes, mysteries, hysterical laughter, the gaps in the relationships between people, lucky finds, and flashes of what was once called boulevard theater. I readily accept that the philosophical notion of Time was Strauss's motivation here; after all, anyone who thinks for longer than half an hour always encounters time, or Time. What I saw in the two hours I sat there (the measurement was unavoidable) was a reflection of the world, familiar and unfamiliar, which I found difficult to shake off afterwards. These too were actors who led you around the brink of delirium.

Once again, the other side, the Janus face of the world, the there and the here. Television, this side. A program about Franz Schönhuber, founder of the Republikaner.* Every country has to have its ultra-right-wing party, so why not the Germans? That is how the argument goes. But what if lots of the police turn out to belong to that party? *"Wir sind eine Polizistenpartei,"* says the leader himself, and immediately it starts to sound different. "We are a police party." Seventy-eight percent of the police force feels let down by politicians. Sixty-four percent believes that the sentences handed out by German judges are too mild. In short, the police are angry, not keen on foreigners, underpaid and unhappy, and they vote en masse for the far right. Film recordings show them advancing on a masked enemy who is dressed in black and throwing stones: "They show more understanding for the *Chaoten* than for us." Then more pictures: rooms full of police gathered around their new hero, the only one who understands. And concerned police unions, who cannot risk losing the twenty thousand Republikaner from their ranks. Then, still on this side, Beijing, Mikhail Gorbachev, Deng Xiaoping dropping a piece of meat from his chopsticks, tens of

* See Glossary.

thousands of students calling for democracy. And on the other side: also Beijing, but no one is dropping any food, and no one is asking for democracy. Speeches, anthems, grand words, just like at home, where Honecker is welcoming Mengistu. The Ethiopian leader has a dream of a woman with him and is wearing a cornflower-blue kind of uniform without insignia. But as his endless anthem is played, he grinds his teeth; you can see him doing it, small, persistent oscillations beneath the black skin. A helmeted officer stands in front of him, sabre drawn, and shouts a long German salutation before walking away, kicking his booted feet towards the sun. Did Mengistu know then that an attempted coup was taking place at home and that the country's two most senior military officers were dead?

May 27, 1989

III

SOMEONE MAKES A JOKE: WEST BERLIN, MORE THAN one million free people in a cage. It does not always feel that way but, oddly enough, it does when you drive out of it, although what I am driving into then is definitely not my freedom. I have to go to Kiel for a reading and have decided to go by car. The Berlin–Hamburg route is one of the three options, and I have not driven that way before. On some sections of the road, which you are never permitted to leave, at any point, not under any circumstances (it is strange how quickly you accept such an alien concept), you are only about seventy kilometers from the Baltic. And, although I cannot quite explain why, that lends a sense of adventure to the proceedings.

There are two kinds of pathos involved in this journey: the pathos of politics and the pathos of weather. Pathos is a weighty word, but today it needs to be said. The weather is wallowing in itself, lavishing lush excess upon itself, having dived into summer in one breathless, senseless swoop. Everything is full, fat; the trees are rounded and plump, the hawthorn is blooming, the breeze is balmy—there is no doubt about it, this is an exemplary summer, the kind that you mention in the future when you are describing how summer should be.

A lot of people in China must feel the same way right now, I think. The images I see on television remind me of May '68, but hugely magnified. Crowds that look like a forest, cars full of flags, the excitement in the voices that hits you even through the mask of a foreign language, the gleaming eyes, the experience against which your entire life is measured, no matter what comes after. In those rare moments, when the articulation of a single idea takes precedence over all other considerations, life suddenly seems to weigh no more than an ounce, because everything else has become so heavy. Every morning I listen to the commentary and interviews on the B.B.C. World Service, and find myself standing in the Square of Heavenly Peace, which, for a few days, has become the town square of the entire world.

There will always be something of the foolish virgin about me (those poor, unwise souls in the parable who have no oil left in their lamps at the crucial moment), and so I want to look at the faces of the guards of the other republic and see what they are thinking. I want to know whether any of that excitement, which should, after all, be their concern as well, is actually filtering through to them. But if it is, you cannot tell from their faces.

I have resolved never to write about this border again, but I have to do it one last time. Together with the dark gate from Macau to China at night, this is the most challenging border I know, one that expresses the very notion of border, to the extent that you cannot believe that those foolish crows can just fly straight over the top of it.

You notice the railings converging, see that you are being channeled somewhere. Suddenly you are inside, yet you have just come out of somewhere else. A forest of lights. The area is bare and wide, but the route you must take is marked out, narrow, severe. There are not many cars around. The weather lends everything a friendly glow, but the forms remain as strict as ever. Do I have children with me? I do not have children with me. Do I have a telephone in my car? I do not. Will I take off my sunglasses and turn to look at the guard? I will, and it is a match. I am me. I am allowed through to the next guard post. Each person processed requires a certain amount of time and no one else has been waved through, so I drive the next section alone, across the concrete. Several watchtowers. More of those tall lights—it must be beautiful here at night. Speed limit thirty, then twenty kilometers per hour. You become your own deceleration, reining in all those invisible horses in your engine. Perhaps you are no longer moving; maybe you are on a conveyor belt that is taking you forward. To my right, a long tube runs from the first guardhouse to the second. That is where my papers are now, travelling onwards, along with me, slow and invisible. I can see a gleaming pulley turning the belt on which my passport must be. Second check, all very friendly. Nothing in those expressions but work. And that is what it is, of course. A job. They are young boys. They are polite but firm, and they are just as strange to me as Jehovah's Witnesses. Then there is a third check, and sometimes a fourth. All that time, you are moving steadily along, like the tortoise Achilles could never catch up with. A sign: "Zero per cent alcohol in the D.D.R.!" Slowly, you flow out, then in. Still thirty, then forty. And then you are in that other country, the same country. I see that summer holds sway here too, see the yellow banks of broom hugging the road. Land is innocent; it knows nothing. Purple lupines, distant views slipping by, rural scenes. Later, farms, villages, church towers. Cars and tractors driving along the other, more distant roads that you sometimes see. I can see them, but I am not allowed to go there. And, of course, that creates a desire. All I want to do is make a right turn and go and sit in one of those villages in the shade of a lime tree.

There is not much traffic. Plenty of time to think. Even the few cars that are around reveal the difference between the two countries, the same country. The Trabant is a silly little vehicle, almost endearing. The others, driving their emblematic Mercedes, Audis, B.M.W.s, must feel so superior. But something is missing here: the hysterical, aggressive rushing and pushing of the West German Autobahn. It is as if all of their national frustrations are played out there. When you are trying to overtake and you see one of those pointless racing drivers looming in your rearview mirror, you know that within two seconds that grim shadow will be pecking at your bumper, flashing his big headlights; given the chance, he would like just to drive straight through you. Murder seems to be constantly on their minds. They disappear over the horizon only seconds after passing you, doing 180, 200, maybe more. They have been bottling something up for their entire lives and now they are burning off that frustration. It feels as though the entire country is permanently furious. But there is none of that on this side. A hundred is not much, and I would feel happier at 120, but within half an hour you are used to it. At least I can look out at Brother Falcon and Sister Buzzard, at the pink blossom of the chestnut trees, at the sensual script of the wind in the corn.

I think about the article I read that morning in *Der Tagesspiegel*: *"Glasnost in der D.D.R. der 90er Jahre?"* Will the D.D.R. always continue to limp along behind the Soviet Union, Hungary and Poland? The D.D.R.'s view is that the Russians needed glasnost to mobilize the population because the economy had fallen woefully behind, an argument that does not apply to the D.D.R. itself, because in that respect they are the mirror image of those other Germans, top of the class. Recently the Aspen Institute in Berlin held a seminar with representatives from the S.E.D think tank, the Akademie für Gesellschaftswissenschaften. It was also attended by Americans, British, West Germans, academics and politicians. The event was intended to pave the way for democratization in the 1990s and was described in *Der Tagesspiegel* as a "contribution from the D.D.R. to the discussion of glasnost and perestroika in Eastern Europe." A couple of quotes: "Socialism needs democracy like we need air to breathe," and "Socialism without democracy or without comprehensive implementation of human rights would be inadequate socialism, or no socialism at all." It was going to take a long time, but the development of a greater sense of personal responsibility and a climate of "criticism and self-criticism" was essential.

But how is that supposed to happen with the Wall still in place? wonders this Dutch citizen, as he drives from one barrier to the next, as though merely contemplating such notions might make all that metal melt away. Words by themselves cannot melt anything; their truth will have to make itself felt in other ways. Perhaps this is the point: it is as inconceivable that it will never happen as that it might happen *immediately.* However, it is, in fact, the *immediate* nature of all those proposals that must matter so much to the people involved. So many Russian soldiers are being withdrawn from Eastern Europe. I watch them on T.V. as they go, soldiers hanging out of train carriages, laughing, arms filled with flowers, their tanks on low, flat wagons, their guns suddenly pointing foolishly into the air. What will happen to all of those men? By the end of the century there will be nineteen million unemployed in the Soviet Union. What is to be done with them? And what are they to do with themselves, once the semblance of activity offered by an army in peacetime has been removed?

Words need to be tapped like a tuning fork. Does it sound the same? Is it really the same? The S.E.D. is based on a "democracy" that politically secures the socialist ownership of the means of production. According to the article in *Der Tagesspiegel*, this should be seen in the light of the *"Grundsatz der Stabilität,"* the principle of stability, along the most sensitive border in the world, the one I am now crossing. According to this principle, the division of Germany is essential to maintain this stability. The Wall is far more than a mere symbol of this requirement; it is an integral part of the need for stability. As becomes evident several times a year, this Wall can also signify death. So how does it work? "Anyone crossing the border in the proper manner has nothing to fear." In 1988, twelve million journeys were made from the D.D.R. to the West and West Berlin, and six million journeys in the opposite direction. Why would anyone choose to cross the border in an "improper" manner? Could it perhaps have been someone who simply wanted to leave, but had not received permission to do so?

I am allowed to leave, that is a fact, just as it is a fact that I will be allowed back in when I return. I pass the guard posts, zigzag over the concrete, inch from barrier to barrier, have no children with me, show my face, and am once again back with the other others. Suddenly the Mercedes begin to race again, as if they have been given a shot of adrenaline. The first Mercedes devours an Audi that was just wolfing down a B.M.W.—the remains are still dangling from its jaws. So this is freedom: exhaust fumes biting into the gentle trees, I am home again. There are five kinds of condoms at the *Raststätte*, ten sorts of trashy magazines, drinks in twelve varieties, but, thank God, there is also that unique, breathtaking summer. I take a side road through the countryside to Lübeck. Woods, lakes, peace. War never happened, the earth was never polluted. I lie in a wood beneath tall beeches and listen to two cuckoos calling out long stories to each other about eggs and other birds' nests.

Lübeck. This is a Germany I do not know. The hotel is on the Wakenitz, languid summer water, rowers, fishermen. It feels northerly here, Hanseatic, mercantile prosperity, Buddenbrooks, old houses, stepped gables, coats of arms, wealth. Everything seems almost Dutch; it is most pleasant. I climb up a tower, let the landscape and the citadel fall away beneath me. The city is a strange jagged shape lying in its own amniotic fluid. In the harbor are the large ferries to Sweden and Norway; to the north, Travemünde, the Baltic; the world is a bowl filled with light. I wander along the quiet streets, eat at the Schiffersgesellschaft: model ships, memories of sailors, ship owners, distant harbors. The Protestant work ethic, the accomplice of trade and capital—nothing that came later would look quite that virtuous and peaceful. The impoverished fishing folk have gone, what has remained are the merchants' houses, the churches with the Hanseatic cog on their weathervanes. Through a closed church door I hear the swelling notes of an organ, and it all sounds like days gone by. Gesellschaft zur Beförderung Gemeinnütziger Tätigkeit, Haus der Kaufmannschaft. In the Heiligen-Geist-Hospital I gaze at the small cabins where the old people used to sleep, like dwarves in their dwarf beds, endless rows of compartments under one large roof of beams and joists that resembles the interior of an upturned ship. Stained-glass windows, benefactors' coats of arms.

In the *Lübecker Nachrichten* it says that Kapitän Harmannus Otten Wildeboer, retired maritime pilot, has died; the first stork of the year has been born in Eekholt; the sale of seagulls' eggs is forbidden because they contain too many toxins; the dollar has overtaken the Mark again; and in the Square of Heavenly Peace the students are dancing, but not for long. I buy a black-and-white postcard that shows the city burning, houses lying ruined in the streets, bells fallen from their towers. That was then. Times are different now. The republic built on that rubble has existed for forty years, and those forty years are also forty of my own years. I could have put together the commemorative issue of *Stern* in my sleep: Adenauer's leathery face, Willy Brandt on his knees in Warsaw, Erhard with his cigar, Uwe Barschel asleep forever in the bathtub of his suicide, his pointless watch still on his wrist. The first student shot dead by the police, Ohnesorg; the successive waves of terror and counter-terror; the suicides of Baader and Meinhof; the construction of the Wall; the fields of rubble in the city where I now live. And all of those lesser nostalgias in between: the first puny little cars, the first wooden television sets displaying their fuzzy grey miracle, the millionth *Gastarbeiter*, so warmly welcomed with the gift of a motorbike.

And so the two histories intertwine, the history of those faces, captured forever, which will go on and on, and that other, smaller history, made up of the memories of the survivors, which will disappear along with them. Michael Jürgs writes in an article that the Germans of today are no better than the others, but just normal: normally good and normally bad. They no longer dream of reunification with the other part of the same country, he says, but are happy to see indications that the Wall was not built for eternity. As always, the Germans have been listening to the voices from abroad and they have heard a lot of things that they do not like. Jürgs (*Stern*, 24 May) suggests some answers. Yes, friends from France and colleagues from *Nouvel Observateur* and *Le Monde*, you are probably right to wonder about this nation of militarists developing into a majority of anti-militarists. But we would rather make you nervous that way than with tanks and cannons. And perhaps, English neighbors, you have still not grasped that we are not like the Teutons in your television series, and that Mrs. Thatcher has no say here, however frustrating that might be for her. The tone is self-assured, including Jürgs' remark that the fatherland matters about as much as Mother's Day. The guilt for the crimes "once committed in our name" has been accepted as "part of our history," and is no longer repressed. And there is no longer a national fatherland of the Germans. So there is no longer any need for others to make the judgment of the past into the prejudice of the present. The whole article is clearly in support of Genscher's politics, and a farewell to the Cold War: "Let us celebrate the future of this troublesome fatherland."

Troublesome fatherland, troublesome neighbor. A country that is hard on itself weighs heavily on its neighbors. On an impulse, I decide to take a detour. I do not have to be in Kiel until late in the afternoon and, on the map above Schleswig-Holstein, I have seen that other border, the Danish one, with the town of Kruså beside it. In my very first book, *Philip en de anderen,* I chose Kruså as the setting for a fictional, embellished encounter, woven out of something that had actually taken place in 1953. That is how long it has been since I was last here. I do not recognize anything, except that same, breathless summer and the foreign language around me. *Soldater slog til i Peking-forstad:* other words, still the same. *Thatchers E.F.-stil kan koste hende dyrt, Alfonsín går før tiden. Tijd,* time, *Zeit, tiden:* what have our mouths done to those words?

It is quiet on the narrow road I have chosen. Blonde children on bicycles, empty houses, thatched roofs. I feel at home here and I wonder why it is that small countries are so appealing. Maybe it is that they have no great weight to place on the scales of the world, but equally no great weight to drag them towards a national fate that is bound up so inextricably with that of its inhabitants. As though that weight is now making itself felt, I turn my car around and drive back towards the north, which is now my south.

---

* *Philip and the Others,* translated by Adrienne Dixon (Louisiana State University Press, 1988).

Bismarck, Kiel

My reading is at the main library in Kiel, a bright and airy space. There are about seventy students there, and we go out for a meal afterwards at Der Friesische Hof. They are friendly, northern, open. Why are they studying Dutch? Dutch people always ask that question, as if they are somehow skeptical of other people's motives. Our language is our hang-up. But the students have their reasons: art history, history, the Golden Age, De Stijl, studying primary sources. Suddenly Holland expands a little; we are not always a secret society. Some of the students think it is a beautiful language, while others were simply looking for a suitable subsidiary subject, and the Netherlands is nearby. One is studying Dutch because a friend of his said it was unfair that so many more Dutch people learn German than the other way around, and he thinks his friend has a point. And he is enjoying the experience. He visits Groningen occasionally and he can talk to his friend now without having to resort to his own language—he likes that. What about the war? When they are in the Netherlands, the students see the monuments: "It's something that our country did. There's no getting around that."

The wind is blowing in Kiel; the sea wind is up to no good. I visit a wonderful exhibition at the Kunsthalle the next morning: *Der junge Lucebert*, 110 paintings, etchings, gouaches, drawings by the COBRA poet and artist. There are a few things I have not seen before, but I know most of them, and I recognize even the pieces I do not know. I reread the words that are already engraved in my memory and have taken up permanent residence in my language. I look nostalgically at the photographs of the earlier, darker man, his eyes glinting then as they do now, walk past the colored animals, the crowned heads, past the earliest, so serious self-portrait from 1942, past all those tattered and vibrant people, the furious pathos of the faces he drew, his riddling moons, mythical creatures. I see how one single painter has taken command of all these differences, characters, forms, techniques, how some of the paintings laugh or mock and others are full of sadness, and I feel downhearted and elated at the same time. *Burdens of the air*, *Thinking animals*, *Heavenly twins*, *The poet feeds poetry*, *In conversation with evil*: the poet's language has wrapped a cord around each of these images, but also around me, a slow, sparkling cord of imagination that remains wrapped, invisible, around me long after I have become a driver again, on the road back to Berlin. A handwritten poem appears in the front of the beautiful catalogue, "Berceuse," the last three lines of which I shall never forget:

Dat je tiert en rond rent
met roestige kettingen dat was
van weleer dat is toch bekend

Het moet ons nu van het hart
je bent behendig in het verkeer
schoon insulair in de weer

Maar wat je ontkracht en verwart
niemand te zijn en nergens
*en dan nog iemand te zijn en hier**

June 10, 1989

---

* Your raging and rampaging / in rusty chains is from / bygone days that much is plain
Now we have to get it off our chests / you are adept in your dealings / yet insular in your feelings
But what weakens and confuses you / is being no one and nowhere / and yet someone and here

IV

Farewell for the summer. Berlin is warm, sensual, but I am leaving for that other, Mediterranean, summer and not returning until autumn. The atmosphere in the city is hedonistic; half-naked women lie around on the lush lawns behind Schloss Charlottenburg and in the park in Kreuzberg, as though anticipating an orgy. Twice I see one of those Germanic figures mounting a humble intellectual lying beneath her, removing his pince-nez and lavishing attention on his thin body, starting at the top and working her way down, not unlike a St Bernard tending to an avalanche victim. Large white breasts gleam in the sunlight, and the man struggles a little, kicks briefly, before sinking into this overwhelming tenderness. This is a matriarchy. The people lounging nearby pay no attention, smoke their joints, read their thick tomes, spill beer down their beards or talk to their dogs. The grass is green; the city draws a circle of noise around these enclaves. It is summer and the thick, sultry air makes the senses tingle. Surrounded by this heathen celebration, I try to remember my arrival in February—the white faces, the armor of clothing—but I cannot. This city surrenders breathlessly to the summer, as though the other seasons no longer count, serving only as an extended run-up to these moments that celebrate a freedom that is usually invisible. The Baroque statues on Schloss Charlottenburg look just as lustful in their graceful petrifaction; it is only when I look closely that I realize some of them have no face beneath their vault of hair, just a smooth oval with no eyes or mouth, like a painting by Malevich or de Chirico. They represent Rhetoric, or Mathematics, but that does not explain why they should have to make do without eyes. It gives them a modern look, in spite of all their eighteenth-century ostentation, which somehow makes them seem false, ominous, their soullessness clashing with their libidinous allure. These faces were not destroyed during some bout of iconoclasm; they were made that way, as elongated, empty spaces, blank coats of arms. I am unable to fathom why, but I realize that the explanation will have to wait until autumn, along with the Egyptian Museum that they are guarding with such vacant expressions.

Some Turkish families have found their own spots in the park. The girls are wearing headscarves and playing with the younger children; the women are sitting in their tents of many clothes, while the men hunker down on their haunches, smoking and talking. De facto, self-imposed apartheid. These families are not lying in the sun; they are sitting. There are two kinds of Elysian Fields here: one with people in various states of undress stretching out and submitting, surrendering to the sun; another with people leaning back or reclining, simply outside in the sunlight. These are two different things. The thoughts of the second group are not as apparent, but I can imagine what they might be. One group is the anachronism of the other, and the trees just stand there, indifferent.

I had said that I did not want to write any more about the border, but that was foolish. With such a challenging cordon, there is

always something going on. This time, it is the Christians. I had
read about them, but had not really been paying attention. Christians were on their way to Berlin, from every direction, even
from the East, for the *Evangelischer Kirchentag*, a gathering of
members of German Protestant churches. More than a hundred
thousand churchgoers were attending this congress. There were
violet-colored posters for the event all over the city, with a slogan
encompassing two great indefinable concepts: God and Time. I
am ashamed that I cannot remember exactly how it went, but it
was something about our time in His hands or His time in our
hands, at any rate something that is true if you believe it and false
if you do not. It certainly changed the appearance of the city. Lots
of people on the U-Bahn wearing crosses, some made of clay;
lots of violet-colored scarves, as though Advent had briefly broken out in the middle of summer; and at the Gedächtniskirche,
amidst all that worldly decay, a religious rock band suddenly
appeared, with their ecstatic faces lifted up out of this world, a
choir that alternated its focus between me (audience, passer-by)
and the sky (Heaven). Plenty of bells ringing in that sky too, particularly early in the morning, including at the church around
the corner from my house, which I never see anyone going into
or coming out of.

I had planned my summer farewell for the Sunday afternoon,
and as usual I had allowed about an hour for the formalities at
the border, not suspecting that I would wash out of the city like a
piece of debris on a gigantic Christian wave until I hit the dyke of
the checkpoints. For one crazy moment, I imagined that the East
German border guards might open the gates on this occasion,
in order to deal with this flash flood. But no. It was business as
usual, and so I found myself in the biggest cluster of cars I had
seen for years, thick, endless, a viscous mass, moving forward,
meter by meter, and splitting into ten slow streams somewhere

around the guard posts, each stream with its own distant exit. People got out and started pushing their cars, and I joined them, which was quite an effort with my old Buick. As we pushed, we took a look at one another. The atmosphere was cheerful. I did not know if it was because of their recent days of devotion, but the Christians all seemed to be filled with charity. Young people dressed in violet had installed loudspeakers on their patched-up old cars. There was lots of shouting and laughter, a mobile party of the people that moved more and more slowly as it drew closer to the uniformed guards, who acted as though this was all perfectly normal and asked the same questions they always did. Children? No children. A quick look into the car. No, no children. As on any other day, no one would be able to leave paradise on earth without permission.

Then the two hundred kilometers to the West, the endless procession of church buses and cars all doing their best to drive at exactly a hundred kilometers an hour, with the same congestion at the exit. Hours behind schedule, I could forget my plans to drive back to the Netherlands that day. I decided to stay overnight in Salzgitter and drive on through the Harz Mountains the next morning.

Salzgitter, salt grating. German places can be deceptive— when you actually get up close to a town, you sometimes find that there is more than one of it. The *Gästehaus* I am looking for is in Salzgitter-Leben-stedt. "Salt Grating-Life Town" looks like America, one of those places you see on a long journey down the freeway. Nothing to remind you of the past. Low-rise buildings, petrol stations, billboards, a pizzeria. Somehow I stumble upon my guesthouse. It is practically deserted and their restaurant is closed on Sundays, but there should be somewhere to eat in the new district behind the hospital. This Germany is different from Berlin. I step through the door of the bar like the stranger in a western. A single question hovers above the seven heads in the bar: "What's he doing here?" Taking a seat in the far corner, I try to make myself invisible. Slowly, the conversation gets going again. I do not know their names, so I just make some up for them, and within half an hour or so I realize that this is a daily repeat performance of the same old thing. Heinz: casually dressed in an echo of Italian fashion, in a silk-look blouson, white socks and loafers, flashy haircut above a face that is in the fast lane to old age even if the driver has not yet noticed. Hannelore: lonely, corner of the bar, encountered old age in the mirror some time ago. Still beautiful, but fragile. A teacher, an executive secretary, teetering on the brink of forty, golden hair in a bun. Lise: firmly ensconced in her sixties, jug of beer in one hand, fag in the other, turning pleasure into work. Minds her own business. The chorus: drunken Ulrich and silver-haired Antonio. Antonio, the worldly-wise Italian, has been here for years, so he is allowed to be part of the gang. Ulrich, fat, scruffy, does not stand a chance with Hannelore, so instead seeks vicarious pleasure in the flashy haircut's love for the golden bun. But Heinz has to go home now; the little woman's waiting.

Don't forget the dog, says Ulrich. You've still got to take the dog out for a walk.

Bloody dog, replies Heinz.

Yeah, bloody thing, agrees the landlord.

Stay and have another one, says Antonio.

It's on me, says Ulrich, because when Heinz leaves, boredom sets in.

Just one more, then.

One or two or three . . .

Hannelore goes to the toilet and, when she comes back, she walks into Heinz's arms. Resistance, but not real resistance. Heinz tries to kiss her, but makes contact with her neck. Ulrich gets another beer in for Heinz. Hannelore struggles out of his clutches and sits down chastely at the corner of the bar again, tidies her bun. She likes Heinz, but there are limits. Feigning reluctance, the landlord slides the glass over the bar. Heinz reaches out to grab it, but misses.

Have I paid yet?

No. This one's on Ulrich.

You shouldn't have done that, Ulrich, says Antonio. Heinz has to go home.

He's got to take the dog for a walk, says Ulrich.

He's got to go home to his wife, says the landlord's wife.

Damn dog, mutters Heinz. Have I paid?

Heinz's large brown hand wanders towards the essence of Hannelore.

No, no, no, says the golden bun, but an inner compass turns her in the desired direction.

Have another beer, says Ulrich. And so the riotous night rages on, a web of increasingly drunken voices and forbidden gestures—it is better than television. Outside, the night air is cool. Damp, misty, the scent of jasmine, sad and lonely traffic lights at the deserted crossing, the night porter startled from his nap.

The next morning, I see that I am not the only guest after all. Two Englishmen in a cloud of smoke talking about contracts and money, a steely businesswoman bashing her egg as she reads the latest news. There is a piece in the *Frankfurter Allgemeine* about *Europa und der Orient 800–1900*, the exhibition I saw yesterday before I left Berlin. Saw: that is the right word. I cannot claim any more than that. The organizers had planted a forest of references in the idiosyncratic space of the Gropius-Bau, and I wandered through that forest, at times in twilight, then in the subdued glow of a harem. The exhibition appealed on various levels: to my more base, hedonistic senses, to my penchant for rapidly acquired erudition, my thirst for everything Spanish, my exoticism, my

Catholic memories, my desire for recognition. A forest of a thousand trees—that is no exaggeration. The catalogue alone, which
was too heavy to take on my journey, contains over one thousand carefully considered, descriptive pages, but the logic of the
catalogue is not the logic of the route through the exhibition,
which is ambling and random, dependent on the gaze and the
flow of other people. This means that you are always turning the
centuries into loops, crossing your own path, meeting yourself,
ascending, descending through time, and that time runs from
the first Babylonian clay tablets to the chastely lustful, absurd
yet wonderful harem fantasies of the Pre-Raphaelites—and
everything in between. Everything? Of course not, but the sheer
mass does suggest that word. Brueghel is there, with his *Tower
of Babel* (another Babylonian tower), and so is Govert Flinck,
with his very Dutch man in a turban, but there are also Catholic
altar cloths with Mozarabic designs, incunabula, the first translation of Aristotle and the commentaries of Averroes, swords and
shields embellished with Moorish enthusiasm, the breathtaking
translucency of the Fatimid rock crystal, the meticulous illustrations of nineteenth-century French Egyptology, and sacred statues from ancient Egypt itself, seventeenth-century Europeans in
fashionable oriental attire, the Andalusian griffin from Pisa, the
cross-pollination between Islamites and Carolingians, between
Venetians and Levantines, the intellectual furnaces of Toledo
and Córdoba, where the Islamic, Jewish and Christian cultures
coexisted until that was no longer permitted, crusades, emissar-
ies, audiences, letters of credence, pilgrimages, cloisters, scripto-
ria, colleges—all woven into a fabric of unfathomable complexity,
which in our age of so-called global communication has been
paradoxically and irreparably torn. Of course, what is on display
here appears, by dint of its beauty alone, to be light years away
from the destructive fundamentalism of the Khomeinis, but

our own burnings of heretics and other barbarisms are equally invisible: the dirt of these encounters has been swept away, and what remains is an image of nostalgia, as if something that was once very close to us has withdrawn into itself, as though we have forgotten that it was the people of Mohammed who preserved the Greek legacy of doctors, mathematicians, philosophers and metaphysicians for the Europe of the Renaissance, and therefore the Enlightenment.

The *Frankfurter Allgemeine* accompanies its article with just one image, but it is not a section of Gilgamesh, and not al-Khwarizmi's astronomical tables. Blood will out, and this blood pulses from an East that never existed, a sensuous nineteenth-century fantasy. And so the image they have chosen is an 1886 painting by Edwin Long, and even in black and white it still achieves its effect: the pharaoh's daughter discovering Moses among the reeds. Flamingos, water lilies, hieroglyphs, marble staircases, lush, oh-so-oriental palms, a sculpted lion, its melancholy head averted and resting on its stylized, four-toed paws. But that is not what this is all about, nor is it about the future law-giver in his woven basket. It is about the naked and scantily clad women who populated that inaccessible realm in the fantasies of the painter and his customers. Visible, available, they sit and stand on those marble steps that run down into the water, their bodies draped here and there to please the breathless libido of the Victorian viewer, their modesty protected only by the varnish of the painting, a transparent, but impenetrable layer of lacquered time immuring them like a five-thousand-year-old tomb.

The Harz, that is where I was planning to go, attracted by the patch of green on my Michelin map. Forests are good for the soul, and I have the image of Goethe's *Harzreise* in my mind's eye. But I am rather naive, as it proves impossible to reconcile the two things: the

romantic, lonely, maybe even dangerous horseback journey that the
poet undertook in 1777, when he was not yet thirty, and the civilized, tamed greenery of the restrained tourist landscape that I drive
through inside my metal shell. He was already famous, even then,
the creator of Werther, a high official at the court of the Duke of
Sachsen-Weimar-Eisenach, member of Secret Commissions, with
a particular interest in geology and mining. He traveled incognito,
called himself a painter and weaver (this was on his first, lonely journey), moving from inn to inn, his head full of Charlotte von Stein,
seven years older, married, six children, the love of his life, to whom
he wrote at least one letter a day.

Strange that this incognito identity should be revealed post-
humously, but that is how it is. The letters, the diary, his reports
have given him away; he will never make that journey alone again.
Every step has been described: the encounters, the stopping places,
the routes he took and those he did not. We know everything,
and so he becomes visible, riding through the snow, through the
dusk, his head filled with thoughts about rock formations, Faust,
his beloved, the finances of the dukedom, a poem, a letter he
intended to write, a drawing he was going to do. The Dutch poet
Roland Holst had a bon mot that he must have been very proud of,
because he trotted it out frequently enough: "Goethe was a plaster Apollo." However, I am unable to see the connection between
plaster and the man riding through the night. Against all advice,
Goethe wanted to climb the Brocken and he went ahead and did
so, absorbing those mysterious mountains and forests, and the
legends that had surrounded them since ancient times, and dis-
tilling it all into his Walpurgisnacht in the first part of his Faust,
and his "Harzreise im Winter":

Dem Geier gleich
Der auf schweren Morgenwolken

Mit sanftem Fittich ruhend
Nach Beute schaut,
Schwebe mein Lied.*

What modern parallels can be found for such poetic genius? A few: Paz, Neruda, Saint-John Perse and Seferis were poets and diplomats; William Carlos Williams was a doctor all his life; Wallace Stevens, the greatest of them all, was vice president of an insurance company. But a diplomat is not a politician, and a politician is not a geologist, and a geologist is not a poet, and a poet is not a minister of state, and the minister of state is not an artist, and the artist is not a tragedian, and the tragedian is not a finance minister, and the minister did not measure elephants' skulls and write letters about it to his sweetheart. So, driving along the bridleways buried under tarmac, I had every reason to think about that twenty-eight-year-old rider who passed this way, turning over a poem in his mind, dismounting to touch the granite (about which he would later write a scholarly study) or to draw a limestone formation and write about it in a letter to his love. Of course, these were the last few moments before general expertise fragmented into specialisation, and of course, he was a one-eyed king in a city where pigs still ran around free, and of course, the dukedom had little power and politics was no more than a pastime for gentlemen, but even so. And that is the "even so" of the later Italian journey, which was foreshadowed by these three journeys through the Harz, when the tension between the poet and his other identities has become too great, the "even so" of the poems and the reorganization of the ducal finances, of the

---

* As a bird of prey / Rests on heavy morning clouds / With wing so gentle / And seeks its quarry / Let my song hover.
"Harzreise im Winter," Johann Wolfgang von Goethe.

dramas he is inventing and the very real political wrangling surrounding the *Fürstenbund* following the death of Prince Elector Maximilian Joseph of Bavaria.

Goethe wanted progress, and he got it. Whether he would have been willing to pay the price in lost poetry is a pointless question. Nature revealed its secrets in the Harz, and the battle between the Neptunists and the Vulcanists was settled (the world of water or the world of fire? Goethe was wrong). Now we know all that there is to know about granite and we can climb the Brocken day or night. Witches, sorcerers, trolls and spirits have no place there; Faust and Mephistopheles no longer wander around through this "Gegend von Schierke und Elend," because today there are signposts and kilometer markers for anyone who wants to find the way from Schierke to Elend. The road has lines down the middle, a smooth surface; the mystery has fled, and, along with it, the restlessness, the inspiration. No Proktophantasmist, or Frau Muhme, no Lilith and no Trödelhexe is going to emerge from this night mist.

One of the roles of this multifaceted individual was that of modern administrator. He wanted to open up the Harz, while I, his retrograde descendant, am trying to wish away this road, the final element in the area's transformation, the progress that Goethe wanted, which would leave no place for the lonely rider-poet. The road becomes a path, and the undergrowth runs rampant over the straight painted lines. The trees grow denser on both sides; they are no longer ordered, tamed, regulated, but forest once more, wild, dark and sinister. Anything could happen here. It is December 9, 1777; the poet-minister has another eight kilometers to go in the snow, the forest and the moonlight. Back then,

---

* From *Goethes Harzreisen* by Rolf Denecke (Hildesheim: Verlag August Lax, 1980).

the forests were darker than the words; now the words have taken possession of the vanished secret. The pedantic future writer of two hundred years later knows exactly what the anonymous traveler was thinking back then: "He remembered his childhood; he thought about the duke, his best friend; again he reflected upon the relationship between nature and adventure"* (and he was right about that, because where nature disappears or is transformed into a pale image of its former self, as has happened here, adventure degenerates into a drive in an Opel). At night he writes, as he does every day, a letter to his beloved, not to me, yet I am the one who is reading the words now. I know that it is perfectly normal, we have the right: Goethe is public property. Yet it seems strange that, without the slightest remorse, we do something we would never think of doing to the living: we read their intimate letters. I cannot help myself—I can see it, picture it before me, this letter, the actual object. The next morning, it leaves the inn, stashed away in someone's bag, up onto another horse, back along the same route the poet once took, his capacious mind filled with words. Perhaps it passes from bag to bag, a piece of paper covered with writing, rolled up or folded into a rectangle, treated with respect, surrounded by the sound of horses' hooves, the creaking of the stagecoach, the whistle of a whip, German voices, shouting, cobbles, gravel; someone carries it up a flight of stairs, gives it to someone else, who places it in the hands of a woman. She waits until she is alone, unties a ribbon or tears open paper, reads it as she lies on a sofa or stands by a window or sits in candlelight, and I, invisible in my present day, read along with her, read the words she read, and yet different—it is *her* living, twenty-eight-year-old Goethe, not mine. I picture her lips moving as she reads his words:

Was die Unruhe ist, die in mir steckt, mag ich nicht untersuchen,
auch nicht untersucht haben. Wenn ich so allein bin, erkenne ich

mich recht wieder, wie ich in meiner ersten Jugend war, da ich so ganz allein in der Welt herumtrieb. Die Menschen kommen mir noch ebenso vor, nur machte ich heute eine Betrachtung. Solange ich im Druck lebte, solange niemand für das, was in mir auf und abstieg, einiges Gefühl hatte, vielmehr, wie's geschieht, die Menschen erst mich nicht achteten, dann wegen einiger widerrennender Sonderbarkeiten scheel ansahen, hatte ich mit aller Lauterkeit meines Herzens eine Menge falscher, schiefer Prätentionen. Es lässt sich so nicht sagen, ich müsste ins Detail gehen; da war ich elend, genagt, gedrückt, verstümmelt, wie Sie wollen. Jetzt ist's kurios, besonders die Tage hier in der freiwilligen Entäusserung, was da für Lieblichkeit, für Glück drinsteckt. *

Goethe went ahead and climbed the Brocken the following day, and even though it can in no way be the same, I would like to do it too, but the Brocken is on the other side, in the D.D.R., and you are not allowed to climb it: it is a *Sperrgebiet*, a prohibited zone.

I am closing the door and leaving Germany behind, on my way to the summer, to Spain. But Germany pursues me, with the duplication I have become accustomed to in Berlin: Honecker in the

---

* I neither wish to examine the unrest within me, nor to have it examined. When I am quite alone I recognize myself as I was in my first youth, when I was drifting through the world all on my own. People still seem the same to me, but today I made an observation: as long as I was subject to the stresses and strains of life, as long as there was nobody who understood what was going on inside me (rather, as it happens, people did not respect me at first, indeed they looked at me with suspicion because of some of the strange contradictions within me) I had with all the integrity of my heart a multitude of false and warped pretensions—it is not easy to say, I would have to go into details—I was eaten up by misery, oppressed, mutilated you might say. Now it is curious, especially the days spent here, in the free expression of what loveliness and happiness lies within.

From Goethe's *Briefe an Charlotte Stein*, Vol. 1, Chapter 22, letter dated 9 December.

Volkskammer in Berlin; Gorbachev cheered by a West German crowd. All the cheering makes Gorbachev look like a general who has won a victory, and maybe that is true: he has surrounded East Germany like a strategist. Victory or defeat, we will soon find out, but faces are tense in this ideologically besieged land. The Volkskammer has assembled to condemn the vandals and "counter-revolutionary" elements in China, as though their own possible fate, surrounded as they are by neighbors who are drifting away, is written on the wall, crisp and clear. Their fate, or the fate of the man who is being applauded? A world is coming undone, and on the screens it looks like a celebration, just like that other distant celebration, only a few weeks ago.

July 15, 1989

V

I AM BACK IN BERLIN AFTER ALMOST FOUR MONTHS
away. The border, the guards, the house—everything is just as I left
it. Except that the city is now clothed in autumn, fitting attire for
all that is happening. Not on this side, but on the other side, the
side you are constantly aware of. It is no more than two kilometers
from where I live. I pass by the Wall almost every day, one way or
another, and the tall television tower of the East is always in evidence. No need to go there; my television supplies the pictures.
On Friday, it was pictures of a celebration. Torches, endless processions, cheering, laughing people, leaders on a podium, waving
and laughing. The eye cannot be deceived by what it sees. We were
not born yesterday; we know what a laugh looks like, we recognize the signs of real joy, and that is what I saw. Maybe the eye can
only be deceived by what it does *not* see. It was a strange evening.
It lasted for hours. The old, emaciated man stood on the podium,
right beside his guest. You cannot stand closer to someone than
right beside them. Their thoughts may have been invisible, but the
invisible thinking, calculating, juggling of political options did not
cease for a moment—and I think I saw it all happening. What goes

on inside you when you see thousands and thousands of people
with torches walking past you, past you and no one else, waving
and shouting? Gorbachev was the very definition of unfathomable.
He held on to the balustrade with both hands, firm hands. If he was
impatient, you could only tell from his fingers, which occasionally
started drumming, as though they had escaped the control of head-
quarters. Women in the crowd pointed at him, pointed him out to
one another, laughed, sometimes ecstatically; you could see it happening, in wave after wave. The others—government, Politburo—
were grouped around the two leaders. The figures in the back row
had no faces, were mere outlines, shadows from Plato's cave.

In the spring, one of the men had been in the West, where he
was applauded as he was now in the East. Back then, for one brief
moment, as he stood waving in a car, he had looked like someone who
was certain that he had achieved something: he had surrounded the
D.D.R. His own country, Poland, Hungary and the West had combined forces to draw a merciless ring around the D.D.R. Inside that
circle, nothing could remain the same. It was only a matter of time.

The moment had to be sealed and now that has happened. With
a kiss. In the moving pictures, it happened quickly; the instant vanished in the clichés of arrival. Aeroplane steps, guard of honor, old
man waiting on the concrete, kiss. It is only when the pictures are
frozen that you can see the intensity of the moment. I am looking
now at two of those images. In one, the light is falling directly on
Gorbachev's face. There is no question about it: this is an intimate
moment. He has closed his eyes, his lips are puckered; they are so
tightly pursed that his mouth has become some strange object. We
have a side view of the other man, the one with the white hair. He also
appears to have closed his eyes; they do not need to look at each other
to perform this action. His face is slightly raised, the left lens of his
glasses catching a curved gleam of light. In the other photograph, you
can see that he has his hand behind the other man's right shoulder,

that his eyes are indeed closed. This is no Judas kiss—you can see that too. And yet this kiss seals the downfall of one of the men, and maybe the other. After all, nothing can be ruled out now; this moment could last for a long time. The kiss is being carried out by people, but it is in fact states, strategies, political philosophies that are kissing each other. The country that was unimaginable without the Soviet Union is being kissed by the country that has made it possible to imagine the death of the D.D.R. The orthodoxy inherited from Lenin and Stalin is being kissed by heresy. The philosophy that broke everything wide open is kissing the philosophy that wants to hold on tightly to the past. The communal house is kissing the divided house. One man represents one of the greatest adventures in history, a revolution that the other man perceives as betrayal of the Revolution.

Mikhail Gorbachev and Erich Honecker: the kiss. © *Corbis*

The others, the ones it is all about, cannot be seen in this photograph. While an oompah band in traditional costume plays on East German television, I see the others on the television on this side. Interviews on the street. Mothers with children, old people, young people. They hope for peaceful change, or they are scared, or furious, or taciturn, or indifferent. They too have been surrounded; their movement within the circle is prescribed, proscribed, circumscribed. They are not the ones who walked past that podium with torches, and maybe even that is not true. Brecht once said that if the people had lost the government's confidence, the government should dissolve the people and elect another. It does not look as though that approach would succeed in this surrounded country.

Today's *Frankfurter Allgemeine* has six headlines on the front page. Demonstrations throughout the D.D.R. Packed prisons in East Berlin. The Hungarian Communists are abolishing themselves and becoming a socialist party. (There were pictures of that yesterday too: red stars being removed from the state buildings I remember from 1956, a statue of Lenin being pulled down, that sharp profile with the pointed beard staring up into the autumn sky, together with a statue of the Sacred Heart in a silent courtyard.) The tide of refugees coming through Hungary is growing. If they are not granted autonomy, all Russian Germans will leave Russia. In the frozen moment of that kiss, all of those angry movements, that pulling and pushing of powers and authorities, accumulated desires, grudges, dogma, resistance and expectation, were invisible, as though the two men stood in the eye of a storm.

That is how it seemed yesterday too, in the deathly atmosphere that often accompanies Sunday afternoons in Berlin, on the border by Lübars: the autumn trees motionless, the lights of the tall security posts mere patches of orange in the misty air, a few walkers, a girl on a horse and, on the sand of the no-man's land between the fence and the Wall, young men with dogs. There were more of them than usual. Watchmen, men charged with watching. But now their watching seems more like waiting, waiting for something that, sooner or later, not now, but one day, will certainly happen.

October 18, 1989

VI

HOW DOES A FISH SEE THE RIVER IT IS SWIMMING IN? It cannot leave the water to gain distance or perspective. Something like that is happening in Berlin. Everything is flowing. Every moment there are new events, reports; whenever I step out of the front door, within a couple of minutes I become part of a swirling crowd, people shouting newspaper headlines at me: Farewell to the island! Germany is one! The people have triumphed! Eight hundred thousand conquered West Berlin! At the banks and post offices, long queues of East Germans stand in line for their "welcome money."* Old people with dazed expressions, in this part of the city for the first time in thirty years, come in search of their memories; young people who were born after the Wall went up, and who live maybe a kilometer away, walk around in a world they have never known, so ecstatic that the asphalt can barely hold them.

---

* Between 1970 and December 29, 1989, each visitor from the D.D.R. to West Germany was entitled to *Begrüßungsgeld*, a financial gift from the government. After the fall of the Wall demand grew so high that it was abolished.

As I write these words, church bells are ringing out on all sides, as they did a few days ago when the bells of the Gedächtniskirche suddenly pealed out their bronze news about the open Wall and people knelt down and cried in the streets. There is always something ecstatic, moving, alarming, about visible history. No one can miss it. And no one knows what is going to happen. This is a city that has been through so much. The tens of thousands of people flowing through the eastern channels to the West all bring their emotions with them as though they are tangible objects. Their feelings are reflected in the faces of the people on this side and boosted by the sound of their own millions of footsteps in the suddenly pedestrianized streets, by the sirens and church bells, by the voices with their questions and rumors, the unwritten words of a script invented by no one. No one, and everyone. "*Wir sind das Volk!*" they called out in Leipzig only two weeks ago. We are the People! Now those people are here and they have left their leaders at home.

The big demonstration in East Berlin happened eight days ago. Simone went, but was singled out by the unerring eye of the border

Queue for Begrüßungsgeld *("welcome money"), West Berlin, November 1989*

guards at Bahnhof Friedrichstraße. No, she could not go through. "So why are all these other people allowed in? I've been waiting here for an hour and a half, just like everyone else." "I'm sorry, but we don't have to give a reason. Try again tomorrow." I was off on another mission at the time, a series of readings in the far West: Aachen, Cologne, Frankfurt, Essen. Even there, Berlin was constantly present in every conversation. Monday evening was Essen, the dark heart of the Ruhr-gebiet. After the reading, a discussion in a dimly lit café, *Erbsensuppe*, *Schlachtplatte*, big glasses of beer. A number of young people, a girl from the theater, a book dealer, a biochemist, a writer. Always the same words, over and over again: *Übersiedler*, *Aussiedler*, *Wiederver-einigung*. Aren't people in Holland scared of German reunification? No? Well, we are. We don't want to be reunified, and certainly not with those Saxons and Prussians. They've had such authoritarian upbringings; they don't know any better. They're at the factory gates by six every morning. How are we supposed to respond to that? They may be Germans, but they're *different* Germans. Of that lot 10 percent would vote for the Republikaner, and 60 percent for the Christian Democrats (C.D.U.). We know that already; we've seen the surveys. Germany will be one big country again, but leaning eastwards, towards the Poles and the Russians. That's sure to make the rest of Europe happy. Is that what you want? The whole balance will shift and we'll have to become one big nation again.

The only answer I can think of is that they already are one big nation, that it is their own relative density that will put an end to this artificial separation. Large countries exert their own gravitational force, which sooner or later draws everything in. It will be up to the Germans themselves to deal with the consequences.

After our conversation, they take me to catch the last train to Cologne, a kind of tram. It is a tortuous journey. The thing is empty, and cold, and stops everywhere, even when there is no one in sight. Outside, the grim silhouettes of heavy industry, hellish flames against the blackness. At Düsseldorf, there is a bomb scare and we come to a standstill in the midst of a silent black void. I am alone in the compartment. I hear the elderly voice of the driver over the loudspeaker, breathing heavily: *Bombendrohung*, a bomb scare. We wait there, endlessly, and whether it is the night, or the absence of other people, or the conversation I had that evening, or simply my age, I cannot help thinking about the war, about the power of attraction exerted by this strange country, which always drags other countries into its destiny, whether it means to or not.

Thursday evening. I am back in Berlin and in a taxi with my photographer and a friend. As we are talking, suddenly I hear something in the sound of the voice on the car radio, a sound I recognize: the

Brandenburger Tor, November 4, 1989

eager, rushed, incredulous tone of major events. I ask the driver to turn up the volume, but that is not necessary; she tells us the news herself now that she knows we can understand her. She is excited, she pushes back her long blonde hair, and she is almost shouting. The Wall is open, everyone is on their way to the Brandenburger Tor, all of Berlin is heading there. If we want, she can take us there now, as she wants to see it too. If we agree to head straight there, she says she will turn off the meter. The traffic is heavier by the second; it is almost impossible to move forward, even from a hundred meters beyond the Siegessäule. In the Trabant beside us, smoke billowing out behind it, young East Germans hold up their visas to show us, their faces white with excitement in the glow of the streetlights. I tell the driver that she would be better off taking John-Foster-Dulles-Allee to the Reichstag. Dulles, Reichstag, war, Cold War—it is impossible to say anything here without invoking the past. The dark ship of the Reichstag lies in a sea of people; everyone is advancing on the tall columns of the Brandenburger Tor and the galloping horses above them, which once stormed in the opposite direction. The viewing platform that looks out over Unter den Linden is swaying under the weight of the people. We fight our way through and whenever someone comes down, we move up, one body at a time. The empty semi-circle in front of the columns is illuminated by an artificial orange light; the phalanx of border soldiers inside the semi-circle seems a weak line of defence against the strength of the crowd on our side. Whenever someone climbs up onto the Wall, the soldiers try to spray them back down, but the jet is usually not strong enough and the lonely figure stays there, soaked to the bone, a living statue within a nimbus of illuminated white foam. Shouting, cheering, the flashes of a hundred cameras, as though the concrete of the Wall has become transparent, as though already it is almost no longer there. Young people dance in the jets of water, the vulnerable line of soldiers forming a backdrop for their ballet.

In the semi-darkness, I cannot see the soldiers' faces, and all they can see is the dancers. The others, the large animal of the crowd, which is growing larger and larger, can only hear them. This is the destruction of their world, the only world they have ever known. The taxi driver does not use the meter on the return journey either. She says she is happy, that she will never forget this moment. Her eyes are gleaming. Her boyfriend is somewhere by the Wall right now and she would like to share this moment with him, but she does not know where he is, and besides, her shift runs until six in the morning.

The next morning, Friday. I am standing in the window of Café Adler, the last café in the West, by Checkpoint Charlie. "You are now leaving the American Sector"—today that means nothing. Everything seems to be peeling away at an incredible speed. A gentle stream of Trabants comes flowing over the border. Someone is handing out money to the people in the cars; someone else

S.E.D. (Sozialistische Einheitspartei Deutschlands) demonstration, East Berlin, November 10, 1989

is giving them flowers. The people in the cars are crying or looking bewildered, as though it cannot be true that they are driving in that place, that those other people are waving and calling to them. The East German border guards are standing on the other side of the street, a few meters away from their Western counterparts. They do not speak to one another, but stand firm in the surging crowd. I find their faces as unreadable as they were in the darkness yesterday. Then I cross to the other side myself, join the line, and I find that everything is the same as ever: visa, five Marks, the desperate exchange rate of one to one, even though the actual rate is ten to one. It goes quickly, and I am through within fifteen minutes, but the queue on the other side stretches endlessly around the corner into Friedrichstraße. I walk to the street where Volk und Welt is based, the publishing house that brought out two of my books. It is quiet there, but the door is open. I find one of the proofreaders and am greeted with Berlin humor: "How kind of you to come and visit, just when everyone else is heading in the other direction!" But it is clear that they have been engulfed by the events. No one has any idea what will happen next. I say that I have heard from a Hungarian friend that after the "change" there—I do not know a better word for it—over two hundred new publishing houses were set up. Of course, they know that already, but their greatest concern if that were to happen would be how to get hold of enough paper. No one has anything sensible to say about reunification: "How would it work economically? No one here can afford books from the West. Our books only cost a couple of Marks." They have a brilliant series of foreign literature—from Duras to Frisch, Queneau, Kawabata, Canetti, Cheever, Calvino, Bernlef, Sarraute and Claus—but what is going to happen when West German publishers are free to operate in the East? Will Volk und Welt still be able to acquire publishing rights? Hundreds of these questions are going around; the whole country is one big question without an answer, and every possible, unimaginable answer, economic or political, intimately affects the lives of millions of people.

"The world has become glass," the proofreader says, a sentiment I retain when I head back outside. It is cold, but the sun is shining on the chariot atop the Brandenburger Tor. Now I am seeing the city where I live from the other side—that is still possible for now. Masses of Westerners are standing on the Wall; cameras from C.B.S. and the B.B.C. are filming the silent waves and cheers, the

Potsdamer Platz,
West Berlin,
November 12, 1989

distant ecstasy. In the classic no-man's land between here and there, officers stride past a backdrop of columns just as they always have done, sunlight glinting on their epaulettes.

Glass: the word will not let me go. I walk across Unter den Linden and see a luxury edition of the collected works of Erich Honecker in the window of a large bookshop. The books are miniatures, thumb-sized, with leather bindings: *Alles für das Wohl des Volkes*. Their tiny format appears to reflect the fate of the vanished leader. They cost 420 Marks. How long ago is it now, that kiss from Gorbachev? On all sides, the buildings are tall, old, powerful. This was once the real center of a major metropolis, but only now do I feel how just big it was, how big it will be again when it is a single, united city. The capital of an empire? Frederick the Great never left; he rides his horse, frozen in his heroic pose. Figures on the Neoclassical build-ings dance their stone dance in the last of the sunlight. Two soldiers stand, so motionlessly, in front of Schinkel's Neue Wache, while opposite, on Bebelplatz, a memorial plaque serves as a reminder of a book-burning: "*Auf diesem Platz vernichtete nazistischer Ungeist*

Potsdamer Platz, West Berlin, November 12, 1989

die besten Werke der deutschen und der Weltliteratur."* And only a short distance away: *"LENIN arbeitete im Jahre 1898 in diesem Gebaüde."†* Can I tell that things have changed just by looking at these people? No, I can see no difference. They are walking and shopping with no indication that half of their city is flowing into the other half at this very moment.

Marx and Engels,
East Berlin,
November 1989

---

* On this spot, the inhumanity of National Socialism destroyed the best works of German and world literature.
† Lenin worked here in the year 1898.

"Socialism with a future—S.E.D."

I cross the dark water of the Spree and come to Das Rote Rathaus, the Red Town Hall, where every Monday evening the demonstrations took place that made the world shake. I walk across the grass in front of the building, towards the backs of Marx and Engels. One is standing, the other is sitting; I recognize them even from behind, by the wavy hair, the wide, jutting beard of the seated man. Their world too seems to be made of glass: fragile, transparent. They are still here, but already somehow departing, disappointed at what has become of their legacy, their backs to the illuminated glass palace of their descendants, the Palast der Republik. A few hours later, the last of their heirs arrive to stage a counter-demonstration. It is dark now; powerful halogen lights shine upon the Reconciliation Door of the Berliner Dom. Another crowd, but this one is not demanding, it is defending, giving itself fresh heart with slogans and banners and mechanical battle songs that come from large loudspeakers. I allow myself to be swept forward across the gravel between the statues, up to Das Alte Museum with its columns and watchful eagles. Members of the press are climbing into Schinkel's giant marble dish in front of the building. From the steps, I have a good view of the banners: *Weiter so, Egon. Sozialismus mit Zukunft: S.E.D.* (Keep it up, Egon. Socialism with a Future: S.E.D.), but also *Für die Unumkehrbarkeit der Wende* (The *Wende*—for irreversible change!) and *Kommt raus aus Wandlitz, seht uns ins Antlitz* (Come out of Wandlitz* and look us in the face). And that is what I do: I look into the faces of the Party members. They are the people who have the most to lose from the changes. In free elections, the S.E.D. would receive only 12 percent of the vote, and most of the people here would disappear into the obscurity where a number of their leaders already reside, has-beens, dispensed with. Some of them sing along hesitantly with the amplified songs about blood-red banners and battle, but the mood is uncertain. The world around them is now a different place. They know what has happened in Poland and Hungary; they have come here to feel safe among the loud voices, but even those voices are saying things they have never said before. Party members are speaking, blaming their leaders for being too late—too late and too slow—they are constantly being overtaken by events. Members who were voted into the Politburo on Wednesday have been thrown out today, and no one knows where they stand. The "monopoly on truth" has been abandoned, and everything sounds like heresy. A few of the speakers say they are happy that they did not have to submit their speeches to the Party for approval, as they used to. Most of them receive more applause than Krenz, who speaks about a revolution on German soil, but the people standing there know that it is not their revolution. He also talks about free elections, but says that the Party will not allow the power to be taken from its hands. *Niemals,* never. What is the validity of such words? Like a group under siege, the leaders appear in *Welt am Sonntag* the next day: raincoats, raised fists, mouths open as they sing

---

* A municipality to the north of Berlin, home to many top East German functionaries.

"Nobel Peace Prize for Gorbachev," S.E.D. demonstration, East Berlin, November 10, 1989

a battle song. By now, all over the city, pneumatic drills are banging the first holes through the Wall. I leave before the crowd disperses. Behind the windows of the Palast Hotel, a palm-court ensemble in dinner jackets plays to an audience of Bulgarians and Koreans.

There is still a queue at Checkpoint Charlie. Foreigners can leave by a separate exit and do not have to wait. The same border guards as this morning, their faces exhausted, pale, tense. I exit as an East Berliner, because a young woman offers me chewing gum and a boy hands me a pamphlet about *Einigkeit und Recht und Freiheit*—unity, justice and freedom—and the Wall having to come down and reunification being inevitable, and McDonald's would like to treat me to "1 small drink, Voucher valid until 12.11.89." So I too am welcomed as a home-comer. In the U-Bahn station at Kochstraße, the thousands wait for a train, offering no resistance as they are pushed through, into the West. When I finally reach Kurfürstendamm, Berlin is one big party. Cars can no longer get through, and the city has descended into madness. The people have become one whirling body, a creature with thousands of heads, undulating, rippling, flowing through the city, no longer knowing whether it is moving or being moved, and I flow along with it, having become crowd, news picture, nobody. News bulletins appear on the wall of a building on the Ku'damm, in lines that quickly fade, as though the news might catch up with them, but nothing can catch up with this crowd, because it is making the news itself. The crowd knows that, and it feels like a mass shiver. They themselves caused what they are reading here, they are the people; after them will come the politicians with their words, but for now those words seem to have the aim of calming, pacifying, more than anything else. No one will ever really know the entire story, but in the past few weeks the people on these streets have turned a page of history, and not only the Krenzes, but also the Kohls, the Gorbachevs, the Mit-

A Mauerspecht (wall woodpecker) pecking away. Potsdamer Platz, West Berlin, November 12, 1989

terrands and the Thatchers will have to wait and see what is written on the next pages, and who will appear on them. Millions of Europeans from the East have caught up with the signatures of Yalta and over-taken them, and we did not assist them.

Thirty-three years ago, I stood in Budapest in a different crowd, one that felt betrayed and abandoned by us. That was history too, the black mirror image of the day I am experiencing now. I watched the Russian army surround the city and wrote my first

*Schlesische
Straße /
Puschkinallee,
West Berlin,
November 11,
1989*

*Checkpoint
Charlie,
West Berlin,
November 10,
1989*

piece for a newspaper, which ended with the words, "Russians, go home." I can laugh at my own ignorance now, but how loud should my laughter be?

There are still Russians in the D.D.R., just as there are Americans in the Bundesrepublik. They are two different countries and the Wall is still there, even though there are holes in it. But the people from that Other Country are walking along these streets for the first time in thirty years, and when I look out of the window, I can see them.

November 18, 1989

VII

BILD, BLACK, YELLOW, RED AND GRUESOME, BUT
with the best headlines, sums it up as though in a song: "GESTÜRZT,
VERHAFTET, VERSTOSSEN, GEJAGT" (overthrown, arrested,
expelled, hunted)—and, between those words, pictures of the
deposed leaders, the same size as the letters of the headline. And
above it all, in the colors of the German flag: "DAS VOLK BEFREIT
SICH" (the people free themselves). It is Monday morning, misty and
grey, and this week has burst apart at the seams. I have seen Kohl in
his attempt to get ahead of the rest of the world; Krenz before, during
and after his fall; Golo Mann in the role of Clausewitz; the simultane-
ity of photographs and history; two female writers; a people embrac-
ing itself; a restive people grumbling and muttering. I have to send
myself telegrams in an attempt to bring some order to it all.

Sunday, 26 November. Café Adler by Checkpoint Charlie. On
the other side of the street, a windowless wall with large letters that were once electrified: *Neue Zeit*. Appropriate words. I
was on my way to a meeting in the East, but the queue at passport control was so long that I realized I would never make it.

This city is still divided. Instead, I stay on this side and visit an exhibition at the Martin-Gropius-Bau. It is raining on the frozen snow, making ice-cold mud. Mitteleuropa. The exhibition is about Jewish sports clubs after Jews were excluded from the "other" sports clubs. The pictures have that awkward look of sports photographs from fifty years ago; you can almost tell just by looking at them that people will be able to run faster in the future. What makes the images so poignant is everything we know now. I read the names, look at the faces. Lili Sara Henoch, multiple champion, deported to Riga with her mother, disappeared without a trace. The list of her final possessions, the eagle she was once permitted to wear on her chest. Alfred Flatow, author of the *Handbuch für Weltturner*, the handbook for international gymnasts, former champion, ejected from the gymnastics association after forty-seven years. In his letter of farewell to the association, he wrote, "Please permit me to remain silent about my own thoughts and feelings." He was born in 1869, but the life he lived after sending that letter was a short one. In 1941, he became an enemy of the Reich; in '42, he was sent to the old-age ghetto in Theresienstadt; by the end of that year, "death from exhaustion." Edmund Neuendorff writes to his "dear fellow gymnast" Naumann (they were both committee members) that he must stand firm on these expulsions; this is first and foremost about Germany. There can be no exceptions. Germany has suffered so much in recent decades; German culture, German society and morality have been "so badly damaged by the Jews, German politics have been so hideously abused by them, that we must at all costs draw a thick line under the past. What we have experienced must never happen again." I look at the robust gymnast in his old-fashioned sports clothes and notice a small sign beside the picture: "The view through the window in front of you is of the foundations of the Gestapo

Headquarters and the remains of the torture chamber." Obediently, I look: a field, a mound, a few bare, black bushes, footprints in the snow, nothing.

Downstairs in the museum, another past is on display: the present. There is something perverse about this contradiction and it takes time to think it through. It is an exhibition of photographs and banners from the demonstrations of recent weeks. After the main demonstration, people were asked to hand in their placards and banners at the history museum (East), which has now loaned them for this exhibition in the West, just as paintings might be loaned. I look at the items hanging there a little foolishly on the plastered wall, the photographs of the familiar scenes, those

Neue Zeit, East Berlin, as seen from Café Adler, West Berlin, November 1989

Checkpoint Charlie, West Berlin, November 10, 1989

same slogans held high above the heads of the people. Maybe this is postmodern: making history and knowing that you will be in a museum that very same week, and then going there to see for yourself. The comments in the visitors' book are mainly from East Berliners: "We want our democracy, not your rubbish!" "The middle class in the D.D.R. only came crawling out of their consumer caves when there was nothing left to fear." "Anything but reunification." "The fear of being embraced by brothers and

Potsdamer Platz, West Berlin, November 12, 1989

sisters." So the story is far from over, in spite of Kohl's ten-point plan. On my way home, I walk by Polenmarkt. Hundreds of freezing people standing in the viciously cold mud, at their feet the pitiful wares that attract the poor and the Turks, ice-cold rain, bargaining and haggling, the underbelly of two worlds.

Monday evening. Hilde Domin is reading at Wolff's Bücherei. Poems, sketches from her life. A long life: she is nearly eighty, with the ruthless indomitability of people who have lived through all sorts of things. Small, fragile, without her spectacles, a voice like glass. Fled Germany in 1933, earned a doctorate in Florence with a thesis on a predecessor of Machiavelli, a rosary of exile, Italy, driven away again, England, Santo Domingo, a life of poems, poverty, endless different houses, nothing could break her. In the book she signs for me, *Aber die Hoffnung*, she underlines the word *Aber* three times. She reads from her poems:

> *Taube,*
> *wenn mein Haus verbrennt*
> *wenn ich wieder verstoßen werde*
> *wenn ich alles verliere*
> *dich nehme ich mit,*
> *Taube aus wurmstichigen Holz,*
> *wegen des sanften Schwungs*
> *deines einzigen ungebrochenen Flügels.* *

Wednesday. I am still thinking about the photographs in the museum. It feels like watching yourself doing something in the mirror. Forms of meta-history. The narcissistic element perhaps lessens the impact. On the other hand, we are confronted every day with a multitude of moving images that, when paused, become illustrations in a history book. But maybe that is just it— perhaps we should not pause them yet. Our obsession with looking never ends. The sinister hunting lodges of the party bigwigs, tasteless, dull imitations of feudal nobility, fat armchairs beneath rows of antlers; you can picture them sitting there with pints of beer in their hands, the marquises of the exploited East in the settings of the class enemy, the accumulated jealousies of the petty bourgeoisie. Meanwhile Krenz is fighting for his life. Every evening, he hangs his big head on the icon that is D.D.R. television, in

---

* Dove, / if my house burns down / if I am cast out again / if I lose everything / I will take you with me, / dove of worm-riddled wood, / because of the gentle sweep / of your one unbroken wing.
   "Versprechen an eine Taube" from *Aber die Hoffnung* by Hilde Domin (Munich: Piper Verlag, 1990).

Polenmarkt, West Berlin, December 1989

department stores, factories, on street corners, beseeching, arguing. But the workers and housewives give as good as they get: they
do not have to go to the West, they will stay right where they are,
but they do not want any more of the mess that he and his kind
have made of things. On the television on this side, Golo Mann,
who is the image of his father, a reincarnation, a sequence of genes

shaken and reassembled; it is a wonderful thing to see. He speaks like Clausewitz about the "glacis" of East Germany, the line of defence that Russia will never want to lose, while also holding forth about the erosion of words, the meanderings through meaning that words such as "communism," "socialism," "democracy" have followed since the end of the eighteenth century. And other images form around these in my mind, images of the falling East: Zhivkov, watching, vacant and open-mouthed, as his statue melts; Ceauşescu, arguing neurotically, a village idiot in an empty palace. It is just a matter of time now—the Maltese handshake of Gorbachev and Bush even had an impact on Castro's biography. And, almost overshadowed by all of those other scenes, there is Dubček on the balcony in Prague, as the ghost of Husák prepares to go in search of Dante's inferno, and the icon of Christ in a Vatican room, averting its eyes as two men without interpreters converse in Russian. *Extra omnes!*

Thursday. A young East German writer, Kerstin Hensel, reads poetry and prose in the Buchhändlerkeller in West Berlin. Small, severe, clean-cut clothing, hair like Brecht's, the shorn head of a nun, born in 1961. Her book of stories is called *Hallimasch*, which is the name of a fungus, the honey fungus, a parasite that lives on conifers, but an edible one, a means of survival in difficult times. Her version of Hansel and Gretel ends with a bitter twist: "'Home,' said the boy, and then the girl looked at him for the first time, for the first time in years, and said, 'How fat you've become, Hansel,' and Hansel saw it too and he said, 'How stupid you've become, Gretel,' and then they started walking, but they did not know where they were going." The next day, I tried to buy her poems in East Berlin, but they were no longer available. "*Vergriffen*," I was told. Out of print.

Friday. This time I take the car; I want to go deeper into the city. Right at the border, the engine of my ancient American automobile starts to boil. "*Ist das normal?*" the border guard asks, and I admit that it is not. "Nothing's normal these days," I want to add, but he helps me to pour a bottle of water into the engine, so I can continue on my way. There is a strange beauty about the ugliness. I drive down Karl-Marx-Allee and Karl-Liebknecht-Straße—evaporated dreams—and then to bleaker neighborhoods. The smog mixes with the mist, the air tastes of Trabant and brown coal; it still feels a bit like after the war. The sun sifts the horrors like an old sous-chef: lumps of tall residential blocks, railway yards. I drive away from the center, along the Wall, which the River Spree must flow behind, the Wall that I so often see on the opposite bank, on the other side of the water. So this is where they live, I think, without thinking too hard about it. But it is true: this is where they live, the people from the demonstrations, the people who watch the same television as me in the evening. They live here, in bare tenement buildings, on wide avenues that dwarf the pedestrians who choose to cross.

Potsdamer Platz, "Holland greets Berlin." West Berlin, November 12, 1989

Suddenly I find myself outside the zoo. I can see the gates and the tall trees beyond, with their clusters of ravens, willful singers who squawk and screech at me to come in. There have been too many people this week; I want animals now. The ticket costs one Mark. Almost the only visitor, I walk tentatively down the paths of frozen snow, listening to the ravens' short, sharp songs. Voles, Vietnamese pot-bellied pigs with peevish expressions, snakes, black panthers, the calm of infinitely recurring forms. I feel the persistent nag of history fade away, and I greet everyone I see, wave at the flamingos in their steamed-up greenhouses, the Siberian bears who are behaving as though it is summertime. Evening starts to fall, casting shades of grey over the snow. The penguins are deliberating about events in the human world, while in the big cats' house the lions are rebelling; they are roaring and clawing, making the whole building shake. Almost as a response, I find myself, half an hour later, watching the changing of the guard at the Neue Wache, as three human animals behave like machines. It is dark by then, so it all takes place by the light of tall lamp posts. These guards can do so much that ordinary animals cannot: they wear helmets and long field-grey overcoats; the soles of their boots scrape the ground as they kick their legs high in their mechanical ballet, do about-turns, raise their rifles, bayonets pointing into the light, as though there are not three men, but only one, a three-person automaton, emitting short, terrifying breaths as it disappears through a secret door. Nearby, demonstrators are gathering at the Volkskammer; the Party will be debating its own fate tomorrow and the next day. And after that the army will no longer be the army of the Party.

Saturday. A play at the Maxim Gorki Theater: *Die Übergangsgesellschaft* by Volker Braun, a reworking of Chekhov's *Three Sisters*. A house full of old junk, failed lives, burned illusions, fear and frustrations, and once again that desire for Moscow, because the wheel of history has turned and hope now comes from Moscow, and everyone here knows it. The play is packed with internal contradictions, psychotic scenes, allusions I do not always grasp. The audience is enthralled, laughing at every reference to recent events. It culminates in a fire in the old house and the death of the Spanish Civil War veteran, the only character for whom life has been clear and meaningful, because of his fight against fascism. All else is confusion for the living.

Downstairs in the foyer, those photographs again, frozen movement, as though the time for reflection has already arrived, the mirror in which we see ourselves standing still. But it must be an illusion; everything is still very much in motion. On a large poster, the playwright asks whether the East must allow itself to be colonized by the West:

> Nothing has been proved yet. Where will we live? And will what comes after us be worth the effort? The Wiener Schnitzel is too small to satisfy our appetites; a dose of Hungarian predatory capitalism will bring about affluence for a third of the population at best, and the new social deprivation will force the Volksrepublik towards the West or into further social unrest. The question is whether there is a more modern option than this circus of parties, something like grass-roots democracy, a democracy that aims to find solutions for everyone.

No one should expect a simple appendage to the Bundesrepublik any time soon.

Sunday. Half past seven in the evening. *Die aktuelle Kamera*, the D.D.R.'s news show, which has become essential viewing:

Mielke, Mittag, Müller caught, Schalck-Golodkowski fled, Krenz deposed, the Party beheaded, Prague '68 regretted—The End. I watch as a politician experiences his own destiny. The expression belongs in old history books, but it seems appropriate here: the people are restless. Krenz stands on the steps, a few meters away from the microphone, pale in the neon light. One after another, they step forward, argue, fulminate, and these are the members of his own party, which in their own lyrical style they refer to as "*die Basis*." They pass their verdict on Krenz, and it is merciless: I have never seen anything like it. He wants to have another go and grabs the microphone, but they are shouting and jeering, a whole square full of people. He is good at shouting too and he shouts about what he wants to do, about what he has never done, about what he would have liked to do, but they just whistle and jeer. So he turns tail and disappears behind the bodies. Later they show him again, the man of a month ago, pinning a medal on Mielke, the former head of the Staatssicherheitsdienst (Stasi), who has now been arrested, a runt of a man in a cream-colored uniform, chest like a noticeboard covered in colored ribbons, to which Krenz makes a new addition, and, even more fatally, Krenz in Beijing after the student uprising. And then he is washed away, disappeared, old news, overwhelmed by a chain of his citizens stretching across the entire country, by two men on a boat, by one of those men in Brussels with Kohl, who was supposed to meet Krenz in two weeks' time in order to lend him some semblance of the respect that has now been taken from him. Egon Bahr sums it up at the end of the evening: "This party has beheaded itself, which is the third stage of a revolution. And we all know that heads do not grow back."

I have been sitting in front of the screen for hours and now I want to go for a walk. It is night, and cold. A few shadows flit around behind the windows of the pubs, but otherwise all is quiet, and I see my city as an enclosed district floating in the middle of a country like a large ship battling upon an angry sea, even though it too is playing a part in whipping up the waves. This may be a peculiar image, but I know of no better way to describe it. There is a storm raging all around and yet it is so quiet.

December 9, 1989

VIII

IF IT INFURIATES THE PEOPLE WHO ARE WATCHING, how must the protagonists feel? Night after night, they come through the screen and into my house with yet more of their harebrained schemes, formations, reactions, edicts, threats, appeals. Every evening, when I watch the D.D.R. news show *Die aktuelle Kamera*, it seems as though the entire country has been participating in one gigantic, uninterrupted meeting for months now, a general promiscuity that gives the round-table discussions, inaugural meetings, press conferences and hearings the atmosphere of one huge bed that everyone, whether they want to or not, has to lie in together, and maybe even sleep together, while the people, where it all began, are leaving that busy bedroom behind, either tiptoeing out or slamming the door behind them. I have become addicted to these television sessions, which sometimes go on all day. I know it is not good for me, that the false impression of proximity can make you forget there is another country behind this one, and beneath and behind that one, there is another and yet another, with a similar kind of pandemon-ium wherever you go, but that is just how life is right now: I am living in this enclave and my enclave is at the eye of the storm.

At Christmas, I fled. I wanted to return to my peaceful homeland, where nothing ever seems to happen, because we did it all a few hundred years ago. The weather was ominous, and peering at the map I saw the word "Hermannsdenkmal" near Detmold, followed by "Teutoburger Wald" in much larger letters. I did not know who Hermann was, but this Teutoburger Wald sounded Wagnerian enough to suit the leaden sky.

As soon as you leave the nonsense of the Autobahn behind, the world mysteriously reverts to being itself: the countryside, where the invisible people live, the provinces, that tough substance that hangs like a weight counterbalancing the contrivances of the city, the *majority*, a region that might differ in terms of accent and dialect, but which you recognize in every country as the largely silent essence of the country itself. I was in Germany here, just as the previous night, when I had spent the night in Celle, I had been in Germany: my dinner had the grand title of *Herzögliche Entenvesper* and the name said it all, the feudal-religious notion of the "ducal duck vesper" on my plate corresponding nicely to the restored middle-class gentility of the city center: signs, timber-framed facades with Gothic lettering, a castle, a Christmas market with *Glühwein* and trees and "*Stille Nacht*." An hour later, I experienced the most silent night in Europe, with only the clock of my feet ticking among the locked houses of people sleeping the sleep of the just.

So, I had gone in search of Hermann, and everyone wanted to help me, because everyone knew where he lived. They were all so friendly, so obliging, and that was just as well, because Hermann did not seem to want to be found. He kept hiding behind hills, forests, squalls of rain, but finally I found a place to leave my car in a vast, almost empty car park beside a few lonely Trabants, shivering sadly as they dreamed of hot Mercedes. If Hermann was their first destination upon being allowed to leave their enclosure after so many years, what did that signify? I still could not see him, so I walked down a woodland path, hurried along by the wind, protecting my face from the whipping rain, until, through my tears, I saw him: a towering beacon of a man on an equally towering pedestal, slicing his sword into the storm, ruling over the world. His scale took my breath away. Walking around beneath him, I studied his irrepressible calves, the huge eagle's wings of his helmet, the curved grey plates of his miniskirt with their ominous sheen of green, the mysterious, solidified space beneath. I climbed a narrow spiral staircase to his mighty feet, but what was just a storm down below became a hurricane up there. Hermann stood firm, but then he weighs more than forty-two tons. Including his pedestal, he stands over fifty meters tall and he does not need to worry about his helmet flying off or his skirt blowing up: he is fastened together with 30,924 copper rivets. I, on the other hand, was finding it all rather tricky. Hanging on to the balustrade with both hands, I peered down at the scrambled syntax of the streets and villages all around and looked out like a bird over the dark forest where Hermann had wiped out three Roman legions in A.D. 9. He did not know that Germany existed, so he could not know that he had liberated it, but now the words are written on his sword: *Deutsche Einigkeit meine Stärke, meine Stärke Deutsch-lands Macht*: German unity my strength, my strength Germany's might. History, that old anachronistic liar, is up to its old tricks again. And now I understand why the former King of Prussia and the later *Alter Kaiser*, who both resided in one and the same body, came to unveil this statue in 1875 (and also why those Trabants are here): it created the impression that a single, uninterrupted line ran from Hermann to Wilhelm, as though the land stretching out beneath my feet had not for centuries been a grab bag of earldoms and kingdoms, with everything that implies. "*Immer zerrissen und geteilt*," said Hölderlin, always torn apart and

Arminius. Hermannsdenkmal (Hermann Monument), Teutoburg Forest

divided—and the numbers back him up: at the Peace of Westphalia in 1648, three hundred German states were recognized as sovereign, each with its own court, its own despot, enlightened or otherwise, and the accompanying officialdom and cult of obedience, which was to have such dramatic consequences even into the twentieth century.

Hermann was of course not called Hermann, but Arminius. A mad classicist made this error in the sixteenth century, and it stuck. After all, what is the good of a national hero with a foreign name? Emperor Augustus sent the wrong man to Germania: Publius Quinctilius Varus, a wimp and a profiteer who had previously been busy plundering Syria. He was not keen on the Teutons, this Varus (". . . he imagined that the inhabitants had nothing human but the voice and limbs . . ."), but underestimating one's enemy is always the best recipe for disaster. Hermann led Varus up the garden path and massacred him. And, had he not appeared in the dreams of the sculptor Ernst von Bandel, he would simply have slumbered on in the history books. For thirty-eight years, this dreamer worked on the statue—ridiculed and impoverished, as is only right and proper. While it may not quite have been a thing of beauty, it was certainly large, so large that even the Kaiser noticed it and decided to turn it to his advantage.

Over the centuries, while France and England became centrally governed units, the German nation was repeatedly blasted by fragmentation bombs of both domestic and foreign manufacture, and everyone was accustomed to this, not least of all the Germans themselves. The arrangement worked well for all concerned: any possible Middle Empire would only disturb the balance; a cordon sanitaire of foreign countries controlled the mouths of all the rivers; and Germany, which did not exist as a state, was locked within the European land mass. The inviolability of those small and large potentates, guaranteed by foreign nations, meant that the once so self-assured cities, with their free citizens, lost power and influence. A Byzantine operetta-cum-nightmare of nobility and titles, privy councilors, addiction to uniforms, heraldic excess, court balls, subjects and serfs, and bureaucracy developed in all of those inward-looking capital cities, and even though there was still no Germany, the kind of people who would later populate Germany were already being bred. Those who do not actually have to live in a state can afford to be sentimental or emotional about the nation that they only have to *feel*, and all that pathos was expressed in the statue above me, which showed every sign of holding its arm aloft well into the next millennium. That was fine by me—I was escaping to the peaceful gardens of my homeland, where the statues may be smaller, but so are the problems.

Not only Hermann, but also other images, moving ones, followed me there: the East German Modrows and the West German Kohls, who together had to try to be a new Bismarck, while Europa, that old woman with all her thousands of memories, jealousies and fears, continued to scrutinize their every movement. The words she mumbles in her sleep are what people once called history; anyone who listens carefully can sometimes understand what she is saying and may hear the word *Gleichgewicht*—equilibrium—and know that she is dreaming about the Peace of Utrecht and the end of the War of the Spanish Succession, but there were so many peace agreements and all of them were pregnant with a future war, which always necessitated a reassessment and rearrangement of the *Gleichgewicht*. If that did not work out, the armies started to slide forward again, because nothing is more unreliable than a set of scales that has been tampered with—and no Rapallos or Munichs can stop that, no peace accords of Vienna or Westphalia, no Versailles and no tango from Molotov and von Ribbentrop: one of the dancers always ends up on the gallows. And who will follow? Or does no one follow anymore? Will all those countries stand like ruminants behind their sealed-up rivers while the European shepherds calmly herd the German flock back together? Among all the willing, the unwilling are scarcely noticed. Reunification resembles a natural phenomenon, and any politician who knows what is good for him swims with the flood-waters while pretending to control the flow.

Now I am back in Berlin, but I have to leave very soon. Poland is roasting, Bulgaria is simmering, Romania is boiling, the Big Country beyond is prodding all of the sore spots and probing the wounds that it caused, and the leader sometimes seems a little like a writer who does not know quite how to proceed with his book, but does not want anyone to notice. And what is happening in Berlin? I am once again a slave to the television screen, watching the endless, entangled discussions, the new openings, connections, enmities, trying to envisage how all those gestures and attitudes stem from recent and more distant history and how a new history should be formed out of these countless crumbs, and yet at the same time my heart is in my mouth. There is one sentence I learned at school that I will never forget: *Senatu deliberante Saguntum periit*—While the Senate deliberated, Saguntum fell. It will not come to that, and there is no other solution anyway, but every day when I look at all those deliberating initials (SEDSDPLDPDBD-CDUDDRSPD and so many other arrangements of the alphabet that I have not yet internalised), I can hear the shuffling feet of the runaways, and it feels as though that round table is standing all alone on the plain of Brandenburg and all of those voices are just drifting on the wind.

Is this a fair assessment? No, of course not, and when I see all those sincere, emotional faces, not yet corroded by years of politics, I know that. Maybe it has more to do with the pernicious influence of television. What that daily spectacle presents is reality, confusion in its full extent and impact, and at the end you want a conclusion, a punch line, catharsis, as we have come to expect from the medium that brings us *Dynasty* and *Tatort*—but there is no end in sight. The series will continue tomorrow—by which time another two thousand or more will have made their escape—with the same slowness, the disagreement, the fragmentation, the pushing and pulling that are all part of the business of politics. It must be incredibly exciting for the people involved, but can the same be said for those watching? The prayers and the copulation of other people can look rather unpleasant on the public screen, and the same generally applies to lengthy political meetings, if only because real time, when inserted into a television screen, comes out as slow motion. I have never entirely understood the secret of this Einsteinian temporal quirk, but it seems pretty clear that anyone who wants to have a longer life should watch plenty of television.

As a temporary resident of Berlin, I have received a *Bescheinigung* from *Der Senator für Inneres* (Internal Affairs, which sounds very intimate) to say that I am registered in Berlin "*mit niederländischer Staatsangehörigkeit*," and, as a Dutch citizen, I can pop in and out of the D.D.R. with no need for any other documents. I do so now, on my way to Munich. A little excitement, because I have never driven this way before. Signs for Gotha, Leipzig, Weimar, Dresden, but I will save them for the way back, when I have more time. Smoke billows from the Trabants, the road surface is ravaged, the service areas look antiquated, and there is none of the dogged luxury that afflicts my part of the world. This is a marked landscape—nowhere else looks like here. The enforced slowness of pace lends it an atmosphere of times forever past, and in a funny kind of way that is not unpleasant. On the other side of the border is Bavaria: an undulating landscape, dark forests, snow here and there, beauty. In my *Gasthaus* by the Englischer Garten, I read Gordon A. Craig's book about this country (*The Germans*) and sink into his illuminating chapters on German history, but when I am outside among the people, with their emblematic hunting attire and vanilla-colored palaces, I am *in* history, the history of Baroque piety and Toller's revolution, of Ludwig I's Athenian dreams and fiery singing in the Hofbräuhaus, of the university where Hans and Sophie Scholl distributed their anti-Nazi pamphlets, and of the mastodontic homes of the Wittelsbachs.

The city touches me somehow and yet feels strange, but I keep coming back. The sun is shining, there is still ice on the pond in the Englischer Garten, where once no Jews were allowed, and that same sunlight has a strange effect on the water behind the Nymphenburg Palace, making it look as though the old ladies out walking are actually floating upon a plain of silver snow. Of course, I have to go inside the palace, and together with the usual Japanese tourists, I wander past the empty chairs, the lonely beds, the silent rooms, the faceless mirrors, the chandeliers and candelabra, the idle geese on the lawns, the swans on the ice; like a bored duke, I stand watching the citizens with their plastic carrier bags and then turn to look at Ludwig's gallery of beauties, dozens of painted young women looking back at us from the realm of the dead, dressed for the ball. Irene Gräfin von Arco-Steppenburg, Markgräfin Pallavicini, the braiding so carefully painted on Helene Sedlmayr's billowing blue bodice, the breathtaking chest of Gräfin Caroline von Holnstein curving perilously out of the picture: may I have the pleasure of this dance? In the restaurant, ladies in green hats munch on the obligatory pigs and the sound of the angelus drifts in from outside, carried on the wind. Twelve noon, the witching hour.

There is a Jim Dine exhibition at the Glyptothek on Königsplatz. The boyhood dream of an old Pop Artist all alone inside the boyhood dream of a Bavarian king, his later echo hanging amongst the gods and heroes, the wise men and the warriors. Ludwig made this Parthenon for his collection, Klenze created it as a magnificent structure, Greece uprooted and planted in the North, and the war completed it by destroying all of the ornamentation and showing the classical structure to its best advantage, with the focus on the statues. And what statues they are! Forty years ago, I saw them in my schoolbooks: the enigmatic smile of the kouros, the youth of Attica; Homer's blind gaze; Aphrodite's disfigured face, denying this desecration; Athene's introspective wisdom, eyes downcast; the seated satyr's troubled sleep. In the stillness of their presence, disturbed by no one, the man of two and a half thousand years later with his sketchbook and other, so much more transitory material.

Jim Dine: I remember his hammers, chisels, lonely objects pulled from anonymity and suddenly called upon to play a leading role, and then the nudes, the endless repetition of his own face, the body first dissected into individual parts and combined with etching tools (*thirty bones of my body*), and later as a single unit, and now, even later, a confrontation with the physical perfection of those classical bodies and the mystical added value that the earlier religious intention and intervening centuries have given them. You need to have some nerve, and he certainly has, partly, he says, because the mutilation and disfigurement of most of the statues have brought them closer to modern art. For him, the work in the Glyptothek was a meditation on beauty and inner calm, but it was also terrifying to attempt to measure up to this cosmic material, as he calls it. What he has added seems at times like a form of assemblage. He has joined statues, such as Homer and Socrates, and his delicate streaks of blue mean that they now belong together, two spirits from the underworld, holy ghosts. He has removed other statues from their context, elevated them, dramatized them with a use of color that is economical, but strategically employed. He is allowed to hang there; his images exist alongside the statues, which lose none of their enigma, which permit these reflections. Walking around the exhibition is a form of happiness, perhaps because there is a connection to my childhood, to what I know, perhaps also because this loftiness remains so close and the divine has here become truly human for once—or the other way round, which is even more beautiful. The museum has held back one surprise for me, with deliberate or unintentional irony: in one corner of a gallery of Roman statues, I find a group of heads of Socrates wrapped in plastic. It is transparent, this plastic, it gleams, and, as though Dine himself had planned it, here too there is intensification, accentuation. The heads become more, not less; the artificial light shining down through the plastic softens the faces, and the philosopher smiles. And that is how I take him with me as I head outside onto the severe square that aimed to be classical in a non-classical era.

On Sundays, there are discussions at the Münchner Kammerspiele: two men and a moderator. They are German–German conversations, and this time it is Wolfgang Harich, Marxist philosopher, with, or rather against, Christoph Stölzl, founding director of the controversial Deutsches Historisches Museum in Berlin. Harich's

Socrates, Glyptothek, Munich

outspoken opinions led to him being imprisoned under Ulbricht
for seven years, and anyone who briefly thinks back to the Stalinist
policy at the time will understand why: there was no place at the
court of Walter Ulbricht for a man who argued for profit-sharing in
socialist companies, for the development of healthy small-scale and
medium-scale agrarian classes, for reestablishment of the S.P.D. in
the D.D.R. and for joint German elections (at that time!), and who
also deserted in '44, becoming a member of a resistance group (anyone born in '23 has lived several different lives in this century). A
hero, you might think, and what you see on the stage is an old satyr
with a viciously high voice, somewhat authoritarian, the advocate
of an eco-dictatorship, still a Communist, against travelling and
tourism and Western consumer society, and actually, you imagine,
still in favour of the old D.D.R., if they had not handled things so
foolishly. His opponent behaves like a Dutchman, by which I mean,
in this case, someone who does not get excited, does not participate
in his interlocutor's ideological capers, occasionally says something
calm about free elections and democracy, and whose worst accusation is that the other man has aristocratic tendencies. I cannot help
it, but I find it hilarious. There he sits, a representative of a country
that threw him in jail for seven years and which is one of the most
polluted places in Europe, and he is speaking out, like some kind of
Marie Antoinette, against the restive people who have been locked
up for forty years, saying that they would be better off just staying
indoors in the future too. You need to have smelled the coal in Weimar to savour such chutzpah. And yet, then I look at him again, old
and fragile, his eyes angry and his head full of Marx and Lukács. He
is arguing against the rampant growth of capitalism, but without
the patience to combat it by taking the tedious route of the steady
drip, a hasty dreamer with delusions, who wants a peace conference
(which should last two years) including all the countries occupied
by Germany, along with Israel and the Arab states. It would be a

most delightful conference, in which the D.D.R. would be spoken of in the past tense, a perverted reunion of old and new friends and foes who are permitted to assemble a catalogue of *faits accomplis*.

Two years! Goodness knows what the map of Europe will look like by then. I do not wait to find out, but decide to head off to Weimar instead.

February 17, 1990

Intermezzo in the Third Person: *Vestigia pedis*

I STILL INTENDED TO GO TO WEIMAR, BUT I PUT THE trip off for a while. Instead, I took a step back in time, transforming myself into a third person: the traveler I once had been, a visitor to Munich, a foreigner attempting to contemplate the history of the city around him.

It was autumn. It is autumn. The traveler, someone, he, I, stepped through the glass door of his hotel on the River Isar. No doubt about it; it had to be morning. But he had not showered yet, probably, he thought, because he did not wish to wash away the night, the province of dreams. Women had appeared in those dreams and he would encounter those women again this morning, but some of them would be without faces. Someone should write a study of the relationship between bedding and national character. Plump pillows, Teutonic titillation.

The clouds are high, but the sky is grey. Later he cannot remember which of the two moving phenomena first attracted his attention: the orange *Schienenräumwagen 303* or the wide triangular formation of migratory geese flying past high overhead. Both represented an element of motion. As a traveler, he was sensitive to movement: like a cat or a child, he was quick to spot moving things. The Euclidean pattern in the sky interested him, because it told him which way was south. If the triangle up there had been the tip of an arrow, and if it had been at the height of his chest, it would have gone straight through his heart. So now he knew that Maximilianstraße, the street in front of him, which the *Schienenräumwagen* was screeching its way along as it cleared the tram tracks, crossed the trail of the geese from east to west. He looked up at the neat, serious flight of the birds as they headed for their goal, and wondered what the seers of antiquity would have read in that flight. At the same time, he felt a desire, as he did sometimes in his dreams, to take off and fly. With slow strokes, like a racing cyclist in a gear that was too low, he would skim over the swirling Isar behind the hotel, setting his course without performing any calculations: a straight line that would take him to his position at the back of the formation in the shortest possible time. None of the other geese would be surprised, the swishing of his large wings would join theirs, and his long, outstretched neck and his flat beak would follow the lonely leader at the front, the one who knew. Did geese see the landscape? Beacons? Hills, curves in rivers, church towers, roads they recognized? The strict order of their flight made him feel sad somehow, with the treacherous longing that military formations can provoke in a man even when he despises them because he himself belongs to the chaos.

Passers-by are all alike: every passer-by is the passer-by of everyone else. At this moment, he is not particularly interested in himself, and so he does not look at them. You can see it in photographs: a group of people waiting for a tram. He is in one of those photographs now, somebody, or nobody, who has taken the ten steps from the pavement to the tram stop. *"Fahrer Wegner, kommen Sie bitte zurück zur Station,"* says the small loudspeaker at the stop, but

Max II Monument, Munich

something else beckons. He can always become *"Fahrer Wegner"* another time. First for the monument.

Opposite his tram stop is another one, the mirror image of his own. The monument stands at the end of the tram stops. The rails sweep in a gentle curve to encircle the monument. The passers-by, the people waiting at the stop, mirroring him and the people waiting at his own stop, are smaller than they should be. This is the fault of the monument, because everyone on it is far too big. First he sees the woman. Whatever it was that he dreamed last night, here it is in physical form. Arousal at the sight of an oversized bronze statue of a woman—there is no denying it. It is all, he thinks, because of her foot. Travel guides are the antidote for feelings that stray too far from the norm, so he does not look at his guide yet. Instead, he embarks upon a relationship with the statue. The woman has a face that might be called Greek, with no further explanation needed.

We all know what is meant by that description: stern forms that retain a sense of mystery. Her headscarf, her shawl, intensifies the effect. Her immense limbs perch on the narrow bench that wraps around the polygon and she has to lean forward a little. Her robe ripples over her implacable thigh in folds that are fluid, yet bronze, and her left wrist rests on a book perched at the point where the thigh comes so close to the stomach (*her* thigh, *her* stomach). A statue is not worthy of contemplation if it does not, at least once, prompt someone to think that beneath that bronze, which depicts fabric, there is a body—genitals, intestines, liver, heart—that can smell and silently respire with an almost imperceptible breath of bronze. And of course this statue is capable of looking back.

But that foot. To start with, it is naked. And so he must assume that the woman's foot may be cold; otherwise there is something not quite right about her. This has nothing to do with sentimentality. He is now standing directly beneath the foot, which is the size of his lower arm including the hand. He cannot touch the foot from where he is standing. To do so, he would have to climb onto one of the steps of the monument, and he is not quite that far gone yet. The grey has disappeared from the sky, as though it was not meant to be there. The sun illuminates the bronze. The big toe shines more brightly than the rest of the foot. He has seen the same effect before, in the Vatican, in Santiago de Compostela. It is from the touch of so many hands, idolatry, paganism. So it would seem that others share his fascination. The steps of the monument have been patched up, like an old pair of jeans—he sees that without seeing it, just as he sees the upturned half-moon in the suddenly blue sky. What is it doing there? He sits down on the ice-cold stone, flesh on marble, and does not allow himself to be distracted. Her stiff thighs are loosely crossed, as only a huge bronze figure can do. Her left foot is to the right of her right foot. The left foot is the one that matters. It is higher. On both feet, the big toe stands out from the other toes, but only the big toe of the left foot is shining. So other people also thought the left foot was the one that mattered. He thinks it is because that foot is in the air. The right foot is resting on a step. Both are half-covered by the hem of her robe. The bronze has turned green, a scaly bronze mould, green with poisonous grey, even white, the rot of excavated copper, oxidation. But that is not the issue now. The issue is what would happen if she were to stand up.

And more than that, what if the ground were soft mud? Clay, loam, mire? The impression made by her feet would reflect her weight, her size. Her marks, her traces. *Vestigia pedis*, the tracks that hunters follow. Size, traces. The Buddha measured out existence by taking seven steps in each direction. Vishnu did the same in three steps: one for the earth, one for the in-between world, one for heaven. Or one for the rising sun, one for the sun at its zenith, one for the setting sun. The hunt for the divine. You can follow the footprints to the Gate of the Sun, and then they become invisible: the Godhead has no feet. But the traveler does not want to travel

Max II Monument, Munich, detail

that distance: it is not his world. He is not hunting, she is not a goddess. Her foot is here. The traveler is interested in movement; he moves through the world. That movement starts and ends with one foot. Not two. One. One foot always gets there first, one is always last, and that is how a step is taken.

And, he believes that this is why, of all that he can see of her, he has chosen her foot. That is where their relationship begins. The dream he dreamed last night, when everything was black and she was hiding in that blackness, continues. She stands up, with a great clashing of bronze. She puts down her book and it sounds like a bell ringing out at one in the morning. No bed he knows would be large enough to accommodate her; with the sound of thunder she would drop her robe, her veil, her sword onto the marble floor beside that nonexistent bed, the Neoclassical severity sliding from her face, her mask of justice disappearing, but her lust would be terrifying; she would crush him with her touch, shatter him with her caresses; she would cross her right foot and her left foot above him and the left one would be on top and the gleaming toe would catch the sunlight. Nothing would remain of him but a handful of scrap metal, iron, bronze, which would look like ashes, a powder, a memory.

Now, on every roof, he sees witnesses, figures, statues. They argue, wave, sway, demonstrate, perform. When did statues first stand alone? They inherited their independence from the Renaissance, the Baroque. The light is in his eyes, so he cannot see their faces, high up above on the edge of the roof, but they are not up there because of their faces. They are empty expressions of ostentation, armed with their attributes, their swords, staffs, laurel wreaths, horns of plenty, palm branches, books, scales, torches, lances—a nation of stone ciphers, symbolising nothing but abstractions, virtues, superhuman qualities, attitudes.

They are a regiment of slaves, platonic servants of ideas, each of them a specified number of meters from the next, actors that may never move from their spot. They nest up above, in a higher realm, the realm that the people waiting at the tram stop must long for, reach out for. This stone tribe occupies bridges, parks, the roofs of palaces and churches in their tens of thousands. Woe betide the world if they ever revolt, if they ever leave their balconies, obelisks, columns, parapets, triumphal arches, belvederes, graveyards, basilicas, parliaments, temples, monuments, a whole nation of Stone Guests out for revenge. The only appropriate musical accompaniment would be the last trump of Judgment Day. The sound of their terrible steps could not be endured.

Liebestraum, apocalypse. Everything is happening too quickly. The traveler steps back to take in the whole monument. His travel guide, a German who is as dry as paper, has made his own opinions very clear. Monuments should not be viewed hysterically. The traveler does not agree. Only the hysterical gaze can perceive the hidden meaning, the origin, what cannot be seen and yet is there. But the traveler is polite, always has been. He listens. "The monument," his guide says, "was built to honour Maximilian the Second, who also ordered this wide, magnificent avenue to be constructed, as well as the Maximilianeum, with its wonderful elevated position on the opposite riverbank." The four seated figures, including the traveler's bronze fantasy, depict the virtues of the ruler. The guide does not say which virtues; he assumes the traveler already knows. What are the virtues of a ruler? Wisdom, prudence, justice, strength? So which one is she? Justice, the guide thinks, but the traveler does not like that idea. Anyway, why does she have to represent something? Simply to honor that long-departed Bavarian king all the way up there on his pedestal?

First, the guide says, there are four putti, but they are a little on the large side for putti. A putto should have something of the suckling lamb about it, a suckling angel, one that has only just learned to fly, if it is even possible for them to fly, with those puny, usually rather idiotic wings on those chubby little babies' bodies. These putti are more like yearlings, heifers—what would you call angels of that age? And then there is that excessively tall pedestal with the larger-than-life king up there, with his robes all the way down to his heels to make him look even larger. Those Wittelsbachs had a pretty high opinion of themselves. Dukes, *Kurfürsten*, kings, they wove themselves into the history of this city from 1180 to 1918— it is impossible to imagine this place without their names. That is the guide's opinion. The traveler agrees. He sets a course for the river that was there even before the people and the dukes came along. He leans over the parapet and looks down into the rapidly flowing, clear water that comes from the Alps. The traveler always wants to find out how the past relates to his own present; he loves to know where he is, and without history we are nowhere. This applies not only to that list of royal names and their deeds but also to the ground he is walking on. Triassic, Tertiary, two hundred million years: he wants to know, needs to know. Otherwise he is not really there. We need a method for being somewhere we do not belong. A million years is one of the most outlandish measures that we apply to the empty contradiction of time, but still he uses that number in order to work out where he is.

All those millions of years ago, the Alps were pushed together, crumpled like a ball of paper ("They came into being," the guide says, preferring that formulation), the highest mountains consisting of hard limestone formations. History that no one was there to see, Tertiary sandstone, glacier walls, masses of rubble, scree. To the north of Munich, the stratum of stone becomes thinner; the groundwater penetrates the gravelly surface and forms bogs, which are called *Moose*. *Das Erdinger Moos*. *Das Dachauer Moos*. The language too, which came so much later, is all part of it. The river, which makes him slightly dizzy with its perpetual motion and constant murmur, dug, ground itself into the earth. It is continuing to do so even as he stands here watching; he can see it, the pebbles lying in its transparent bed. Later that day, in an antique shop, he stops to look at some maps, including the oldest street plan of the city, and he is surprised by the consistency of the rivers, by their strength. Everything changes: the settlement around the monastery (München, monks) becomes a village becomes a town becomes a city and blows up like a balloon, and the river continues to carve its way through the earth in the same place it always has and still makes the same sound it did when no one could hear it. How do you know that? That its sounds are the same when no one can hear them? He does not want to think too hard about that right now. He leans over the other parapet, and sees a modern, tarnished statue: a horse biting its rider, who is tumbling to his catastrophic fate with hands outspread.

The traveler can now choose between two directions. The river is the border, the wall. When he walks towards the Maximilianeum, it feels like leaving the city, which remains behind him, growling. The greenery along the water on the other side gives him a sense of being outside-the-walls, *extra muros*, so that is where he heads.

High above everything, a golden angel waves, but, still on the bridge, a new female form inserts itself between him and the panoramic view, someone else forcing him to stop in his tracks: Athene. What is she doing here? What does she want to say to him? Whom is she guarding, protecting? "Dating from 1906," the guide says, but that only makes it even more absurd. Someone dragged her out of her own time into this century, but what is the point of such brazen anachronism? What right does anyone have to bring an obsolete goddess into their city? Is it to prove that if she belongs with you, then you belong with her, that you are part of some everlasting antiquity, a new Athens? This statue too towers above him, full, Nibelung-like, luxuriant, a woman who might just burst into song. Just yesterday he saw a more relevant depiction of this goddess in the Antikens-ammlungen. In that version, her peplos hung straight, with verti-cal folds, and her face had a simple-minded, unworldly expression, a Buddha smile. There were two holes between her barely existent breasts ("her almost boy-like chest") for the missing Gorgon's head. The goddess on the bridge also wears a peplos with perfectly straight folds, but these are not hieratic; they flow over the voluptuous curve of a rounded stomach. It makes her less mysterious, more approach-able. There is something about this Athene that he likes, and he is afraid that once again it is the superhuman size, the exaggeration in stone. Is it because endless sets of stairs and skyscrapers make you smaller, while statues make you bigger, because they represent the platonic possibility that you yourself might be that size? Her right knee is slightly forward, but there is no way to touch it. Even so, you can imagine the possibility and that is probably the secret. He decides to leave her where she is and to walk on to the angel, standing so high up there that he or she is part of the airspace. The statue shim-mers above the trees like a golden flame. Everything is green where he is walking, although the first leaves are starting to change color. It is quiet too. Just an old lady with a long tuft of chamois hair in her green hunting hat, like a strange sort of Native American headdress. Dogs too, with their noses buried in the hidden scents of other dogs, zigzagging, sniffing out truffles of canine lust.

The way the light streams through the trees onto the ground makes him notice, perhaps for the first time, that beech trees have leaves on their feet; he sees the light shining through them. He hears the sound of a shovel hitting earth, with a pleasant regularity. He cannot see where this shovelling is happening, but hearing it means that he can still picture it somehow: the sharp metal edge slicing open the damp soil, a brief moment of silence, then a thud as the dug-up soil falls. It is a natural spectacle, this park, but a calming one. The sound of the river, the digging of something that could be a grave but is not, the footsteps of the few passers-by on the gravel, now and then a breath of wind in the leaves, the distant traffic muffled, smothered. *Herbst, herfst*, an autumnal harvest of thoughts. The traveler, we, you, he, has sat down on a bench, and is replaying what he has seen, his bronze beloved, *"errichtet von seinem Volke,"* erected by his people, the waving laurel wreaths, the biting horse, Athene. That was today. The Glyptothek, the propylaea, the Doric and Ionian facades belonged to yesterday, illusions of a Greece reborn, the nostalgia and the claim. The nostalgia is understandable, and he is also familiar with the notion of staking claims; appropriating a past to make the present more bearable is an option. The softness of Romanticism calls out for the severity of Neoclassicism. But here it is mixed with power, power and nostalgia, perhaps a Germanic variation on the theme. The past, once stripped of the blood and filth of history, tidied up and titivated, is a most desirable possession for rulers. If you give yourself a Greek past, if you build the constructions of another age, you distort the present. But if that is so, what about the Renaissance? That is the point: there is a difference between rebirth and appropri-ation. It is all just so much theatrical scenery: the old gods are already dead and can no longer harm your own. Erecting statues of impotent, obsolete gods, what can that mean? But he realizes that is not what is bothering him. After all, gods never die completely; they continue to make their presence felt, even if only because they are still visible and therefore convey something of their earlier selves, their effect, their origin, the luminosity of their deeds, so exemplary that they still have something to tell us about ourselves. No, it is the special relationship that the German language claims with that earlier world, made manifest in the grandiose reconstruction of König-splatz. Was it not true that the traveler himself thought the flavor of antiquity had been preserved and reborn nowhere better than in Hölderlin's German, that none of his other beloved languages was capable of the same achievement? Was he not himself a victim of that grammar-school culture, of the Germanic echoes in Boutens and Leopold? Of inverted word order, convoluted conjugations, purist orthography, such as the spelling of Plato's name as "Platoon," which meant that the American movie about Vietnam always made him think of the Greek philosopher instead of just a military unit?

All that is true, but German *was* the only living language the traveler knew that had retained the declensions that even Italian and Spanish, the descendants of Latin, had done away with. No, it was the claim staked by a new Athens, a presumption that was so sinister because it would culminate in Heidegger's claim that Western philosophy had foundered in nihilism, and that those first, hazy visions that the pre-Socratic philosophers had of the mysteries of Being had been overwhelmed by totalitarian technology, and that it was his, Heidegger's, calling to lead European culture back to that original mystery, and that the German language should play a decisive role in this *"anderer Anfang,"* this new, second beginning, because it had a unique relationship to the language of the *"erster Anfang,"* the first beginning, which was hidden in the mists of time.* It was only later that the traveler saw, like some missing piece of evidence, a photograph of one of the Ehrentempel, the two "temples of honor" that Hitler had had constructed on Königsplatz, in commemoration of his followers who had fallen during his march on the Feldherrnhalle.

---

* This is how the philosopher formulated his opinion: "I am thinking of the special relationship between the German language and the language and thinking of the Greeks. This is something that French people have repeatedly confirmed to me. When they start to think, they speak German. They assure me that they cannot succeed in their own language." Translated from an interview given by Heidegger ("Nur noch ein Gott kann uns retten"), published in the 31 May 1976 issue of *Der Spiegel*.

The Americans later blew up the Ehrentempel, and rightly so. In comparison, Ludwig I's Greek dream had been little more than nostalgia. Hitler's temples made his claim very clear. Those hard, square columns with their plain capitals might seem like touching echoes of a Doric past, but the temples represented the new age of fascism, which claimed a link to a civilization that it was in fact trying to destroy.

Now, as usual, the traveler is overcome by doubt. The golden angel stands at the end of the imitation woodland path, waving down from on high, and it seems as though he can hear the wind in her (this angel has to be a female) wings. The contradiction within himself has also become more turbulent. He might call the Königsplatz "grandiose," but he has to admit that when he walked around the moonlit square, like a figure in a watercolor from 1830, all that severity, now veiled in darkness, gave him some kind of extrasensory emotion, a sensation that briefly made him think he was somewhere else, not just a different place, but a different time. It was a feeling he remembered from reading Simon Vestdijk's *Aktaion onder de sterren* and *De verminkte Apollo*[*] when he was young and thinking that the writer must possess mysterious psychic gifts that allowed him to be in ancient Greece when he wrote: not merely *there*, but also *then*. The traveler had never experienced the same kind of sensation in front of the Palais Bourbon or at La Madeleine, and certainly not when reading the cut crystal of Corneille and Racine, and yet simply Hölderlin's lines: "*Blüht Ionien? Ist es die Zeit? Kehren die Kraniche wieder . . .* ,"[†] or however it went, still made him swoon with schoolboy delight. On the other hand—and now his internal debate took a less high-flown direction—was it not those same German-oriented classicists who had imposed their

[*] "Aktaion under the stars" and "The maimed Apollo."
[†] Is Ionia in flower? Is this the season? Are the cranes returning? (from "Der Archipelagus")

relentless "K" over his Catholic "C," so now there were not only idi-ots who said "Kikero," which made the philosopher sound like a particularly pretentious footballer, but also "*ekke homo*."

Suddenly he could see them in his mind's eye: the two monks who had taught him Greek and Latin over forty years ago. The Greek teacher had forever vanished behind his nickname and in the traveler's memories he was called only Pa, because of the way he used to sigh and say, "*Ach, kind,*" to everyone (it was true—once, in that unrecoverable past, the traveler had been a child), and always gasped in such a peculiar fashion that it was almost as though Homer's sculpted lines were written in the air in front of him, or as if an invisible Plato were feeding him his dialogues, like a special kind of pet. The Latin teacher had been Ludgerus Zeinstra, old, fat, white-haired, and always with ash on his habit. Admittedly, his Latin may have come with a Friesian accent, but it never had that spurious "K" of "Kaesar" and "Kikero," no matter if the Germans repeated "Kaiser" one hundred times. The traveler had never cared who was actually right, even now. The sensual-ity of Rome's seven hills would not permit the staccato of those harsh "K"s, that was all the traveler had to say on the matter, and the notion that Ludgerus Zeinstra might ever have been obliged to stand at the altar and say "*Ekke kalix sanguinis mei*" was anath-ema, nothing less. It was as unthinkable as the thought that he, the traveler, who once had been a soprano, surrounded by other sopranos, might ever have lent his high-pitched voice, created for innocence, to the words, "*Regina Koeli, laetare, alleluia.*" And so he brought his train of thoughts or what passed for thoughts to an end, because he had now arrived within the angel's territory, and his history ensured that, here too, he was not free to think what he wanted to think.

Beside him, the guide's murmuring started up again. It was not simply chatter, but sounded more like a litany. What he was

seeing was the crowning glory of Prinzregentenstraße, and everything was an allusion to something, as though postmodernism
had preceded modernism. The emptiness of such labels. He saw
peculiar leaps and feats: architecture based on old motifs, which
still had been new at the end of the previous century, and now, in
spite of all those Greek, Roman, Florentine references, undeni-
ably had a *fin de siècle* flavor. The eye would not be deceived. In
the same way, one day, regardless of the professed polyvalence of
styles, postmodern architecture would no longer look like something new, but would somehow reflect the era in which he had
lived. It was a kind of contamination. Of course, nothing existed
that did not involve borrowing, except in those days when there
was not yet anything to borrow, but now that he was walking
here, among all of these re-creations, that Corinthian column
again, more medallions, mosaics, pilasters, Florentine landscap-
ing, this repeated, cobbled-together *déjà-vu*, all those things
that individually he found "beautiful," a feeling of resentment
crept over him. But it *was* beautiful, there was no denying that,
and the idiotic thing was that it would become more and more
beautiful. Give it another century or so of snow, hail, föhn, Isar
mist and Alpine sun, and people who knew less and less, and this
architecture would appear inconceivably, immortally old, hark-
ing back to a dim and distant prehistory of mythological figures:
Bismarck, Kaiser Wilhelm I, Moltke. They might even join the
same incomprehensible ranks as those eight adorable caryatids which had to bear the weight of the column supporting the
golden angel, which was not an angel, but a Nike, a goddess of
victory from Olympia, a doppelgänger, borrowed from 400 B.C., a
winged woman who was supposed to embody peace, which then
was as far back in the past as the next war lay in the future, which
in that same future would be followed by another war, which for
him now was past. Confusing.

The sun smeared a brazen layer of gold on the broken sheen of the mosaic, and he never could resist gold—it was his color—just as he could not resist the immobile womenfolk of the caryatids. If they took one single step to the side, that whole edifice, with its twenty-three-meter-high column, would collapse, and that golden figure, which of course was once again much larger than he thought, would lie in pieces at his feet, dead, a fallen angel. That was quite enough of that, he thought, and so he sat down on a park bench, among Rilke's roses. The scent floated, literally all around him, the irresistible sensuality of a thousand sonnets. It seemed as though the archaic effect of the monuments was extending into everyday life. The tramp on the next bench, his bottle fallen over on the gravel, was not just any old tramp, but a vagabond from a fairy tale. He had kicked off his worn-out shoes and lay there with his bulging plastic bag, his sleep, his matted hair. Within the context of the clipped acacias and the classical laurels, he assumed an otherworldly allure; he was a man who might suddenly sit up and start reciting an endless poem about tournaments, star-crossed lovers and miracles. Now the traveler himself lay down and gazed up at the angel through his eyelashes. That was dangerous, because he could so easily be drawn up there, where anything might happen. This angel was a woman, after all, and that was strange. As far as gender is concerned, angels are usually neutral. He had once wondered what an angel's skeleton might look like, and if anatomy lessons might demonstrate how the joints of the wings fitted in with the rest of the angelic bones, but of course immortals do not have skeletons. Anything that must remain invisible for all eternity does not exist.

The woman up there was filled with momentum, and for the second time that day he felt the urge to rise up, to take off, in spite of the danger. You could see the wind tugging at her. She leapt over the Isar, raced into the city. Her speed made her golden dress cling to her stomach and her breasts, folding between her golden thighs, a woman dipped in sunlight. Which golden man visited her at night to couple with her in the air, as birds do? If he closed his eyes almost completely, he could transform the gold of her statue into long, piercing streaks, stars of near-blindness. The scent of roses, golden stars; before long he would be an unreadable poet from a one-Mark anthology, Richter von Engelstein (Munich, 1876–1899).

The guide shook his sleeve. There was more. They had work to do. They stood at the base of the column for a moment. The caryatids had not moved. "Peace, war, victory," mumbled the guide, pointing. "The blessings of culture." But, once again, the traveler did not look where he was told to look. As always, his attention was drawn by something that signified nothing: empty ornaments, rosettes, helmets without any heads inside, cuirasses without bodies, visors without eyes, the uniform of the Hero, but without a hero. Things around something, and that something was nothing. As though, with one click, he had shot back into his own time. That was as it should be. Now he would walk across the bridge, ignoring the stones that were supposed to represent the German peoples, and head into the city. There were other Munichs to see.

Second Intermezzo: Ancient Times

Some cities fulfil their obligations. They present the traveler with the image he has of them, even if that image is false. This traveler, who has left the Angel of Peace behind (he can still feel the golden flourish of her farewell on his back) and is now ambling through the green temptation of the Englischer Garten to Prinzregentenstraße, is sensitive to the martial element of the city around him. Field Marshals' Hall, Victory Gate, Hall of Fame, the cenotaph of Ludwig the Bavarian, with its black marble, described by the sculptor as a *"castrum doloris,"* a "castle of grief"— the military is never far away. It shimmers even in the clothing of the passers-by, their dramatic hats, their trophies of feathers and fur, their green loden coats. It is as though the wearers of these garments, perhaps precisely because they form a minority, are moving through the city with strategic goals, all on their own missions. A German friend has explained that this is traditional attire, not a uniform, but even so. These people appear to be clad in iron, laden with loden.

They are surrounded by the air of ancient times. Tally-ho, muffled shots in a dark forest, campfires at night, incomprehensible songs. The traveler has seen a photograph of Heidegger in traditional costume. He does not wish to draw any modish conclusions from this; after all, he has himself posed in the traditional costume of the burghers of Volendam, but he found that he looked comical rather than anything else. Heidegger, however, did not look comical. Was it possible to don some kind of uniform, because that is what it was, for thinking? And was this the same man who had written about boredom, angst and time, and who had dared to wrap strings of words around *das Nichts*, nothingness?

You see what you want to see, his friend had said, and that was precisely the point. It was hard to remove oneself from the equation, and before you even wanted to see something, memories of what you had seen before imposed themselves: other uniforms in these settings, still so familiar and recognizable, the marches, the demonstrations. And yet when he caught vague snatches of marching music from the direction of the Hofgarten, he quickened his pace. The traveler was ashamed to admit it, but military music had always excited him. He crossed a temporary bridge over a main road and came to a ruin. The music had stopped; a group of young soldiers was standing there, as still as could be. Words came wafting over to him: death and remembrance. They were about the war that refused to die, which would only disappear when the last person who had tasted it in his own mouth was himself dead. And not until then. He saw old men down there too, people who could never have been young, not the men of the wartime broadcasts, not the soldiers he had seen on the streets as a child following the same kind of regimental colors, yet different, and the same kind of banner, yet different. The eagle on this flag was silver, but the mysterious symbol had fallen from its claws. That symbol no longer existed. He felt his own age flowing together with that of the old men standing down there in a sort of square formation. He had more to do with those men than with the young soldiers, and that was strange. He could not catch the words, but he did not need to; he knew them anyway: honor, loyalty, sorrow, sacrifice, once, then. These men nurtured the past so they could have a present, and that past took the form of flowers, flags, blue-and-white ribbons. All of this was happening within an enclosure, beside an excavation, in front of a ruin—the fumbling of people who are tugging at time.

The traveler goes slowly down the steps and walks to the Hofgarten. This leads to an encounter. As he reaches the bottom of the stairs and enters the Hofgarten, the young soldiers are rounding the corner, as only soldiers do: rather than take a curve as normal people would, they turn at an angle of ninety degrees. And no, these are not the same uniforms, and yes, the man who is carrying the standard with the eagle, the sunlight reflecting on its silver, is tall and blond, and no, the orders are not yelled or barked, but almost spoken, and no, the music does not sound martial, but instead is played *en sourdine*, as Couperus would say—muffled, veiled—and no, there is no stamping of feet, because when the music stops, he watches the big, clodhopping shoes, still marching in time, treading almost tentatively upon the stone chippings of the path, and it sounds almost like a rhythmic rustling. He thinks himself back into his earlier life, almost fifty years ago now, soldiers marching in, more men, the uniforms a deeper, more fundamental grey. The men back then had helmets that almost covered their eyes, so that all expression vanished from their faces and they lost their individuality, exchanging it for an unbearable similarity in which each of them became the other.

And, thought the traveler, who could feel how time was at that very moment coloring his hair grey, pressing him down, ageing his bones and veiling his eyes until they became those of a man searching the horizon for the distance from whence he himself must have come, in the past those standards were held higher, there was brass, those mouths had sung something to a tune he would obviously never forget. These heads wore no helmets, they were almost *pueri imberbi*, or so it seemed to him, beardless boys. They had difficulty keeping in step and their uniforms belonged to some tiny, forgotten principality, the grey far too pale, and it felt as though choruses should have been sung, but no one was singing, only those rustling feet and the shy faces passing by, and the old man in front of him removing his hat and bowing to the banner. When the man straightened his back, the traveler felt a twinge in his own spine because the pain was clearly too much for that other back. And then it was over. He took a step back into the trimmed privet, the mutilated flowers and plants that were meant to express the national colors here in this spot, and let the old men pass, wrapped in their vague, untranslatable thoughts, and then he turned around. The angelus began to ring and he caught himself thinking a sentence in Latin. It seemed as though his life simply did not wish to move on to later things.

The traveler walked past the benches where people were sitting in the autumn sunshine, as if trying to stock up before the Alpine winter. They looked peaceful, absorbed in dreams or meditation, their eyes closed. Soon they would again become anonymous passers-by, but now, in their vulnerability, faces surrendered to the light, they were their own fragile selves, big-city dwellers in a garden, that regimented imitation of nature. As he turned away and started to walk towards the colonnade to look at the poems on the walls, an apparition came along that lent the new afternoon a different hue. Again it made him think about the past, where most of his points of reference were evidently anchored. But this man too came from a different era. He wore a white straw hat and pale clothes and had one of those dogs that consist mainly of hair. The two men greeted each other as though they were acquainted, or at least knew that they were of the same kind. "What nonsense," the old man said, and the traveler knew he was talking about the military ceremony.

Where do I know him from? the traveler wondered, immediately realizing that he did not know the man as a person, but as an idea, a type, a species, or however one might put it. Not a species, as in an extinct species. An actor perhaps. Boulevard theater, operetta, or—who knows?—maybe Schnitzler. Someone who had survived it all. Photographs appeared in his mind's eye, ones he must have seen in the past, during the war. They were in color; even back then the rose in the buttonhole of the white Palm Beach suit would have been red. He heard names too: Hans Moser, Heinz Rühmann . . . Moser's nasal voice, the strange Viennese accent. He had not replied to the man and there was no need to do so. Memories. Paul Steenbergen in a play by Anouilh, the great days of the Dutch stage, a world that now appeared to have fallen into the hands of talented children. The old man laughed, as though he knew what the traveler was thinking. His face was distinguished, joyful, ironic. They spoke a few sentences that someone had written for them, which signified nothing other than that they appreciated performing this semblance of a conversation. Then the other man removed his straw hat, gave it a little wave in the air, said "*Sehr verehrt*" or something similar, and turned, exactly in the middle of the wide path, just as a director would have instructed him to. There was no one else on the path. The dog followed him, and the traveler watched them go, as they steered a straight line over the shadows of the trees and the intervening pale patches, keeping midway between the expanses of grass on either side of the path. This man knew how he would look if someone was watching him from behind; he knew his *Platz*. He also knew he would spoil the effect of walking away if he looked around or chose one side of the path. What was it that moved the traveler so profoundly? An apparition from a vanished world? He thought about other old men he had known, one of whom had just died, the father of a friend, Jewish, cosmopolitan, as old as the century, from this very country, maybe even this very city, hounded out in the 1930s by those others whose memory still haunted this place. Maybe it was the sheer mass of the memories that moved him—all those notions that resided in names, parks, statues, triumphal arches, and which had also interfered with his own past, until it seemed as though you could not take a step anywhere on this continent, his own part of the world, without being presented with fragments, allusions, exhortations to mourning or contemplation.

The past as an occupation—it must be a disease. Normal people occupied themselves with the future or with the drifting ice floe they called life, that moving station that belonged nowhere, that was always on the move. He was standing on that floe and looking back. Everything in Europe was old, but here, at its center, the age seemed to have a different relative density. He was walking through a vanished kingdom, but that in itself did not summon any particular emotions—no, if he carried on walking to the east, that was where it really began, the shattered world of Musil, of the Austro-Hungarian Empire, all that debris, the fragments, the power become impotence, the closed world of Poland and Czechoslovakia, which seemed to have been torn away from this continent, and Serbia, Croatia, Slovenia, Trieste too, the gravitational pull of what had happened to those regions in this century, of what was still happening, the doubly lost worlds of Isaac Bashevis Singer and Vladimir Nabokov, of Kafka and Rilke, of Roth and Canetti. It seemed to him that this was a vantage point from where one might look deep into time and see just how much those remote areas had once belonged, how deep the wounds were. Retrieving them would mean descending deep into a mine. He did not have the same feeling in France, in Italy, or in his own country. Those places had enough past, but somehow it had transformed more or less organically into a present. Here, the transition was not complete. The past had become stuck, bogged down, coagulated, curdled, been torn away. But it was still there. Perhaps it was just waiting. The wind he felt on his face came from that direction, warm, scorching, as though it too had something to say. The old man had long disappeared. "What nonsense," he had said, and now that he had gone, in his light-hearted disguise, those words hung in the air, so much less innocent than when he had spoken them. What had happened here, in this city, that beginning, already over sixty years ago, could never be described as *Unsinn*, nonsense, unless you took the word literally, as non-sense, the negation of sense that had nothing to do with *Wahnsinn*, madness, even though that is how people often chose to refer to that era, because of the word's suggestion of insanity as an excuse. The lack of sense, then, once. That had been the end, an end that still continued and one which, if he was to believe his friends, was going to be turned around. But the servants of the past do not make good voyagers into the future, the traveler thought, and he set course for the towers of the Theatinerkirche, their color reminding him of the custard at boarding school, which the boys always said the kitchens made on the first of January, in one big batch for the whole year.

Boarding school, Augustinians, custard, food. Busy bustling beneath the matt glass dome of Restaurant Augustiner in Neuhauser Straße. The waitresses are dressed in traditional costume, low-cut, white, billowing blouses. They slip the bills into their bodices, between those Bavarian breasts. Embroidered aprons, red sashes, puffed sleeves, the chorus for *Die Csárdásfürstin*. The traveler appears to have no objection to women wearing traditional costume.

"*Karpfen im Bierteig, aus dunklem Bier und Kräutern, mit Butterkartoffeln. Rapunzelsalat mit Würfelkartoffeln. Fränkische*

Blut- und Leberwurst im Naturdarm. Fränkische Kartoffelsuppe mit Steinpilzen und Majoran, 1/4 Fränkischer Gansbraten mit handgeriebenem Kartoffelkloß, Blaukraut oder Selleriesalat, 3 Stück Reiberdatschi mit Apfelmus, gefüllte Dampfäpfel."

Peasant food in the big city—that is something that does not exist in his own country these days, but then there is very little actual country left in his country. The list of dishes sounded like an incantation of national peculiarities. Why was that so repellent, yet attractive? *Volkseigen*: peculiar to the people, the people's own—a word that might refer to scabies, but at the same time to tradition, preservation, conservatism in the sense of conservation, not throwing things away, allowing them to occupy a longer space within time, delaying the death of the familiar world. Why were some forms of preservation permitted (brown bears in Spain, goshawks and badgers in the Netherlands), while others (traditional costumes, languages, dances, food) were viewed with suspicion? Both types of preservation involved a dogged struggle against time, impotent last-ditch efforts. The suspect element was probably the trouble caused by the involvement of human affairs, or when the word *Blut* was invoked, together with its twin brother, *Boden*: blood and soil. It seemed to be impossible to think about such things without first working through what he called the "repertoire." The mind, that thinking and feeling authority, cannot get to work until its more or less automatic surface, where the repertoire is situated, is activated and satisfied. The repertoire contains the *idées reçues*, the things that everyone has to say about everything, a series of clichés that have to be worked through and dismissed before the real thinking begins.

He knew that he would not reach that stage that afternoon; there was too much to see, and seeing, because of the superficial categorization it involves, is all part of the repertoire. There was a young punk in the restaurant, stiff black Mohican above her innocent face:

a plump girl dressed as a gladiator. He noticed that she kept asking for more apple sauce, children's food. The waitress was kind to her, motherly. Categories, the limbo of what he called thinking. To see, that was why he was here. An older man in traditional costume, with a fat book and a font full of beer. If he kept looking for long enough, he would see them all, like a list of characters in a play: "Some Soldiers, the Priest, the Lady, an Aristocratic Family." He looked at the old man, who was absorbed in his book and who naturally reminded him of Heidegger again. Traditional costumes were perhaps no more than a mild form of anachronism: some people wearing something that other people no longer wore, even though everyone had worn it in the past. Heidegger had refused to accept time as a series of successive present moments, seeing it instead as a link, a connection between what had happened once, before, back then, and what would happen soon, later, sometime. The traveler, who had never felt really at home in the present because, by his very nature, he always saw it as colored and determined by a past, could identify with that thought. Even the past that did not belong to your own life made all kinds of demands on that life. That was inevitable, although most people seemed perfectly capable of living without any thoughts of the past, and entire countries were able, when it suited them, to forget their past with the greatest of ease. He never had a great deal to say about the future other than that, no matter how dark the past often appeared, there was no way he could ever be a pessimist. As far as he was concerned, humanity was a collection of mutants on their way to an invisible goal that might not even exist. The problem was that they were not moving towards this goal at the same speed. While one person was still locked in medieval fundamentalism, another was working away on a computer or travelling to Mars. There was no harm in that; it was the mixtures of the two situations that was so explosive, the instruments of one in the hands of another, the terrorist who wants to take his enemies with him when he commits suicide, because he thinks that will get him into some kind of heaven.

But was it true that he had never really felt at home in the present? That would be a romantic idea, but somewhat infantile. It was more that he did not feel at home among people who felt at home only in the present, who had such high expectations of it. If you were not able, at the same time, to detach yourself from it—which was perhaps paradoxical—you could not really experience it. The past was desiccated, everything superfluous had been stripped away; the same could not be said of the present. For the last time (and only because that man with his book and his traditional attire was sitting opposite him), the traveler thought about that photograph of Heidegger in his peculiar costume. Nietzsche had said that philosophy often had a physical cause, and the traveler wondered if the philosopher's body had felt comfortable in that traditional costume which, like the doctrine he devised, was so fixated on the past. Maybe that was going too far, but now, as he ordered an Oberberger Vulkanfelsen, he came back to blood and soil, because the wine was blood red, and that, combined with the name and its suggestion of volcanoes and rocks, made him feel as though he was drinking the earth. Seeing wine as blood—it had to be his Catholic background. And why had he chosen that wine in particular? Language reflects the psyche: after all, he could have gone for a Randersackerer Ewigleben '86, or a Rödelseer Schwanleite. The deconstruction of wine names—someone really should do a study. He looked at the ferns, the bronze busts, the baskets of dried Alpine flowers hanging from the ceiling. Deer antlers, house plants, ornamental shells. He was somewhere else. Around him he could hear the Bavarian variety of German, and for the first time he realized that German must have been the first foreign language he had heard.

Sixteen years before, in a white wooden country house in Maine, an old man, also white-haired, who looked like his friend's dead father and therefore also like the old man who had just greeted him in the park, had asked the traveler to read Rilke to him. That man had the same accent in English as his friend's father had in Dutch. A German accent, but more than German, an entire past in Mitteleuropa was contained within that accent, an ineradicable, thick, attractive accent; even his friend, who had been living in the Netherlands for so long, still had traces of it. That request back then, there in Maine, had taken him by surprise, not least because he was full of admiration for his host, who had won the Nobel Prize for a discovery in biochemistry. As soon as he heard that the traveler came from the Netherlands, the scientist had started to talk about Multatuli, ignoring the Americans who made up the rest of the party. The traveler had often met people over the age of eighty who would strike up a conversation about Multatuli or Couperus; the Netherlands had truly existed in the past. As for Rilke, his host had insisted. The traveler had protested that his German was not up to it, but the old man would not take no for an answer. Thanksgiving, November, Indian summer, the garden stretching down to Penobscot Bay, leaves aflame. The traveler had opened up the book, yellowing, falling apart, signs of homesickness on every page, and he had read. The Americans had been very quiet, and he could hear the fire crackling in the hearth, but he had not read for the others, only for that bowed white head, which was thinking about who knows what, something from fifty years ago, before he had been banished or fled, something *old*, and as he read, it was as though a bubble of old air burst open, like in the story by Mulisch, and his own voice mixed with that rare air, decanted for the first time:

Herr: es ist Zeit. Der Sommer war sehr groß.
Leg deinen Schatten auf die Sonnenuhren
Und auf den Fluren laß die Winde los.

Befiehl den letzten Früchten voll zu sein;
gib ihnen noch zwei südlichere Tage,

dränge sie zur Vollendung hin und jage
die letzte Süße in den schweren Wein

Wer jetzt kein Haus hat, baut sich keines mehr.
Wer jetzt allein ist, wird es lange bleiben,
Wird wachen, lesen, lange Briefe schreiben
Und wird in den Alleen hin und her
Unruhig wandern, wenn die Blätter treiben.*

He would have read more, that late afternoon, but as he read the last lines of that poem he had seen his host's lips moving along with his, and he had felt the same emotion that swept over him now, as though there was no fracture between that then and his now. The old man was dead, as was his friend's father, along with a few more of those men that life constantly seemed to place in his path, as though some strange sort of predestination was involved. They had all lived to over eighty. A cellist, a restorer of paintings, a banker. Survival had rippled around them like a second soul, not survival itself, because they were dead now, all five of them, but what they had survived, something that none of the five men had ever spoken to him about.

Wasn't this Munich? He had not come here to remember, but to look, but as he sat there so peacefully with his glass of volcano wine

---

* Lord: it is time. The summer was so large. / Lay your shadow on the
  sundials, / unleash your winds upon the fields.
  Command the last few fruits to ripen; / grant them two more balmy days,
  / urge them now unto perfection / press lingering sweetness into wine.
  He who has no home will now build none. / He who is alone will long be
  so, / will wait, and read, and write long letters / wandering to and fro
  along avenues, / restless, as leaves tumble all around.
  "Herbsttag" / "Autumn Day" by Rainer Maria Rilke

he found himself in the eye of a storm of memories. How strange it was. Time itself, that weightless thing, could only move in one direction, no matter how you defined it or tried to pin it down; that at least appeared to be certain. No one knew what time was, but even if you gave every clock in the world the shape of a circle, time would still keep on going in a straight line, and if that line had an end, humans could never imagine it without being overwhelmed by giddiness. So what were memories, then? Time left behind, which caught up with you later, or which you could pull back towards you, against the flow of time, doing the impossible. And not only your own memories, but other people's memories too. His friend's father, who had been a friend of Toller's, had once told him that he had been there during Toller's failed revolution in Munich, the city where the traveler was now, with all the accom-panying violence, shouting, death. Toller had gone into exile afterwards, first in London, then in New York. Once, in New York, the traveler's friend had pointed out the Mayflower Hotel to him: "That's where Toller committed suicide." But the supreme irony was that, long after Toller's death, his friend's father had gone to see a play about Toller in Amsterdam. The survivor went to watch an actor playing his dead friend, but that evening the theater was besieged by members of the "Actie Tomaat" movement—protesters yelling, tear gas, performance cancelled—and the old man had left the theater with tears in his eyes, the real revolution supplanted by an imitation. The traveler could still picture his friend's father now. Even well into his eighties, he had been a handsome man, someone you noticed, slightly stooped, dark eyes, the face of an elderly Native American, a white mane. He was often mentioned in Thomas Mann's diaries. "Dr. L. came to visit. We had some delicious spinach." "Yes," his son said, "but what did you talk about? It doesn't say."

When a memory fails to appear, it seems as though the time when it was created did not really exist, and maybe that is true.

Time itself is nothing; only the experience of it is something. When that dies, it assumes the form of a denial, the symbol of mortality, what you have already lost before you lose everything. When his friend had said something similar to his father, his response had been, "If you had to retain everything, you'd explode. There's simply not enough space for it all. Forgetting is like medicine; you have to take it at the right time."

At the right time. Time. As he headed outside, through the large dining room, he could not help laughing at himself. How on earth could you ponder a concept that had forced itself into the language in a thousand different ways, obfuscating any image that you might have of it? Time has always been confused with the instruments that are used to measure it. Always. In one of the Scandinavian languages, that word, "always," was expressed as "the whole time," as if you could really say that about something that was not yet complete. Human time, scientific time, Newton's time, which progressed uniformly and without reference to any external object; Einstein's time, which allowed itself to be bewitched by space. And then the time of those infinitesimally tiny particles, pulverized, immeasurable diminution. He looked at the other people moving so solidly around him on Neuhauser Straße, each with their own internal clock upon which the little clock on their wrist vainly attempted to impose its wretched order. Watches were idle boasters; they claimed to be speaking on behalf of an authority, but no one had ever seen that authority. But they could inform him when the church doors would open, and a few moments later (later—there was no avoiding that tyrant) he was standing in the cool space of the St Michaelskirche. One of the first words he read was, of course, *Uhr*, hour: "*Am 22.11.44 kurz nach 13.00 Uhr wurde die St Michaelskirche von mehreren Sprengbomben eines amerikanischen Fliegerverbandes getroffen*"—and at the thought of those American bombs hitting the church, more memories hit home, the drone of bombers flying overhead during the war to the adults' eager delight: "It's the Americans. They're going to bomb the blasted Krauts." That noise was part of the soundtrack of eternity, an accompaniment to death and vengeance, filling the entire sky with a continuous bass tone, made by a musician who was bent on destruction. But he did not want to think about that now. The dead were dead, the church had been rebuilt, and a woman was walking through the filtered light of the pale-grey space, heading straight for her goal. She was impeccably dressed. Everything she wore was black, and her fair hair was tied back in a chignon with a black velvet ribbon. She knelt down and buried her face in her hands. Her patent leather shoes did not touch the floor, but hovered just above it. At that moment, the sun disappeared, the plaster of the vaulted ceiling grew dull, and the traveler saw three Japanese people staring at the woman. At the back of the church, a bronze angel leaned on a large font, casually, like someone who walks past a piano and stops for a moment to play something on it. He could see praying figures everywhere, confirming the scale of the edifice, dwarven supplicants in red, in hunting green, a man in traditional costume, hand on his heart, saying something to a statue. The traveler walked back to the angel and stopped beside it, just two random churchgoers, a man and an angel, one with wings and one without. The angel was larger and its bronze gleamed, but that was beside the point. He looked at the spread fingers, and then at the wings. It was his second angel today, but this one was not a woman.

Angels were officially men. They had men's names—Lucifer, Gabriel, Michael—and yet they were not men. They were myriad, he had learnt, and they came in all varieties. Angels of darkness, of death, of light. Guardians, messengers. They had ranks: cherubim, seraphim, powers, thrones. Heavenly legions. He could not remember whether he had ever really believed in them, but he thought not. The idea was appealing though. Someone who did not

Michaelskirche, Munich

have to be a human, but still looked like one, who did not need to get old, and, moreover, who could fly. Of course, there were all sorts of things they were not allowed to do, which was only logical when you considered their proximity to God. What he liked was that they were still around, and not only in churches. Made of wood, stone, bronze, on monuments to the Dead and for Peace, on secular buildings; they had maintained their position everywhere. The Arabs had them too. Did people still see angels these days? Or had they become invisible, in spite of their superhuman scale and presence? He thought not, but maybe other people did not make a point of seeking them out, of consciously seeing them, as he did, but instead perceived them as something that appears in a dream, and so the winged ones could make their way to those secret, inner places where our nameless ancestors reside without the recipient of the dream ever noticing. That brought him back to the idea of time, but he really did not want to think about that subject anymore. He had promised himself one more church that day, a church that he felt had more to do with this actual city rather than the rebirth of a wounded Athens, inspired by false nostalgia, and that is where he meant to go next. That church was in Sendlinger Straße, but then his guide popped up again, trying to send him in another direction.

He snapped at the guide. "Where do you want me to go now?" The guide must have been hiding under the table when the traveler was eating, because he had forgotten all about him. Could this kind of guide hear every thought that passed through your mind?

"The Viktualienmarkt," the guide said.

Markets, along with churchyards, were the traveler's weak spot, so he changed his plans without complaint. Eating is perhaps the act that is furthest removed from evil. Radishes, carrots, cheese, bread, mushrooms, pumpkins, eggs evoke the idea of nature, and therefore calm and patience, in the middle of the city, reminding the city of its origins as the marketplace for a rural district. The traveler wandered among all of those piled-up wares for half an hour or more: fresh herbs, sausages exceeding the imagination in their absurd variety, silky bacon, fish from rivers and from lakes, things that had looked exactly the same a thousand years ago, a thousand-year empire of tubers, carp and onions, surrendering themselves time and again, without protest, to be crushed between the grindstones of human molars.

The street outside the church was busy, but once he was inside the noise fell away. "St John of Nepomuk," the guide whispered. A Bohemian saint. The traveler loved that word: Bohemia. Not only because it sounded so beautiful, but also because of all the misconceptions associated with it. The first Gypsies in France were seen as followers of Jan Hus, the Bohemian heretic, so some painters and poets were still referred to as Bohemians even now. A combination of prejudices based on a misconception—what could be better?

Poets being identified with vagabonds, Gypsies and heathens never did any harm.

"Nepomuk," the guide repeated. Once the most popular saint in Bavaria, after the Virgin Mary. A martyr's death, drowned in the Vltava, six hundred years ago. The traveler felt a little as though he came from Bohemia himself, and so he decided to adopt Nepomuk as his patron saint. Now the guide wanted to tell him all sorts of things about the saint's life, as it is carved on the wooden doors of the church porch, but the traveler was transported by the wondrous space around him. He would listen and read later, but not now. Now he wanted to be swept along by what he would once contemptuously have referred to as frills and furbelows. The Baroque, like opera, was a late discovery in his life; there had been a time when he could not understand what people saw in it, and even now he found it hard to put into words. There was no need for him to feel embarrassed about this failing; everyone makes mistakes. But this place? Maybe it was the sheer extravagance, combined with the contrast of the rigid framework in which this profusion was permitted. Luxuriant. Lush. And, what was perhaps the most difficult thing for an admirer of Romanesque churches to admit: *lively*. Even if you were alone, you had a sense of things going on all around you: angels jostling, clothes flapping, wind whipping around the stones, the marble, the gilded plaster, bustle, hustle, a cave in which faith and piety clung to every stalactite and stalagmite. Festoons, twisting pillars, lavish crypts, curving lines: maybe here he was looking into the soul of the Bavarian people for the very first time. The Athens of the Königsplatz was imposed from outside, dreamed up by other people, but here you could even yodel if you wanted to, because the building itself was doing something similar: trills, jubilation, crazy high notes. The Bohemian saint was also commemorated in the altarpiece, an eventful biography, in which the narrators had not headed straight for their goal. Carving, polishing, embellishing, adorning, interrupting—even though the altarpiece was perfectly still, it was full of life. In fact, it was as busy as a heavenly road junction. God in his crown leaned down over the cross, flanked by two angels with their wings pointing straight up like donkey's ears. No one else was around, so the traveler walked backwards away from the altar, looking up. He realized that when you tried to look directly up, past the pilasters, over the golden capitals, the garlands of flowers and the round-bellied pillars of the balustrade, and slowly moved your head sideways, more and more of those innocent babies' heads came into view. This was where they lived. When he moved, they moved too, gazing at him with inappropriately ecstatic expressions on their plaster faces, a look that was far too old and knowing. It was, he thought, as though the wall up there had started to foam and froth, and that froth had taken on human form. Out of nowhere, a line by Goethe, which he knew only from a Schubert-lied, popped into his head: "Was bedeutet die Bewegung?": "what does this movement mean?" And perhaps the answer here was that the movement meant only itself. It was the ultimate in reproducing motion in material that cannot move: movement and stasis, the solidification of supreme exuberance.

Does he know the city any better now? He is not sure, but decides that this is the moment to leave. And go where? To the south, following the birds that beckoned him this morning. To some Bohemia, to the mountains, the watershed of Europe, where the languages, the states, the rivers flow in every direction and his own continent feels dearest to him, with its chaos of lost kingdoms, conquered territories, conflicting languages, clashing systems, the contradiction of valleys and mountains, the old, fragmented Middle Kingdom. He walks through the grassy meadows of the Englischer Garten, sees the trees in the last fire of autumn, feeds the swans, lies in the grass and watches the clouds heading for the Alps. No, he does not know this city yet, but other cities are calling him now, and that call that no one else can hear, the secret singsong of the Bohemians, is one he cannot resist.

IX

Yet again I did not do as I had promised myself, because I drove northwards. My "third person" wanted to head off to all the Bohemias of this world, and I knew where to find them, even those in the past. But for me, it was now January, and 1990; I had to go to Regensburg and Nuremberg, not to Bohemia. There was already enough to think about. There was, there is. These are exciting days. I often hear the words, "We're living in historic times." I have caught myself doing it, not just saying those words, but also displaying the slight air of smugness that is attached to them, as though we have all suddenly become a little more important ourselves because we are no longer able to keep up with the pace of events. Everyone knows that Unity is coming, and yet we are all surprised on a daily basis about the speed with which it seems to be happening, as though these developments have a dynamic of their own that resists any attempts at control. What was unimaginable yesterday is suggested today and amended tomorrow, and what I am writing here will have become old news by the time it is published, just one tiny piece in a constantly spinning kaleidoscope. The ones who are perhaps keeping quietest about it all are the organizers and the entrepreneurs, who are busily working around the political palaver to stake their claims in the D.D.R., while at the same time keeping a close eye on the newspapers. And when you spread out those headlines like a pack of cards, you are baffled by the combination. All trumps! To the astonishment of his own party, the man called "Modrow ohne Land," Modrow Lackland, by the *SüddeutscheZeitung* one day, embraced German unity the next day, albeit with neutrality, only to claim, the day after that, that he had added the part about neutrality only for the sake of discussion. "Modrow surrenders," *Die Tageszeitung* announces, but then proceeds to wash away that news the next day with "NATO is looking for *Lebensraum* in the East." Meanwhile, West German politicians are swarming over the future new *Bundesländer* in order to secure the position of their parties. I do not know whether it is a consequence of all that turbulence and historical awareness that is still evidently in force, but events are conspiring to make it seem as though there is no longer a present: the fleeting moments of all those U-turns, negotiations, decisions and conflicts already appear to belong in a history book or to have been swallowed whole by a voracious future that will only be satisfied with more and more changes. Thatcher and Mitterrand might as well be living in Australasia and even the neighboring countries have disappeared in banks of fog. Only Gorbachev is still being watched on his lonely adventure, because everyone here, according to the old laws of *Gleichgewicht*, equilibrium, is well aware that the place he is still in charge of is the *other* focal point in Europe.

I am in Regensburg, on my way back from Munich to Berlin. With the new history still simmering in the pot, or maybe even burning, I search this country that I still do not know too well, trying to find relics of the past. After all, this collection of regions, which together were once called Germany and soon will be called Germany again, after a little adjustment, also intervened in my life fifty years ago, and the buildings and the cities I want to visit on this historic pilgrimage are the illustrations for the story I am reading. The "little adjustment" I am referring to involves the borders, of course, which have prompted so much discussion and so much silence. A map on the front page of the *Tageszeitung* depicts Germany in its entirety, with the eccentrically located Berlin suddenly looking very close to the eastern border.

"It could actually do with another chunk of land behind it," jokes the person who shows it to me. "A capital city should be closer to the middle, don't you think?" You can see where that middle might be on other maps, with dotted lines indicating the claims of a nostalgic minority.

The foreigner has a rather peculiar role these days for some enlightened groups of Germans: they want to know what he thinks about it, to measure their own agitation or aversion or angst against the foreigner's reaction, suspecting that, for historical reasons, he will somehow have a natural disinclination towards "dangerous developments." It is as though they are frightened of themselves and would like to see that fear confirmed by an outsider, but then again perhaps not. But it is hard to find the border manipulators and the Republikaner more dangerous than you actually find them, in spite of the historical reflex reaction and the nausea they provoke. In that respect, I liked a sentence I read in the *Frankfurter Allgemeine* (which was in fact about something else): "History shies away from repeating itself." Most of the people I speak to don't agree. It must be strange to be scared of your own compatriots, but it is not unusual here. That fear is sometimes accompanied by a sudden reverence for the D.D.R., as though "in spite of everything" a sort of utopia existed there, where things "may, admittedly, not have been right," but where life had "in a sense" been simpler, more human, not corrupted by greed, materialism, the flashiness of the Bundesrepublik. Seen from that point of view, the people who want to hand over the D.D.R. to a united Germany are of course traitors. But the people who say this are usually already in the Bundesrepublik, and what they, in their hypocrisy, do not realize is how much the others have had to pay over the past decades for their violated utopia.

Puns are always irritating, particularly when nature is involved, but of course it would have to be raining in Regensburg, the fortress of rain. It is a pleasant city, though, and resolutely old. I look at the gargoyles on the Dom, stretched-out monsters drooling rainwater from their maws, see the stones of the Roman fortress tower and, in a hidden side wall of the Dom, bulging like a hernia, the crude remains of an earlier, ancient church, irregular giant boulders hoisted up there by the Devil. I also find foods that the rest of Europe has forgotten: catfish from the Danube, roasted hearts, braised lungs. Even eating can be an ecological issue: I can never understand why the same progressive conservative who would give his life for the preservation of the twelve-toed Saxonian Ringworm Eagle would allow a certain McDonald's to remove the lungs from his plate.

In a bookshop, I spot something that looks like the Greek temple of Segesta, a mighty building on a deserted coast in Sicily. Here it stands among northern greenery, high above the Danube, and is called Walhalla. At first, I refuse to believe my eyes and then I decide I want to go there right away. Fred Strohmaier, the owner of the Atlantis Buchhandlung, offers to drive me there.

Walhalla seems more like Atlantis, but then the rain stops. The last part has to be walked and climbed; these heights will not allow themselves to be conquered easily. In the distance below, the low landscape gleams, with the towers of Regensburg, the river lying like a broad strip of flat iron, the marble of yet another royal dream, shining through the bare trees. The king and his architect—Hitler must have had similar thoughts when he stood with Speer at night, leaning over the drawing board. After the Glyptothek in Munich, this is the second building by those two gentlemen that I have visited this week.

It was 1807, and the king was not yet king. His father had sided with Napoleon in the Confederation of the Rhine. The emperor had conquered Prussia and whipped his way across Europe. Four kings and thirty princes were required to pay homage to him in Erfurt—the same Erfurt in the D.D.R. where Willy Brandt met Willi Stoph in 1970, so laying the first public brick for his policy of *Wandel durch Annäherung*, change through rapprochement, the *Ostpolitik* whose consequences have been so much more far-reaching than anyone could have envisaged, and also the same Erfurt where the old visionary was allowed to return this week to address his new, old party. German unity also shone through in the dreams of the Bavarian prince. This German temple had to be big, "not only colossal in terms of space. Greatness must also be in the design, extreme simplicity, combined with splendour." And who, given the lack of gods, was supposed to live in this Walhalla? "Walhalla's fellows should be of German tongue . . . laudable and distinguished Germans." And so, when I enter, in a state of awe, I encounter a noble company of faces turned to stone: a gaunt Kant, and a youthful, somewhat bloated-looking Goethe, who looks like a movie producer, all double chin and Gorgon locks. Row upon row, the white busts occupy Klenze's light and lofty space, staring with blind eyes at their shuffling descendants. In his mind, the royal founder had already annexed the Netherlands, because I encounter Boerhaave, William of Orange, Hugo Grotius and Maarten Harpertszoon Tromp in the company of Bach and Leibniz, of Mozart and Paracelsus, of remembered generals and forgotten *Kurfürsten*. Up at the very top float the faceless heroes and saints, their memory consisting solely of letters: Eginhard, Horsa, Marbod, Hengist, Teutelinde and Ulfila. I do not know who they

Walhalla,
Regensburg

are, but I can imagine the most wonderful musical accompaniment for them, made in Bayreuth. The king himself sits there, as relaxed as marble will allow, crowned with laurel, bare feet in sandals, his robes wrapped casually around him, a Roman senator flanked by winged lions. Lola Montez and the 1848 revolution forced him to give up the throne, but his Walhalla remained. Outside, 358 marble steps lead back down, and it is easy to see why Hitler did not like Walhalla: there was nowhere for a crowd of people to congregate, nowhere to make a dramatic entrance. You came to this marble tomb when you had done everything you had to do, not when you still had so much ahead of you. Once you were in Walhalla, there was no escape.

Walhalla,
Regensburg

Hitler went about things differently. I once saw some black-and-white films of the *Reichsparteitage* in Nuremberg, atavistic rituals already darkened by time. There is no need to describe them; they belong to our eternal sorrow. Of course, now that I am in this part of the world, I have to go there and, of course, once I am standing there I have the greatest difficulty picturing anything at all. Everyone else has already left—it is that kind of feeling. Empty places, the leader departed, vanished, but his image is still there if you call it to mind, along with the memory of his voice. One voice screaming, a voice with a name, and all those other nameless voices screaming back, an ancient chorus with a limited script. I am old, but I can still hear it. It is a sound that came from Bakelite radios; the adults

Goethe, Walhalla, Regensburg

turned it off, but it always went on playing somewhere else, the shouts fading away and swelling again, in an orgy of rhetoric. I did not understand it because I was a child, but it was associated with doom, and also excitement. Nothing remains of it on this rainy day. I am there alone, the others are dead, or old. A quarter of a million people used to gather in this place, a cathedral of light was built around them, and they were together, and that made them happier. Flags; cohorts, twelve men wide; banners; a cult designed to charm fate. I can imagine this empty field full again, populate the cracked, broken, dirty tribunes with the ghosts of the past, and wait with those others for that one man, that perfectly orchestrated moment, the ejaculation, the orgasm of the world-giant.

Nothing remains but the place itself, intended to demonstrate absence. It is a pitiful *genius loci* that occupies this site. I climb over a broken fence and make my way up the steps where they sat and stood. Beer cans, sodden copies of *Bild-Zeitung* like filthy old rags, covered in blood and snot as their ink runs. The Walter Mitty in me cannot resist climbing up to the tribune, to the dilapidated bronze door, on which someone has scratched "Nero," and then down the few steps to the small rostrum where he once stood. My audience, my people, consists of my beloved and two lorry drivers who are unhooking a trailer. They are pottering around on the wet tarmac and have forgotten to pay attention to me. Nothing else, just grey clouds, bare trees, the secrets of the soul, chimaeras.

Tribune, Nazi party rally grounds, Nuremberg

I return to the town center, to the real Middle Ages, recover from history within an older history. The churches lie at the heart of the city like boats that once sailed on a long-gone sea and are now stranded in a world that can no longer read their icons. Who nowadays knows the identity of the female figures in the portals of the Frauenkirche? The inwardly focused piety of those faces excludes them from the surrounding world; they have not heard the cries of the market traders for centuries. They have faces as we do, but they do something different with theirs. They are remote and self-absorbed, like female Buddhas, which is how the tumult of time has passed them by. Frauenkirche, Sebalduskirche, Lorentzkirche: over and over again that lofty Gothic space that draws my thoughts upwards to the ogival arches, the spandrels, the ribbed vaults, the keystones—all those elevated things that my body cannot reach because Newton has declared that it must remain down below. And against the pillars, beneath the arches, in the windows, in the niches, the stone nation of statues that lives alongside us, in parallel, not hearing us or seeing us, the stained-glass evangelists in their animal forms, bishops resting on their tombs, the panopticon of martyrdom and Judas kiss, of mythical creatures and crowned heads, tyrants and winged people: a language that speaks to itself because hardly anyone listens anymore.

I wonder what kind of heathen Glyptothek these images might reside in one day, and I receive my answer that same afternoon from the statues of saints and the tombstones in the Germanisches Museum. They stand there helplessly, deprived of their context, obsolete, art. I am back where I started, because the museum is showing an exhibition about *entartete Musik*. My brain does not wish to make that leap twice in one day—I can feel it baulking—but the earnest faces of the schoolchildren and students around me make me stay, and I look at them as they look at the evil in the world, at the wretched injustice. This is not something that can be shared: we must all look, read, process it on our own, and this happens in silence. Like me, they read that despicable letter from Wagner to Meyerbeer in which he offers himself as the other man's slave, and later, when he no longer needs him, his equally despicable anti-Semitic statements about that same Meyerbeer and about Mendelssohn in his essay "Das Judentum in der Musik," an essay that will stink for all eternity, along with the name of Wagner. No, it is not a happy experience. The photographs of Schönberg and Adorno, Weill and Eisler, the awful caricatures, the paranoid regulations, the obsessively bigoted mindset that believed it needed to destroy in order to survive. Nothing remains of it now, only sorrow, death, emptiness, division and, of course, row upon row of display cabinets. You stand in front of them in order to understand, but still you cannot grasp it. Why is evil so much more difficult to understand than goodness? How could the Strauss of the *Vier letzte Lieder* stand next to Hitler? Why did Wagner's notes become poisonous and discordant as soon as he wrote that grim nonsense? I do not know, and the girl standing beside me at the display cabinet does not know either; I can tell by the way she is standing. And I am certainly not in the mood for Rococo tableware, hoop skirts, suits of armor and dolls' houses. I drive to Bamberg, sleep in a hotel beside the fast-flowing river, listen to all those bells in the night, walk through the rain and the silence, watch the Kohls and the Modrows on television, and know that I have to return to the demanding present. I say farewell to the Bamberger Reiter, a serious young horseman looking into the twentieth century with a troubled expression, and head back to the D.D.R.

It is now possible to drive from Bamberg to Weimar on secondary roads; Coburg is the last major town before the border. I have checked to see if I am allowed to cross the border there, and according to the A.D.A.C., the German automobile club, it should not be a problem, but once I am there the border guards appear to object to the combination of a Dutch passport and residency in Berlin. They keep turning the piece of paper over, staring at me and then at my mug shot, without asking me any questions, but discussing at length with one another. For a moment, it seems as though the old days have returned, but then they let me through. After that, everything is different and everything is true. Now, for the first time, I am not driving along the Autobahn, but through the country itself, and it feels as though a veil of sadness has descended upon the car, almost as if it has a new windscreen that makes the world more faded and dilapidated. Does that even apply to the trees, great traveler? No, not to the trees, and yet, dear friend, there is something different about the roads and trees, houses and trees, a process by which those trees have surrendered a little of their immortal selves and taken on the color of their surroundings. Even in the forests? No, not in the forests. Snow, wet snow, panoramas, beauty, slate houses, few cars, Eisfeld, Saalfeld,

Rudolstadt, Kahle, industry, dirty smoke, peeling paint, crows in the fields, a world without color. It is winter, I tell myself; it will all look different with the sun shining, and in a few months the trees will be green again. But the people living here do not want to have to wait even those few months.

X

MARCH 9, 1990. WHERE I AM NOW, EVERY PLACE HAS
two names. "Oder," I say to the water in front of me, which looks so
blue today; "Odra," says the soldier on the other side of the bridge.
Neisse-Nysa, Lerida-Lleida, Mons-Bergen: the contradiction of
two words for one place, the mingled whispering of languages that
both want something different. Claims and bloody histories are
concealed within them, nostalgia and memories. Double naming,
double meaning, and always with some sense of longing or loath-
ing. I drove out of the city through the gloomy blocks of East Berlin, a light mist veiling the worst of it. The Autobahn to Szczecin,
exit at Finow, into the countryside: cobbled roads, nature, Kerkow,
Felchow, Schwedt, the border, the iron bridge. I follow a path down
to the river, and look at the village on the other side: Hohenkränig,
Krajnik Górny. Though I am a frequent traveler to the other side,
it is not possible this time; I am not permitted to travel on into the
East. There is no sign of movement in the Polish village, but on this
side a man is screaming out his fury at two others who look a little embarrassed at the scene he is making. There are two kinds of
writers: *voyeurs* and *auditeurs*. Armando, with whom I am making

this short journey, is an *auditeur*, and has the slightly stern, legal-istic aspect that the word suggests: I can see him making an inter-nal record of the conversation, of the fury at forty years of wasted time, the cursing, the gesticulating at the other side of the river. Odra-Nysa; a spoonful of tar can spoil a vat of honey. Jaruzelski said so this week. Viewed from the side, the bridge is a tall iron skeleton. Once there must have been ferries to transport all of those armies to the other side: French, Russian, German. Border rivers, bridges—in some places, the fate of countries takes visible form.

The weather changes, the leaden darkness above merging with the decay below. In Stralsund, the rain whips the paper faces of Modrow, Gysi, Kohl, the promises of a new Unity. The city seems deserted, but the hotels are full; we cannot even find anywhere to eat. Through the storm, we see churches, merchants' houses, an antiquated Lübeck, a city that was frozen in time just after the war. The power of belief: how was it possible to live surrounded by such obvious failure? At the Baltic Hotel, a helpful receptionist calls a seaside resort on the Baltic, on the island of Rügen. They have a room for us, but it is an hour's drive, it will cost almost 300 guilders, and we will have to pay in West Marks. When I say it's expensive, she replies, "You just wait. You'll see. All the important people have stayed there. Hon-ecker, Mielke . . . They practically had the place to themselves." She is right. The hotel is surrounded by a ring of Mercedes and B.M.W.s, and all of the doors display a threatening notice: *Nur für Hotelgäste*. An ordinary person cannot even get a drink here, but an entire con-ference of people would be able to dance in the dining room, where the prices are in East German money, which means the Mercedes are once again eating for free. The storm is now a hurricane, and I know the invisible sea must be out there somewhere. I see Kohl on televi-sion looking like some immense marsupial that could easily accom-modate the entire D.D.R. in its pouch, although lugging the country around might prove more difficult than he imagines.

Bridge over the River Oder. German–Polish border

When I wake up, I hear a woman's voice on the radio frantically asking, "But what's going to happen about abortion if we join up with the B.R.D. via Article 23?" "Well, that means abortion as we know it will become illegal here, in accordance with the West German constitution," says the man she is talking to. He goes on to list all of the other babies that will be thrown out with the bathwater: crèches, security, women's rights. Real, harsh, capitalist society is on its way, and she is just going to have to learn to live with it. There is almost a threat in his voice, and she finds that hard to take. "Yes, but . . ." she begins, and the dilemma and the ever-increasing speed of the changes are encapsulated in those two simple words. The metaphor of a train ploughing ahead, unstoppable, has frequently been used in recent weeks, but in fact there are two trains: there is also a slow train heading from East to West. The atmosphere of love and togetherness that reigned on the ninth of November has already evaporated. People from the East are saying that people from the West want to buy up their country at bargain-basement prices, while people from the West are saying that the East is a bottomless pit into which their hard Marks will disappear, after they have sweated so much to earn them. What is actually happening is of course extraordinary. Wilhelmine Germany races into the First World War, is bloodily defeated and mercilessly and short-sightedly punished. Then comes a brief opportunity for the oppressed working classes: Weimar, with its good intentions, chaos, inflation, scheming politicians and arrogant rejection of politics by so many intellectuals, the rise of fascism, Hitler, another war. And even though that first unity only came about under Bismarck, they had been one nation all that time, one people; it was only *afterwards* that they split apart. And then one became rich while the other became poor, one was helped and the other exploited, one was forced to carry the mental burden of the past, and the other the material burden, with all the mutual resentment that created. To what kind of music should these two peoples, who are almost one, but not quite, dance their duet? Beneath the loud, impulsive waltz of the new Unity, that other music still plays, so much more slowly, the music of forty years of separate lives, which no one can forget, not for money and not by decree, music that suggests different, incompatible dance steps, so that the moves of the superior dance instructor no longer look quite so masterful. History is a substance that is made of itself. If you turn away from the staccato of newspaper headlines and listen very carefully, you can hear the sound of large wheels grinding exceeding slow without letting a single grain of history escape.

Ostseebad Sellin, Ostseebad Binz. I look at Armando eagerly watching the death throes of the big villas, the Kurhaus amidst them like an old lady with no money left for make-up. "Dear Pensioners, Don't give the fearmongers a chance! Say yes! For freedom and prosperity!" shouts the C.D.U. in black, red and yellow. "Into the future with optimism: 44% for the S.P.D. on Sunday," the S.P.D. shouts back. We, the outsiders, drive through the storm in search of a mythical place in German art, the Königstuhl on the Stubbenkammer promontory on the island of Rügen, where, in 1818, Caspar David Friedrich painted his *Kreidefelsen auf Rügen* (Chalk cliffs on Rügen): three figures, two men and a woman, one sitting, one leaning, one on all fours, their backs to the viewer, with high chalk walls on the left and the right, looking out over the infinity of the sea. Goethe did something fiendish with that painting; he turned it upside down to create a gruesome ice cave with the three figures clinging like bats to the jagged vault. It makes me feel dizzy and I do not want to picture this scene upside down, because with Simone here, we are that group of three, and we can position ourselves in exactly the same way. I, of course, take the part of the curious fool leaning over the abyss; disapproving German voices call me back: you mustn't do that, it's not allowed. How should I explain? Should I say that the rail that is there now did not exist back then? Can't they see my tall hat beside me in the grass? No, they cannot, just as they cannot see the piercing eyes of my friend the painter, or my wife's red dress and those two white sails that, once upon a time, on that day in 1818, in that other Germany, made the sea so much larger.

And so we continue on our *Winterreise*: Danish and Swedish voices on the radio, lighthouses, black-tarred fishing boats upside down on the beach. Then, having wandered away from the others, I find myself standing at the end of a small road beside an iron gate with a red star. I cannot read the sign, but I do not need to. I already know what this is: it is a sentry box with a Russian soldier inside. The window of his shelter has blown away and now he has only a sheet of flapping plastic to protect him from the ice-cold wind. He is wearing a winter hat with another star on it, and he is looking at me. I can sense that we both want to say something, but then decide not to, watchman and wanderer, two foreign species in the territory of a third.

Leipzig, 13 March. A short piece in the *Leipziger Volkszeitung*: "HUNGARY: Soviet soldiers return home. The withdrawal of Soviet troops from Hungary started on Monday with the repatriation of

Election campaign, Rügen,
March 1990

a Motor Rifle Brigade." Some things keep coming back again and
again until they encounter their own echo. I have talked about this
before, but it is a notion that does not seem to want to leave my system. In 1956, I went to Budapest. It was more a coincidence, a desire
for adventure, than any sort of well-defined conviction: a photographer called to ask if I would go with him, as he had heard that there
was an uprising. I left Budapest a few days later, just ahead of the
Russian troops. I had smelled the scent of war and realized that I
was still familiar with the stench of burning. Candles in windows at
night: a wake for the dead. Hanged busts of Rákosi, of Stalin. I came
across this image again over thirty years later in György Konrád's
The Loser, encountering confirm-ation of reality in a novel—and it
proved that my memory was correct. Corpses lay in the streets and
people spat on them. Banknotes in their mouths, they were agents
of the secret police. Later I saw a photograph of their execution,
faces you do not want to describe, that split second as hands try
to ward off bullets. The world behind this world returned in Péter
Nádas's enigmatic novel *The End of a Family Story*, the Stalinist uni-
verse seen through the eyes of a child; betrayal and death woven
into an imagination that distorts the world of adults, mercilessly
exposing its unbearable truth.

They had to stay there, while I could go home. People had asked
when we would come, when we would help, and there was no answer
to that question, because you could not utter the only answer that
there was. We would never come. I wrote my first piece, probably a
bad one, for a newspaper. It ended with the sentence, "Russians, go
home." I had been given a lesson in violence and shame. Other than
East Berlin, I have never visited an Eastern Bloc country since then;
it was impossible for me. When I returned to the Netherlands, the
mood was one of hysteria. The very fabric of The Truth was under
attack, that kind of thing. The PEN Club, which I had just joined,
debated the idea of expelling Communist members. That seemed

to be the same thing I had just experienced, but on a small scale, and I was against it. When it happened anyway, I left the PEN Club. The Mitteleuropa I had just returned from began to turn to stone, and that stone did not shatter until recently. In the coming decades, that era will be documented—the indignities, the nonsense, the betrayal, the pettiness, the fear, the pride. But nowhere will it be captured so tragically, so cynically, so ironically, so solemnly, so hilariously as in the novels of Konrád, Hein, Moníková, Kundera, Nádas, and their ilk. Scores will be settled, as happens after every war, and profiteers and hangers-on exposed. The shining founder of the new party is the Stasi informant of yesterday; those who stay will attack those who left, and vice versa. The television pictures of the congress of the East German Writers' Union offered a foretaste: disoriented former people of privilege watching their houses and subsidies and boltholes by the water disappear, without any idea of what was going to happen next, and gazing with envy at those whose talent or political courage had already won them a place in the West. Each of those East European communities is small enough for everyone to know everything about everyone else, but once the dust has settled, alongside the world of files, photographs, minutes, reports, another world will exist, the so much more apocryphal but also more accessible world of letters, diaries, memoirs, poems, the truth of fiction, that last refuge of the subversive imagination, of resistance.

In Leipzig, the sun is shining. I walk around the Marktplatz in front of the old town hall, read the golden letters listing the grand titles of Goethe's duke, breathe the hazy, all-pervasive smell of brown coal and try to think about the past, but find that there is too much present. Are my memories correct? I am no longer sure. I can still see the face of a girl in Budapest, very intense, asking me when we will come. She is not the only one. What does that mean, "we"? Pincer movement: I remember that expression. The Russian tank divisions performed a pincer movement, closing their pincers on the main road to Vienna. Was it the tank divisions? What I should have seen was invisible to me at the time; I am reading it only now, courtesy of Konrád. Pre-war Hungarian Communism, collaboration, Hungarians on the Eastern front, defections to the partisans, the horror of Communist mutual surveillance—even back then, during the war, still ongoing in Russia—torture, executions, the return of the survivors, the power, Stalinism, more torture, more executions. All of that was already going on before those few days when I found myself walking among the burned-out cars, the shoot-outs, the people hunting down traitors. What makes Konrád's book so unusual is not the litany of human cruelty and stupidity, but the studied nonchalance, the *tone*, which suggests that it is possible to survive anything. Torture and cynicism, the apparently unfathomable depths of evil, are described so vividly that I often have to stop reading, and sit there helplessly, a little foolishly, with my hand over my mouth, because it is unbearable. And yet, by some kind of Manichaean magic, something like hope shines through that panorama of horror, as though someone were smiling throughout, and there is healing in that smile. So now I understand what kind of world I was blindly wandering through back in 1956, where it came from, what was yet to come. The end of that era brings a sense of joy to which an outsider like me has no right, but I feel it just the same.

In the Marktplatz around me are other people who have more reason than I to be thinking about their past. After my return home, I still had choice, freedom. There were conflicts of opinions, the Cold War, people who continued to condone the system, friends who, for whatever reason, expected everything to turn out well, disappointed expectations in Cambodia and Vietnam. We were free thinkers, and literally so, because whatever we thought, we were still free. It all seems so far away now, those embittered ballets of right and left on the Dutch stage, but here, in this marketplace, they still continue and, for the first time, the performance is at full volume. Large circles gather around small groups who are debating about Sunday's elections, about Gysi and the S.E.D.'s gold, about Böhme, Schnur, Modrow, about traitors and bloodsuckers, about intellectuals who think they know it all, about *Stasis* and *Bundis*, about the Bundesrepublik and how it is waltzing all over them, about money and rents and unemployment. They hold forth among the posters of Kohl and Brandt and Schmidt, the kiosks of Western newspapers; they get excited and shout as though making up for all those years of silence. The circle round them mutters approval, and disapproval.

Who were they yesterday? What novels, libretti, diaries stand beside me? The streets of Leipzig are busy, even cheerful. Paint is peeling off the houses, antiquated trams squeal along the rails, large groups of travelers stride through the enormous station on their way to a trade fair. Who are the judges, the informers, the people of last year? The question applies both to this country and to the other one. Where is the judge to whom Václav Havel made his concluding statement, ending with the words, "That is also why I trust I shall not be convicted groundlessly yet again," whereupon she once again sentenced him to however many months? What does she think when she sees him on television with Bush or Gorbachev? Where are the officials who often decided not to hand over the letters his wife wrote to him (". . . because, as I have been informed, you went beyond the scope of family matters and sent me various greetings") when he was in prison from 1979 to 1983? Where are "the young men in the car in front of the house" in the latest, as yet unpublished, story by Christa Wolf? Did they see her reading that story on television? This is a reversal of fortunes of the kind that belongs in fairy tales or seventeenth-century comedies: frogs as princes, prisoners as kings, stokers as ministers, hangmen scared, judges accused. And fairy stories are grim tales: it can be fatal to

"Wailing Wall,"
Leipzig, March 1990

end up on the wrong side. But the time for the great unmasking has not yet arrived, and maybe people do not want it to; they have other things to do.

Few novels succeed in fictionalizing reality in such a way that you are certain you have met the protagonists before, or that you might just bump into them tomorrow. One such character is Orten, from Libuše Moníková's novel *The Facade*. Orten, a painter, undertakes an insane journey with his friends through the Soviet Union, heading for Japan, which seems to retreat as they move closer. Laughing at misfortune would appear to be a Czech character trait, as their journey becomes one huge, enforced delay and everything that can go wrong does go wrong, but the picture that Moníková paints of Czech–Russian relations, of absurd enclaves of Russian scientists in Siberia, the extraordinary nonsense of the system, is something I cannot get out of my head, so much so that I wish Orten were here to tell me what is really going on in Prague these days, as only a fictional character from an exemplary book can—such as Cervantes' *Novelas ejemplares*—so constructing a truth out of the semblance of reality that is the world.

Clichés involve things that everyone notices, but which still need to be said. "It feels like the war just ended," Armando said on Saturday, and it feels like that here too. It is not just the peeling paint, the antiquated cars, the bad roads; it must be something else, as if, even though the grass is green and the roof tiles are red, everything has been photographed in black and white, as though this world does not entirely want to become *now*, the present. And there is that slight sense of nostalgia that some people seem to feel, those who would rather things stayed as they were. It is perhaps what Günter Grass means when he says that people here live more slowly, and that is exactly what Monika Maron resists, just as she resists the dreams that Stefan Heym still wishes to salvage from the nightmare of the past. I have caught myself thinking the same way too, but it is impossible. On Sunday, the people will make their own decision about what is possible next Sunday. "*Die Stunde der Wahrheit naht*," says *Der Sachsenspiegel*. They are right: the hour of truth *is* approaching. It is too early, but still I head to the Nachttanzcafé at the Hotel Astoria for a coffee. It is only ten in the morning, but those ancient times are here again: men in white dinner jackets playing ballroom music, swishing percussion, sweet violins. I become my own dead father and sit down on the plush seats. Huge chairs arranged in regiments, nooks, clusters, velvet-covered bar stools, '50s-style, the Volksrepublik version, a backdrop of swirling, bulbous plastic, wall lights in colored frosted glass, rectangular, yellow, blood red. A sanctuary, a trolley of *Kuchen*, a willowy blonde, a life of privilege. I read *Die Geschichte ist offen*: Volker Braun, Günter de Bruyn, Sarah Kirsch, Monika Maron, Günter Kunert. Voices, dissenting opinions. I am hooked by Maron's beautiful autobiographical piece, which, more

successfully than anything else I have recently read, presents a picture, with such clarity and compassion, of what has happened to
people in this century in Germany: Jewish grandfather, Catholic
grandmother, Communists, deportation, neighbors who are Nazi
sympathizers, but still help them, a mother who, in spite of everything, clings to the old Communist beliefs, the rift, some who go
to the West and others who stay in the East, the grandfather who
never comes back, reconciliation, seeing lost relatives again, fate,
history that is its own explanation.

Outside, the sun denies the past. I walk through the city to the
Thomaskirche. Bach is buried there, Mozart played there, and so
did Schumann. Mendelssohn performed the *Matthäus Passion*
there for the first time since Bach's death. A photograph of Wilhelm Pieck, Walter Ulbricht and Dmitri Shostakovich at Bach's
grave. And that too prompts a memory: Ulbricht in 1963, with
Khrushchev, at the S.E.D. party congress. Snow at the border, men
with dogs, a blizzard on the squares where I saw the uprising last
year. In front of the congress building, old women working away
at red carpets as though they want to lick them clean. That high,
thin, Saxon voice, the hundreds of people, their applause. That
church has been dissolved; this one is still standing. Anyone who
promises to accommodate not only the living, but also the dead,
will himself have a longer life. The space is high and cool. I look at
the stern clerical faces of the eighteenth-century *Superintendenten*,
men in pious black, their heads served up on white ruffs. Someone
is playing the organ, a form of eternity. Then someone else speaks,
and eternity crumbles. I walk past political posters of Women and
Greens to the book fair, where publishers from the West are busy
staking their claims. On the stairs, photographs of Christa Wolf,
Christoph Hein, Helga Königsdorf, Stefan Heym, Walter Janka,
and I think about Janka's trial, the betrayal of Johannes Becher
and Anna Seghers, his seven years in prison and his book about

it, *Schwierigkeiten mit der Wahrheit* (Difficulties with the truth), and then about Hein's plea to fill the gaps in the past with the truth about those years. *Autoren als Vordenker und Wegbereiter des revolutionären Aufbruchs*, declare the large letters beside the photographs: "Authors as prophets and pioneers of the revolutionary awakening." Is that really true? Or was it in fact what they had written at home, alone, without the crowd, that later, someday, would explain why those equally lonely members of that crowd, why the abstraction that is called "the people," had gone out onto the streets of this city to do some writing of their own?

Berlin, Alexanderplatz, 16 March. Gysi is speaking. I saw him working his way through the crowd surrounded by a swirl of photographers. He is much smaller than I imagined, and his cap does not help. What is it that makes him so appealing? It must be his courage; what intelligent person would wish to inherit the burden of such bankruptcy? They are all waiting to see him and the crowd is growing by the minute. They are young, carrying flags, and they fill the large square all the way into the distance. The little man is lifted up onto a truck and I see those morello eyes flashing behind his small glasses. *Und doch wird dieser schlaue Judenjunge es nicht schaffen*, I heard someone say in West Berlin: And still the clever Jewish boy isn't going to make it. That was at the beginning, but even then I already liked him. Too bad about the party he belongs to, though. On the other hand, a politician who puts you in a good mood when you see him—how often does that happen nowadays? "So do you agree with him?" someone asks me. "Hardly, but he's got a good sense of humor," I say, and that does not go down too well. So I add, "You know he's received all sorts of fantastic offers from big law firms in the West." That improves the atmosphere a little. A person who refuses money on principle is always somewhat sacrosanct. It means that he is serious.

The crowd is patient, still growing. So it looks as though he is going to win more votes than the 5 percent of the unions. One speaker after another, last but one is Janka, who did not lose his faith when he was in prison. Then comes Gysi. It is dark, the tall buildings have shed their irrepressible ugliness and are casting a circle of light around us. He speaks about the mistakes that have been made, the renewal of the party, which is far from complete, about what, in spite of everything, has been achieved over the past forty years, about the reparations that the East has been obliged to pay, but the West has not, about property and rent control, about the certainties that will disappear. I look at the faces around me. They are listening, all seriousness. He does not shout, barely argues, employs no demagogic tactics, neither does he suggest how the problems might be solved. Here is someone who is talking against the flow of history, but that does not mean that he represents nothing.

Two days later, I see him again. The cards have been reshuffled. The C.D.U. has waltzed all over the country. The socialists, led by Ibrahim Böhme, only achieved half of that 44 percent; his eyes are sad. Around midnight, I head east again. It is quiet at Checkpoint Charlie. I do not know exactly what I was expecting, but it is not

Elections,
S-Bahnhof
Alexanderplatz,
East Berlin,
March 1990

Marx, wall relief, East Berlin

here. There is a sort of party going on at the former head-quarters of the Central Committee. People are walking in small groups around the large squares, while at the Palast der Republik the television companies from the West are starting to pack up their things. I walk past a wall that says *nein nein nein nein*, and then past a bronze plaque with a very large head of Marx and lots of little men whirling past beneath him. Walking back along Friedrichstraße, I hear some noise coming from a building. I open the door and find myself among the heroic pioneers, the small parties of the big demonstrations, the forerunners who were abandoned by the voters. A large group is standing around someone I cannot see. When I climb up onto a chair, I realize that it is Gysi. "Where were you last year?" someone yells at him, drunk and aggressive. Before he can reply, someone else has climbed onto the podium and says that Gysi defended him four years ago. He is followed by a student who wants to stand up for Gysi because he heard him years ago saying things that no one else dared to say. I wonder why he is still here, why he has not gone to bed. What does he still have to say to this handful of people after an election night like this? But then, through the greyness of exhaustion, I catch that flash of laughter in those cherry eyes again, and I know that this man, together with Modrow and his rasping seriousness, can still provide a decent opposition, and not only in this Germany. The debate continues, machines that you cannot switch off. At Checkpoint Charlie I am the only one going through. I have those neon lights, guards, corridors, doors, the whole labyrinthine route all to myself. *Neue Zeit*, it still says in those old-fashioned letters on the wall high above me, but that too will have gone within a year.

March 24, 1990

XI

IN 1810, MADAME DE STAËL LAMENTED THE LACK OF Gothic buildings in Berlin, feeling that the city was not old enough: "*. . . on n'y voit rien qui retrace les temps antérieurs.*" That cannot be said now; over the past two hundred years, particularly the last fifty, so much history has been made in this place that the very air seems saturated with it. I am not only talking about what has been built, but also about what has disappeared: the power of empty spaces, the force of attraction exerted by vanished squares, ministries, *Führerbunker*, torture cellars, the no-man's land around the Wall, the deadly sandbank between the two barriers that was called the *Todesstreifen*, the death strip—all of those places where people and memories have been sucked away. Berlin is the city of the negative space, the space where something is not, the bombed-out-of-existence, the closed-off, the mysteriously forbidden. The symbol of this is the bullet holes that you see so often, small indentations, places where stone or brick should be, but where they are conspicuous by their absence, just as people are absent from closed metro stations. You pass through those stations and find yourself in a realm of ghosts, a world where everyone has fled or died of the plague.

The platforms are empty, eerily illuminated; even from inside the train you can sense the breathtaking silence that fills those spaces. You know that if you were to step off the train, you would instantly be transformed into an ancient man, someone with a newspaper from 1943 in his bag. "Old" buildings, like the Reichstag or the Pergamon Museum, look a little strange, as if they ran aground on a submerged rock back in some distant past, as if they have difficulty remembering their past or their function.

These thoughts come to me at Schloss Bellevue, as I am waiting for Richard von Weizsäcker to introduce his guest, Wolfgang Hildesheimer, who is about to give a reading. I have found a place at the back of the room, so as to have a better view. This is not my country, so I recognize hardly anyone. It simply remains a rather large company of abstract ladies and gentlemen who somehow seem suited to the refurbished anonymity of the room. One man is wearing a few absurdly large sculpted rings, and that is as far as the extravagance goes. I see Stefan Heym, perched like a bad-tempered old heron in the front row. Only recently he spoke out about the West German *Freibeuterstaat* (pirate state) and now he is here, chatting away with the white-haired president. In this week's *Die Zeit*, Marion Gräfin Dönhoff writes about von Weizsäcker, about his dignity, his authority. While Hildesheimer reads, I use the opportunity to drape a silver wig over the president's head and give him the uniform of a privy chamberlain at the court of Sanssouci. His stateliness remains intact; it is the aristocracy of an earlier Germany, something from the age in which Hildesheimer's story is set, the fake biography of an English aristocrat who goes to visit Goethe in Weimar. I listen to the invented dialogue, which, having read Eckermann's *Conversations with Goethe*, seems entirely authentic, and at the same time I reflect upon the constancy of bodies. The president's body looks solid, yet fragile; I have difficulty imagining that this is the same body his soul inhabited when, together, they found themselves outside Leningrad in 1943. Not that I know exactly what his soul is, but I think it must be what I see shining in those cool, bright eyes when I am standing beside him later. Constancy: I can find no better word for it. What I mean is the body as the bearer of memory, experience, the way it has lived in one single uninterrupted line, incorporating memories of the war, of his regiment, nineteen officers of which were put to death after the attempt on Hitler's life, while the majority of soldiers in the regiment were killed in action, until here it stands, in a room that was destroyed back then, a glass of champagne in hand, smiling, talking, listening.

Only later do I realize that this meeting had another purpose and that a number of the faces I vaguely recognized belonged to politicians from the D.D.R., with whom informal discussions had taken place before the start of the reading. I do not see Modrow until I reach the exit; he is almost hidden among a jogging cohort of bodyguards. It feels as though a chill runs through the room, not because of the man, but because of the event. He is still *Ministerpräsident*, and I see it all as a rapid series of film-like images: the twelve men surrounding him, the awkward trot they seem to be forcing him into, his forlorn expression, as though he also feels that he is being made to run too quickly, the step I have to take to clear the exit, the three black, gleaming, elongated cars that are waiting a short distance away, the slamming of the heavy doors, the lights disappearing down the driveway, the lack of reality, the silence. This man will govern the D.D.R. for one more week, after which the same fate probably awaits him as Suarez in Spain, even though there is no king here to make Modrow a duke. Exit Modrow, but without the Elizabethan glamour of the true royal drama. He is present, and yet already gone, along with his Byzantine curiosity cabinet of politicians from all points of the compass and eight ministers without portfolio. And no, it was not a farce. This bizarre court with its rectangular round table spent five months squaring the circle, all that time wandering through the mud of history and carrying in its arms a real country, which, finally, at the request of the people, it deposited on the steps of the Bundesrepublik, with a piggybank beside it. Von Weizsäcker, Modrow: two parallel German lives that have barely anything to do with each other except for this one remarkable moment when their paths intersect. They have both made the long march through the institutions of their estranged twin states, and now the scriptwriter has written Modrow out of the next episode, but the show goes on.

The cars have disappeared into the distance and behind me in the hallway, I hear a voice asking, "Were they all Stasi?" and another voice answering, "No, there were six of our lot too. They're working together these days."

Conversations: words you pull out of the air and, just as you sometimes hear a few notes and immediately know which tune they are from, you can instantly place them within a greater whole, because they are key phrases: Stasi, one-to-one, Poland, this side, that side. An old man in a bar in Ost: "If they think they're going to shaft us with one-to-two, blood's going to flow. You mark my words. They've been buggering us about for so many years, but it's not going to happen again, whatever happens with that de Maizière and all that mess. Honecker's harmless in comparison. We'll take to the streets, and I'm telling you, it won't be with candles this time. You can be sure of that."

In West, in Kantstraße: "I wish they'd just clear off, the bloody Poles. They're all over the place, and they're buying everything up, and you know it's all cheaper for them because they don't have to pay sales tax. You should see them! So much stuff, videos, radios, televisions, and then they go back home and they sell it there and make a packet, but all they do here is piss in doorways."

"But it's good for the shop-keepers."

"Yes, I'm sure it is, but I can't do anything, go anywhere. I have to queue for a bloody hour in my own local supermarket! That lot buy enough for an entire village. You should see them lugging it all back."

In front of the Stasi build-ing, on Normannenstraße. I stand there, gazing at it from across the street. It is quiet, the morning after Easter, and the building basks in the sun, large and evil. A passer-by on the other side of the street laughs and calls out, "They got

Dream exchange rate, East Germany, May 1990

something of yours in there too?" No, they do not have anything of mine. Because the street is so quiet, I can imagine how it was: betrayal in the form of sound, voices distorted by the telephone, accusations, whispers about the neighbor, the doctor, the pastor, the rattling of the telex, the quiet machine guns of the typewriters, the hum of the computers, the words of an observer echoing in a room. The Stasi had more people in its service than the army and it cast its net even into the most distant villages. Anyone could spy on any-one, every word could be taken in someone else's mouth and car-ried until it arrived here, in this building, where it was transformed into a file, into a report, into a weapon that would remain loaded even after everything had changed, a weapon that, because you had been used or allowed yourself to be used, could now be used against you. What did your father say? What did the teacher say? What did the student say? What did that colleague in your department say? Words, allegations, sentences, true or false, wrapping themselves around people, slowly pulling them into this building, fabricating meanings, determining positions. And where did she go next? How long does she usually stay there? Who does she meet? Hundreds and thousands of people were involved; if you heard all of the voices at the same time, it would sound like a hurricane, but that is the point: betrayal does not sound like that; it sounds like silence, a thousandfold silence, an eerie, chilling murmur of names and dates solidifying to form ever-expanding archives.

I have seen so many faces this week: Böhme, Schnur, Hirsch, faces that are not guilty, maybe guilty, guilty, of manipulation, revenge, lies, maybe another file, a fine dust that gets into everything, the dust of doubt, betrayal, double betrayal. The photo of Schnur was the worst: the giant figure of Kohl standing on a balcony in Dresden or Leipzig while, down below, the people must be calling "Helmut! Helmut!" but the people cannot be seen in the photograph, and the mass of Kohl's body is outlined against the sky, an implacable silhouette. A few meters behind him is Schnur, also seen from behind. He is standing some distance away from Kohl, the dutiful servant, and that is precisely what he looks like, caught in the act, hands clasped tightly behind his back. He knows that Kohl already knows and that soon everyone will know—the end, the disgrace. And what about Hirsch, and Böhme? Is it possible to have done something without being aware that you have done it? Might there be a file that says you are someone other than who you think you are? Or might something be found that you never imagined would ever be found? Or is it just doubt that is being sown to damage you, to destroy you? The smug face of the man from *Bild* saying to Hirsch, yes, but they could still find another file, couldn't they? These are the conversations of a falsified world, the legacy of forty years of tainted thinking; it is in the language, the behavior, the memory, the files, a past that forces its way into the present, seeking a foundation for the future, a skeleton that has stepped out of the closet, one that can eat, smoke, drink, vote and is sitting beside you at the bar or in the Volkskammer.

I am the foreigner here, but I try to understand. I am at a council with millions of bishops; I listen to the debates, read the transcripts, the monetary theology, the political casuistry, the scholastic reasoning of article 23 versus 146. Whose doctrine is right? Who is the heretic? What punishment should there be for which sin? What is the canonical rate of exchange? Two-to-one means a dissatisfied nation, and a dissatisfied nation could turn nasty. One-to-one means unemployment, and unemployment means dissatisfaction. But some dissatisfaction is not as bad as general dissatisfaction, is it? The people want unity—is that a sin? I remember, a year ago, when it was unthinkable, that people you spoke to in West Berlin said they did not want to be united with "that lot over there." Some of those same people are now arguing for a confederation, which would mean, for the umpteenth time in history, delaying or frustrating something that cannot be prevented or denied with impunity, a desire that flows like a river through the German past: the longing for a national, political unity of the kind that France and England have known since the Middle Ages, but which did not come about for Germany until 1871, and which was never entirely accepted by France. Even then, internal developments meant that German democracy did not function properly until 1918, and even after 1918 the power actually remained in the hands of a small but powerful minority of army men and industrialists who, after the humiliation of Versailles, were out to get revenge and to regain power. They certainly were not planning to give the people the democracy and unity they wanted, even if those same people had chosen their own leaders and there was a social-democratic majority in parliament.

There is ample material to study about the appalling intellectual confusion of those days, the metaphysical dreams that Spengler, Jünger, Hitler, disguised as secular ideas, the cynical calculation of the von Papens, the Hugenbergs, the Thyssens and their unholy alliance with the National Socialists, which began in 1929 and culminated in 1933 with Hitler coming to power after, or rather *because*, he had *lost* two million votes to the Left. In his book *The Origins of Modern Germany*, Geoffrey Barraclough calls this a conspiracy against the German people, and those who keep repeating that the Germans voted for Hitler (even using this as an argument against democracy) would be well advised to take another look at the figures. In 1924, under a million people voted for the National Socialists; in 1928, it was even fewer; in 1930, after the Wall Street crash and the collapse of German industry, it was 6.4 million; in July 1932, 13.7 million (there were over six million unemployed people at the time); and in November 1932, that figure fell to 11.7 million.

Social-democratic and Communist votes remained relatively constant over this period, a rising line of 10.5 million in 1924 to 13.1 million in 1932. The Catholic Zentrumspartei also remained stable at just over four million. The other middle-class parties fell from 13.2 to 4.2 million but, all told, there were over twenty-two million Germans who did not vote for Hitler at the last free elections in 1932.

We know what came after that, and we also know what came after *that* for the country we still call the D.D.R., but the problem is that this knowledge can be used by both sides in the debate about unification, for and against. One remarkable fact is that the economic argument is always cited as something sinful or scandalous, as though it were completely independent of all the other considerations. In that sense, the West German desire could be seen exclusively as a longing for a new colony, while the desire of the East

Germans is most akin to the final days of a pregnancy, but with the opposite aim: to get *inside* as quickly as possible, via a reverse Caesarean if necessary, and to connect directly to the sacred supplies of placenta and amniotic fluid in the larger body. This second view has its naturalistic imagery in its favour, but perhaps "natural" is not a category that can be applied when *das Volk* is involved, because fundamentally the thinkers do not trust the people, or maybe they even fear the people—that is another possibility. So those who favour immediate unification (article 23) are accused of D-Mark nationalism, while members of the cautious minority who are backing article 146 (*Dieses Grundgesetz verliert seine Gültigkeit an dem Tage, an dem eine Verfassung in Kraft tritt, die von dem deutschen Volke in freier Entscheidung beschlossen worden ist*: "This Constitution loses its validity on the day when a constitution that has been freely decided by the German people enters into force") are labelled as constitutional patriots. That immediately makes the others non-patriots and, in these wars of words, it sometimes even seems as though all the ghosts of the past would be summoned if the quick route of article 23 were chosen. The word "Auschwitz" regularly puts in an appearance, and even if this is done with the noblest of intentions, it still seems like blasphemy to me, because that past is untouchable and what people intend to say by bringing it up cannot be proved.

Perhaps it would be better, as Grass and Habermas are advocating, to allow all Germans to speak out about the alternative of a single, shared state *or* a federation of the two existing republics. After all, the D.D.R. is still economically crippled and dependent, with a different social structure and historical burden, and, with a population of sixteen million, it would be in the minority in a joint Bundestag, which would mean too few representatives to protect the citizens of their former republic from all kinds of unpleasantness. But if this path were chosen, at least it would be with eyes wide open. The minority would have a chance to justify its position, and the document providing that justification would always remain on the table: see, we could have done it this way instead. But the people are singing faster than their thinkers; they have already sung their former leaders into ignominious oblivion, and they have come to like the sound of their own song. And who knows those singers well enough to claim that it is not in fact their song?

It is raining and the sun is shining at the same time; there is a funfair on in hell. I am standing in the right place to watch the fake, brassy sunlight glinting off the blind, reflective windows of the Stasi building. It is odd that it has taken me so long, but I have only just noticed that this building has no doors at the front; the whole wall, covered with words of anger, is tiled to above head height with speckled, dung-colored stone; the four floors with their faceless windows begin above that, as though the architect took a perverse pleasure in expressing the function of this building in his design: the dehumanization, the disaster, the place of the skull. You cannot imagine anyone ever drinking a glass of water in this building, and yet of course they drank water here, just as they stepped off the tram on Jacques Duclosstraße, which then traveled on to Lenin Allee and Ho Chi Minhstraße, just as they walked past the newspaper kiosk with its embroidery designs "*für die D.D.R.-Frau,*" past the purple display windows of the shop selling household appliances, past Reni's Getränkeladen, the Tierfreund with the live parakeets in the window, just as they heard the voices from the Hans Zoschke-Stadion, and then entered through a side door somewhere and went to work, normally, just like everyone else. They looked out through the window, knowing that the people walking by could not see them; they took out folders and put them away, made notes in files, listened to recordings, drank coffee; and in the evening they went home and took Wolfgang the dog for a walk and tested their children on their homework. *Liebe und Wahrheit sollen siegen über*

Falkplatz,
East Berlin,
April 1990

*Lüge + Gewalt** (*Václav Havel*) is written on the walls, words that were not there back then.

Two weeks ago, I went to Falkplatz, a square that had recently been vacated by the D.D.R. border troops. Trees were to be planted in this saddest of all neighborhoods; everyone could bring something to plant, and the Prenzlauer Berg parks division and some other organizations were contributing a hundred trees. To coincide with the event, a demonstration of cyclists was riding to the square from Alexanderplatz, and as a "special treat" (*Besonderes Bonbon*) they would be allowed to cycle along the former *Todesstreifen*, or death strip, the empty space between the two lengths of Wall, a flat and bare piece of land, which made anyone running across it an easy target for the guards. The sun was shining, everyone was busy hacking into the ground, and even the member of the People's Police was lugging around saplings with roots packed in hessian sacks. The atmosphere was friendly, someone was playing a flute, the color purple was present in abundance, and some of the cyclists had more hair individually than thirty soldiers combined. A boy in overalls tried for hours to scrape a PDS poster off a watchtower using a spade, not yet old enough to know that everything

* Let love and truth triumph over lies and violence.

disappears by itself in time. The residents of the dilapidated buildings around the square sat on their balconies, sullen or apathetic, watching the idiots down there sweating away to turn the barren wasteland into a park. I am not very gifted botanically, but I thought that the many different varieties of trees were being planted awfully close together, yet the earth was fragrant and girls were digging small hollows with their hands for little plants with yellow flowers, and a young man cycled past with a handmade watchtower on the back of his bike. There was singing and laughter against the backdrop of that all-consuming Wall and the abandoned watchtowers and, with the once so deadly sand all around, I felt an intense pleasure, maybe it was simply happiness, as I stood on their side of the Wall and looked over at my world on the other side. I tried to imagine these two districts snuggling up together, but I could not. It was too much of a challenge. First the towers would have to go, and those walls, and that sand, and new things would have to come, things I could not yet see. I knew that something would fill that space, but I did not know how. I am not a town planner; my task is documentation.

And that is why I have now returned to that place, a different now, two weeks later, and why I got off at Schönhauser Allee and walked here down Kopenhagener Straße through a neighborhood that looks so much sadder in the rain, and made my way along the Wall to Falkplatz once again. But there is no one here, no flute and no voices; the P.D.S. poster is still on the tower, challenging the rain, and the young trees are there too, bare, stiff, awkward, limes and spruces and pines and chestnuts, and for a moment I think about how, in fifty or a hundred years' time, I would like to shelter under the mighty crowns of this forest in waiting, and how I do not want the planters to be disappointed.

April 21, 1990

Falkplatz,
East Berlin,
April 1990

Death strip, Falkplatz,
East Berlin, April 1990

XII

Political speculative fiction—that is what it would have been if, a year ago, you had produced a novel in which a C.D.U. *Ministerpräsident* of the D.D.R. with a French name had flown to Moscow to talk to Gorbachev about the possibility of NATO membership for a united Germany. Imagine the Honecker of a year ago, with a copy of today's newspaper in his hand, flicking on the television to see de Maizière descending the stairs of an aeroplane in Moscow. What kind of reality is it that is real, and yet absurd? I live in a city, I take the bus, I go to the Reichstag. The Brandenburger Tor has been stripped of its horses and chariot and is in scaffolding, a building emasculated. The surrounding square is wide and open; they are demolishing the Wall by night. People walk across the space, East German soldiers in boots, a child, windswept figures with the Charité in the background. I go to the other side, am permitted to walk straight through, and in a wooden hut I exchange West Marks for East Marks: three to one. You can change money illegally as well; wherever you look, there are grubby moneychangers with bundles of banknotes in their hands. You get a lot more money that way, but there is something unpleasant about it;

the situation is bad enough as it is. You are ten minutes away from your own house, the weather here is the same, you can hear the same language around you, but suddenly the money in your pockets has miraculously multiplied, because not only is one of yours worth three of theirs, but soup costs 1.50, goulash 3.95, a pils is 1.20, and you can divide all of those amounts by three again and, feeling a little peculiar, head back outside and go to the bookshop, where you can buy a beautiful bilingual edition of poems by René Char for six Ostmark = two Westmark. It is not right, but that is how it is. You only have to pay in D-Marks (*Westgeld*) at the big hotels, and when you buy petrol you sometimes (but not often) have to show proof that you changed your money officially. There is a huge amount of fiddling, speculation, calculation going on. Everything tastes, smells, reeks of money. It beats and buzzes in the conversations, and drifts off into the realm of fear, insecurity: what is going to happen soon, after the second of July, and what will that mean for individual citizens?

A journey through the D.D.R. I drive down a road I have driven along so often, on the way to the Netherlands, but now I am allowed to leave it, to head off into the countryside. Magdeburg, Halberstadt, a cathedral, another one, monasteries, dead aristocrats lying on top of their tombs, a world that was kept on ice, but which is now being defrosted. That can't really be the case, can it? So why does it feel that way? A war, bombardments, restoration, and these churches stood here all that time. The English wife of one of the Ottonians lay here for centuries, hidden beneath an enigmatic smile that suggests she can hear something a long way off in the distance, but what? The sculptor designed her epitaph as a rebus, weaving together the letters of her titles and virtues, but still I can decipher her name. I read her, just as I can read the language of the pillars, of the images carved in the wood of the choir stalls, a language that told the same story everywhere, so that these churches somehow gave a semblance of unity to eternally divided Europe. This land was closed off, and it seemed as though these churches no longer existed, but to me it feels like they went elsewhere for all that time and have only just returned, as though they have reclaimed their place amidst these peculiar piles of socialist architecture: migratory birds returning to nestle among the dilapidated cardboard blocks; paradoxical forms, foreign bodies that belong here.

Magdeburg Cathedral, May 1990

I look at the medieval faces, the Holbein figures on the tall, upright tombstones, the sooty, corroded angels, the black cliff faces of the high buildings. Then I follow a group of children whose teacher is giving them a guided tour and I listen to his soft, melodious sentences as he tells stories about that former empire. It feels as though it is not only the stories, which are so old, that are being given back to the children, but also the German language that these stories are told in, a German that such children have not possessed for quite some time. It was simply not available. Another variant of language was in use, one in which other words had taken root and divergent forms of history had concealed themselves, absent without ever truly disappearing. Maybe that is what we are experiencing here: beneath all of the material copulation and gluttony that is taking place on the surface, a submerged, *deferred* Germany is giving itself back to itself, and no one knows quite what to do with it. But whatever occurs, it will happen in language, and that will not be the language that is used for "ordering socks from Taiwan" (Peter Sloterdijk), nor will it be the language of the *Neues Deutschland* editorials of two years ago, nor that shared, earlier variant that was valid from '33 to '45 and which was used for so many lies that a lot of words will never recover their former strength. Where words are missing, speech falters and fails, and forms of reticence, obfuscation, silence develop. *Sprechen, versprechen*: to speak, to promise. This German connection between speaking and promising does not exist in Dutch. We certainly know all about *verspreken*, but the Dutch word means only to say the wrong thing, to make a slip of the tongue, to put one's foot in one's mouth. The Germans are capable of doing that too, of course, but when we Dutch people *verspreken*, we never promise anything. That sense of "to promise" is what the philosopher Sloterdijk is talking about when he says that being German means having to reflect more carefully than any other nation about what you can promise yourself and the world.*

As I continue to traipse after the schoolchildren (they have now reached St Maurice, and the teacher says, "Have you seen this? The black saint?"), my thoughts stray somewhere I cannot follow: is a language, as well as being everything that *is* written or said in it, also everything that *can* be written or said in it? And if that is the case, what does it mean? Are some languages less capable of expressing evil than others? Are some languages better suited to lies? And, if so, how long does it take for a language to recover from its lies? Or, if the language itself is innocent and therefore just a victim, or just another victim, along with the people it has been used for lying to, how can we help her (language has to be feminine) to heal? And who should be the healer?

The children are laughing about something. Their high-pitched peals ring up to the vaulted ceiling and, shocked at the sound, they start shushing themselves, and yet, because they are here and I am here and their laughter is now part of my thoughts, it seems as though they are saying, "You need a healer? We can do that." At the same time, it occurs to me (as you suddenly find yourself able to express something that you have actually known for a long time) how peculiar it is that we are born into a language, as though, for the arbitrary span of our lives, we are immersed in a river. But the river never remains the same, and you play a part in changing that water yourself. After you, the river is never the same. For me, that river is Ruusbroec, Hadewijch, the words spoken by the judge against Oldenbarnevelt, Vondel, as well as more modern figures like Max Blokzijl, and beneath and behind all those written,

---

* Wer auf deutsch etwas versprechen will, muss sich über das Was und das Wie seines Redens in der Zukunft radikalere Gedanken machen als irgendwer irgendwo sonst.

articulated words, the endless murmuring of generation after gener-ation, the mass of words and sentences constantly accumulating around us. For the schoolchildren now stroking the devils and animals of the choir stalls, it is the words that Luther translated from the Greek on the Wartburg, but also the Germanic echoes of the *Nibelungenlied*, the surging waves of Hölderlin and the forgotten words that Handke gave back when he described the landscapes of his youth in *Die Wiederholung*; it is the cries of the Thirty Years War, but also Himmler's protocols and Goebbels' roars, or Gottfried Benn's response to Klaus Mann and his later remorse, which he captured in words. It is a living, never-ending intermingling of spoken and written words, the conversation that a nation has with itself: language, who may perhaps even be able to purify herself once the pressure of the systems that abuse her is removed, just as lungs can cleanse themselves when you give up smoking, even after many years.

I am on my way to the Harz. Friends in Berlin laughed suspiciously when I listed my destinations: the Hexentanzplatz, the Rosstrappe, the Brocken, the Barbarossahöhle, the Wartburg, the Germany of those lonely pilgrimages in search of the Holy Grail, the dragon's blood, the witches' screeches, the legends, the nostalgic memory. Why is it that the witches from *Macbeth* and the ancient twilight of the Druids and Celtic heroes do not elicit the same ironic shiver as Richard Wagner's "*Wallala weiala weia*" or the shrieking females in Goethe's *Faust*? The answer can only be that this world died a gentle death with the anemic English Pre-Raphaelite movement, while here it has made a comeback and has merged with symbols of death and destruction. After all, Kniebolo (the childish code name that Jünger came up with for Hitler, as though it might somehow render him harmless, like some sort of Pinocchio) also relished the *Nie-wieder-Erwachens wahnlos hold bewusster Wunsch*; language as the anaesthetic of thought, an escape from the rational world.

I am rewarded, as though the set designer is looking kindly upon me. I have not even reached Thale, the location of the Hexentanzplatz—the witches' dance floor—when the white mist starts swirling around my car. I see a sign for a *Schwebebahn*, a suspension railway, and although the idea of taking a floating train seems like a suitably magical approach, I would prefer to walk the last part: a little fear never does any harm. What I think is mist turns out to be clouds; sometimes they are there, sometimes they disappear. The trees are dripping. There is not a soul in sight. But commerce has already had its wicked way with the legend: when I finally reach the top, I find a parking area for coaches, a restaurant with an amusing painting of a witch above the entrance, a *Bratwurst* stand, all of it empty, deserted. I walk around this tainted legend and then, at the far end of the site, I find it, the actual site of the Walpurgisnacht ball. I climb the slippery rocks and stop at a rusty railing that would have caused a few landing problems for the witches. Some of the genius of this place still remains; the abyss before me is deep, with ragged fir trees growing against bare rock faces, shreds of mist, mystery. Now that all of that commercial nonsense is behind me, it really is quite beautiful.

There is a whistling of wind in the trees, but otherwise the silence is dense, dense enough to make you imagine all kinds of things, but before I can picture anything that might make me shiver, memory intervenes once again: an actor wearing a peculiar green pyjama-like outfit, dancing on a small stage. It was a few months ago and I had read that someone was performing a one-man version of *Faust* somewhere in East Berlin, both parts, in a tiny theater that was aptly called "Unter dem Dach," Under the Roof. Both parts of *Faust*, I thought, how was that even possible? It would take ten hours, and yet I was intrigued. There were twenty of us and, as usual, I must have been the oldest person there. The others were serious young people who wanted to wrap themselves up in Goethe for an evening. The actor was in his forties and was dressed in the aforementioned garment, which was clearly handmade and gave him the freedom of movement he required. As he was playing several roles, he had rather a lot of leaping around to do. And, of course, the winds had to blow, the choruses had to be spoken, the witches had to screech evilly, and so he had cunningly hidden a cassette recorder behind a curtain, but he had to keep going over to switch it on (after all, the machine could hardly come to him) and he concealed this repeated movement with a fascinating variety of dance steps. It was terrible and wonderful, all at the same time. He had mastered his lines and kept up his performance for hours, but sometimes he tried to shout along with himself on the cassette recorder and that did not work: a failed twinning of natural and mechanical voices. By the interval, I had had my fill and wanted to leave the attic, but some fiendish spirit had locked the cloakroom. However, it turned out fine, because the man in the green pyjamas, with all of his histrionic posturing, managed yet again to draw me into his Faustian world of darkness, the search for light, the lewdness and the lust for knowledge; he was his own devil and his own doctor, his own Gretchen and his own witches. All by himself, he had enchanted me and now, here in this gloomy place in the forest, I thought of him again, a man who had surrendered himself to Goethe and wound his lines around me and sent me home, bewitched, after the earnest youngsters and I had called him back three times for one more round of thunderous applause. I walked slowly back past the *Knödelbüffet* and the *Selbstbedienungsgaststätte*. Witches, dumplings, Goethe: without irony, it is no longer possible to endure the world. It is not the writer who is postmodern, but the world.

From deep in the valley, I had seen a hotel and that was where I wanted to go now. The clouds turned into ordinary rain and then the road began to climb again, and finally I ended up at the same height, but on the other side of the gorge. In the cloud of mist surrounding the hotel, I could make out two Western cars and two Trabants, so I knew there must still be vacancies. The young man at the reception desk decided that I should pay in West Marks; an accent costs money here. The room had a balcony that must have looked out over the valley, but the door was locked. A shabby orange rag hung at the window, there was no shower or toilet in the room, and any complaints were to be made to the collective. The reading lamp did not work—call the collective! The communal shower was grimy, and there were splotches of paint all over the rest of the bathroom, not important in themselves, but because of what they signified. Tap, mirror, curtain, hallway all expressed the same sentiment: to hell with you, we are long gone, and we were never really here even when we were present.

Rosstrappe, this is where Brunhilde once fled from Bodo the knight, her horse taking an almighty leap and flying across the gorge; you can still see the mark left by its hoof. I can even go and stand inside it. So I clamber up to it along a muddy path, and on the way I meet another hotel guest, who says that it's *"mystisch"* up there. His glasses are gleaming in the rain. I think he might be a little mystical himself, but when I am standing in the spot where Bodo plunged into the abyss, the weight of German Romanticism descends, and the unspoiled landscape down there calls something, languishing or pining, as a white-masked bird I have never seen before comes and sits on the inaccessible rock in front of me, singing its heart out without expecting anything in return, and some inconceivable mountaineer has planted a cross up there atop a dragon's tooth, the mist wrapping around it like a cloak. I see a path zigzagging down to a river that I can hear but not see. Chinese hills, Japanese trees, the German landscape as an oriental wash drawing. As I descend, the birds grow louder, throwing themselves into the depths and hovering there, writing letters in the air and perching on more distant rocks to continue delivering their orations. I try to understand what they are saying, but one sounds like a Chinese person discussing tasty food, while another seems to be translating Hildegard of Bingen into the language of the birds, so I am never going to work it out. As evening falls, I climb back up again, to a hotel and dining room with ficus and ferns and burghers tucking into boar meat, mountain air, contentment.

Before I go to bed, I take a quick look outside, but there is nothing to see. I am living in a cloud, Niflheim, the abode of mist, the camouflage clothing of Germanic mythology or, as Gottfried Benn puts it, "Always and eternally, ribbons of mist and veils of fog and a need for the bearskins of the 'glorious old Germans,' as they are called in the radio broadcasts [of the Nazi era]. From a place such as this, Taine would surely have postulated a geophysical explanation for the fact that our nation, deep in its very essence, has a strange relationship to clarity and form, or, one might say, to honesty." As a counterbalance, I try to read some of Heine's *Harzreise*, but I have just reached the point where the poet sits down at the foot of the Brocken with a shepherd, *"ein freundlich blonder junger Mensch"* for a *"Déjeuner dînatoire"* consisting of bread and cheese, while the little sheep snatch up the crumbs and the sweet calves leap around them, with their big, happy eyes. Such shepherds no longer exist and, besides, sleep is creeping up on me, but I put my Walkman on for a while and fortunately, or perhaps un-fortunately, find a D.D.R. station with the voice of an older man who is arguing, trying to persuade *"ein junger Freund."* There is no doubt about it—these men are writers. You can recognize the type immediately. The man he is addressing is not present;

the voice remains alone, an intelligent, lonely sound, disillusioned, mournful. The younger man has apparently written something about Anna Seghers' betrayal of Walter Janka. He has expressed suspicions and mentioned the names of Christa Wolf and Stefan Heym, and the voice wonders whether the young man really knows enough about all those things, if he knows about Seghers' conversations with Ulbricht, if he knows about the pain and the moral conflicts. So, once again, this is about the rift between belief and conscience, and the man to whom the voice belongs knows what he is talking about because he too was imprisoned under the regime for several years ("so many years of my life were stolen from me"), and condemned by people who had themselves been in prison for many years of their lives, under a different regime, and now this young friend had attacked Seghers, but had gone on to argue, of all things, that the work of "anti-Semites such as Céline and Pound, Gottfried Benn with his fantasies of eugenics, of a warmonger like Ernst Jünger, who still has on his desk the perforated helmet of an English soldier he shot dead in the First World War" should finally be published in the D.D.R.

What is going to happen, I wonder in the fog of my drowsiness, to those who are faithful to the old doctrine, who have suffered so much through their practice of that doctrine and been pilloried as heretics and yet still have not lost their faith? Last week I read a lovely little book by Stefan Hermlin, *Abendlicht*, in which he writes about his youth and his father, his wealthy Jewish background (what the French refer to as the "*haute juiverie*," a term that makes you wonder if they are talking about some extremely rare sort of bird)—liberal, musical and, above all, German, people with horses and paintings (later, in a museum in Oslo, he sees the Munchs and Redons that used to hang on the walls at home).

One day, as a schoolboy, in the summer of 1931, he stops on his way home to watch a couple of unemployed men who have no money to buy a newspaper and so are reading one in a shop window instead. He listens to their conversation and keeps returning to the same spot, until finally one of the workers speaks to him and, gently mocking his appearance (a dutiful schoolboy from a well-to-do family), suggests that he should join the *Kommunistischer Jugendverband Deutschlands*. The man hands him a piece of paper with pale letters that are hard to decipher: it is a badly printed membership form for that organization, the Communist Youth Association, which he duly signs. The sentence that follows might have been spoken by Saint Paul on the road to Damascus: "The street started spinning around me, slowly and steadily." That one moment defines Hermlin's life. He flees to Switzerland in the Nazi era, while his father stays behind and dies in Sachsenhausen. After the war, he chooses the D.D.R. and he remains a Communist, like the man whose voice I can hear without knowing who he is. I am in that hopeless moment of near-sleep, when everything is very faraway, but also very large; the voice is inside my head now and it feels as though the split personality of these people, with their high ideals and the Stalinist mould that has eaten away at them so viciously, is attempting to take up residence in my brain, to seep through the two tiny sponges of my Walkman, as they deliver increasing doses of their soporific drug. When it is finally over, I hear the name: Günther Rücker. Later, back in Berlin, I make enquiries: he is a filmmaker in his late sixties, who has made some wonderful things, and who wrote a very fine debut novel in 1984, *Herr von Oe*. I still have no idea who the young friend was.

Morning, more mist. I hear the sound of birds flying past; they must be operating on automatic pilot. The morning newspaper is singing about two to one, one to one, the state arts subsidy is no more, and at breakfast some gentlemen from the East and the West are busy either tearing apart a sand-mining company or setting one up. The men from the West are dressed in leather, the men from the East are in Nikita Khrushchev suits—something else that will soon disappear. I go down the same mountain path as yesterday, but this time I reach the river and cross the Devil's Bridge (what better name for a bridge in this place?). Down at that level, the fog has dispersed. I lean out over the swirling water and watch as a white-throated dipper disappears into the rounded form of its nest, which is glued to the rock face, and then reappears and flies off, low over the water, a small propeller without a body. The path rises and falls, the leaves of the chestnut trees are curled or unfurled, depending on how high or low I am. The walk to the next village is twelve kilometers, but I do not meet a soul. Somewhere, someone has carved Goethe into his own granite; there is no avoiding him: *Der Geist aus dem wir handeln ist das höchste. Zum 200sten Geburtstag, Kulturbund Thale.* It is midday by the time I arrive in Treseburg, muddy and soaked through. After lunch, I ask if there is a bus that goes back to Thale, but I am informed that it does not leave until late in the afternoon, and a taxi costs forty-three Marks, which works out to fifteen. When I say I'll take a taxi, the boss says he will drive me himself. On the way, he gives me a lesson in socialism for company owners: the penalties for making more money, the harassment from state officials, the countless forms you have to fill in just to paint a windowsill, the fines for putting in extra effort, all the things that are supposed to be in the past now, "but, honestly, I'll have to see it for myself first, because the same people are still in the same jobs." I keep hearing this refrain in the days that follow, no matter who I speak to: owners or staff, teachers or students, waiters or customers waiting in the long queue for the restaurant. The feeling of resentment is huge. People do not know where they stand,

---

* The spirit that guides us is the highest. On the occasion of his 200th birthday, Thale Cultural Association.

if their company is going to close down, if their child will be able to study, if their qualifications are still valid in the West, what Grandma's savings are worth, if they will be able to keep their job, if the Party-appointed leader of the government enterprise will still be its owner tomorrow. Politicians from East and West are rowing against this tide of uncertainty, with faces and statements full of confidence; they are talking about three years, five years of hardship at the most, and about the golden future that will follow. But four thousand people a week are still leaving for the other Germany.

May 5, 1990

XIII

QUEDLINBURG, STOLBERG, THE GERMANY OF PIC-
ture postcards. A lick of paint and then the coach parties can come.
Some places were built for tourism centuries ago—timbers in the
walls, crests above the doors, money in the tills. Anyone who lives
in these places must be perm-anently scarred: they become scenery,
bit-part actors, their bartered souls wandering through thousands
of anonymous photographs in albums in Tokyo, Saint Louis, Düsseldorf, a population nourished by the nostalgia of other people.
This is how we imagine history; this is how the past should behave.
I drive in and back out again, impressed yet resentful. This is other
people's idea of the picturesque, a museum of the living, unbearable.

But Nature could not care less. There is very little industry here,
the fruit trees are in blossom, and the landscape rolls and arches
into view. It is all pleasant enough, but charming is not my territory,
and certainly not when it goes on for too long. I would rather have
a chunk of desert or a slightly seedy metropolis; I have never imagined paradise as perfectly raked and tidy. Many of the roads are
still cobbled, which at least prevents that gentle, soporific rocking.
The landscapes in the other part of the Harz, over the border, have

already been tamed for good. All of the locals appear to be pensioners, and before long it will be the same here too: unification as homogenisation. Leaden clouds, the occasional shower, bright spells that make the green look garish: this weather is setting the tone for my destination, the Kyffhäuser, a landscape of mountains, where, according to legend, the restless spirit of Emperor Barbarossa lies in a cave somewhere, waiting for German Unity. It no longer matters that this legend was originally not about him, but about his grandson Frederick II (known as *stupor mundi*, the wonder of the world). Of course, Barbarossa was a better fit for the nationalists who were striving for unity at the beginning of the previous century; he was, after all, the last leader under whom the Reich had apparently still meant something. He had, admittedly, gone to Venice in 1177 to kiss the feet of Pope Alexander III (nations have long memories, and the popes of Rome would pay for that kiss during the Reformation; nothing is ever lost, not only in the material world, but also in history: every atom of insult and humiliation is accounted for and remains in existence somewhere), but still he had strung the republics of Italy in a long line after his name while, at the same time, working from his Swabian and Burgundian territories to rally the German princes to his crown by means of a cunning game of give and take.

In his essay "De toekomst van gisteren," Yesterday's Future, Mulisch sees this Hohenstaufen as a link in a chain (Hermann—Barbarossa—Bismarck—Hitler), but that is projecting the nineteenth century onto the twelfth, a process that works the other way round too. If the Staufen emperor had succeeded—like the Capets and Plantagenets, his French and English contemporaries—in establishing his empire as a lasting entity, the history of Germany, and therefore the history of Europe, would have been different. If . . . would . . . —as ever, those weak-minded words do not prove anything, but still . . . After Barbarossa's death, his legacy foundered, and ever since then a fragmentation bomb has been lying beneath German history; it is enough to make any country neurotic. Germany was incapable of becoming a healthy or organic entity under Bismarck, not only because the ridiculous fragmentation that followed the Thirty Years War had become institutionalized (even with only six million Germans left out of an original twenty million!) but also because, as the *Markgrafen*, *Kurfürsten*, dukes and royal offspring had modeled themselves on the Sun King, the bourgeoisie did not get a look-in and the revolution ultimately remained a piece of news from abroad. If you wanted to be blunt, it could be said that the constipation of all those centuries is only finally being processed now. That is why the unity of the present can occur without fanaticism or dynastic fantasies: it is simply the right moment for it. The Hohenstaufen in his cave would understand that better than anyone; he was after all a political realist of the highest order. Carlyle, of course, puts it far more elegantly, in the kind of English that evaporates when you try to transfer it to this century: "No king so furnished out with apparatus and arena, with personal faculty to rule and scene to do it in, has appeared elsewhere."

I go to visit the great emperor in his grotto. A strange cave system was discovered under this mountain in the second half of the last century, which lent even more luster to the legend. He must be down there somewhere, with his beard, still red, wrapped around the table nine times, among his dreaming horses and his sleeping guards. Some say every hundred years, some say every thousand years, a raven wakes him and tells him if German Unity has finally dawned; according to another version of the legend, a dwarf who lives down there with him is sent up to the surface every hundred years to see if the dread ravens of German division are still flying above the mountain.

The leaflet I receive at the ticket desk (a legend with a ticket desk—it is only to be expected) remains blissfully buried in

dialectical times. It waffles on about the ruling class of exploiters who abused the legend for their own aims and about German
imperialism and militarism and the upper bourgeoisie and all
those other despicable types who are unworthy of legend. I am
rather enjoying it, but then there is a sudden panic, because it
turns out that the previous group of visitors is already some way
inside the cave and if I want to see it today, this is my last chance.
The lady at the ticket desk purposefully locks up her till and leads
me by the hand into an endless tunnel. Her *Kollegin* should still be
nearby, she is sure we can catch up with her, but the tunnel grows
longer and longer, and as I hurry after the cashier in the dim light
and see our scampering shadows on the wall, I think that this is
the kind of moment when someone should be filming you, as you
run along deep beneath the ground, following a woman you do
not know, in search of her colleague and the ghost of a thousand-
year-old emperor.

Pause, shout, echo, echo, no answer. The tunnel opens out into
a cathedral-sized cave; it smells of sulphur and I can see pools of
deathly still, reflective water on the left and right. "You just wait
here," my female Virgil says, rather mysteriously. "I'll go back and
phone her."

And so I wait there, all alone, as her footsteps disappear into
the darkness. If Redbeard ever wishes to put in an appearance,
now would be the time. Snow White is welcome to join us. Jagged,
vicious limestone sculptures stab down at me from the vaulted roof,
the stone is stained by strange substances, and even though I can
see the bottom of the water, it does not reveal its depth. I softly say
something to myself and the cathedral mumbles a response. Then
Virgil returns with her lamp and leads me onwards, to a group of
damned souls who are listening to the high, clear sound of a young
woman chirping and babbling about Barbarossa and his dog and
his table, and also about the early bourgeois revolution, because her

psalm still smacks of doctrine. I realize that the others can hear that doctrine too and that we all know she cannot hear it herself, but we forgive her because she is young and we are deep under the ground, where the living have no business being.

Only a few kilometers separate this place and the monument that the nationalists (not the innocent liberals of the beginning of the last century, but the hungry Prussians who came later) erected to Frederick I Barbarossa, and of course that monstrosity sits on the highest point, where the castle used to stand, and of course, immediately above the old emperor, brooding on his throne, they installed a statue of Wilhelm I on a horse, flanked by the god of war and a woman with voluptuous bronze breasts, but the avian symbolism around him comes from the Aztec pyramids. I actually wish they would consign the whole pile of nonsense to the legions of toppled statues who are morosely making their way through Eastern Europe in search of a final resting place. Only Barbarossa should be allowed to remain seated, liberated from the monument above him, where you can climb Escheresque steps to reach the dome and look out over the landscape like a raven. He would still sit there alone, brooding, at the mercy of the wind, pondering the alchemical arithmetic that turns four plus two into one and without his Wilhelmine *Über-Ich*, who had vanished, complete with horse and helmet, into the darkness of the posthumous world.

My pilgrimage is not yet at an end. Erfurt, the Dom with its painted golden unicorn resting its goat legs in the virgin's lap and with those other, dancing, foolish virgins outside, swaying in stone with their dangerous smiles; the Wartburg, where in 1817 the *Burschenschaften*, the student fraternities, gathered in nostalgically restored rooms to dream of restoration. I am led in a surge of visitors past bad-tempered attendants, past saccharine bad taste and former greatness, past von Schwind's murals, whose pallid

*Emperor Frederick
Barbarossa,
Kyffhäuser Monument*

nostalgia for days gone by cannot outdo one single medieval love casket, past the Cranachs and the Dürers and the manuscripts and the first editions and the tiny room where Luther translated the Bible from Greek and threw his inkpot at the Devil. Every time I tarry, I feel the resentment of the attendants as they rattle their wretched keys. No one will come between the guardians of this world and their highest goal: to shut up shop twenty minutes before closing time. And no *Arbeiter- und Bauernstaat* can do anything to change that.

Weimar. I have been here before, last winter. I should identify the city with Goethe, but instead it is brown coal. That is, of course, nonsense, because one will remain while the other will fade, and yet the smell of that coal is unforgettable. Ultimately, I am sure that whenever I smell brown coal anywhere, I will be reminded of Goethe. It is a smell that you encounter wherever you go in the D.D.R. Some days it comes wafting over from East Berlin and into my house in the West, but nowhere did it seem as strong as during those days in Weimar, and I do not know whether it was a result of the climatic conditions of those winter days or something else, but I remember waking up in the middle of the night in my hotel feeling like I was suffocating, as if someone had left the gas on somewhere. I staggered over to the window and opened it, but that just made things worse. Even my saliva tasted of it; I had gas in my mouth. The following day, I saw heaps of coal lying in the streets all over the city, just tipped out, the way a milkman might deposit a bottle of milk at the front door. I had taken up residence at Goethe's Hotel Elephant, a hotel that now shared only the name, the rest of it consisting of a new development: overpriced, anemic rooms, a restaurant that was a haven for Party bigwigs, a failed attempt at grandeur. The city seemed melancholy, like an impoverished aristocrat who had withdrawn for the season and was eking out her reserves and her memories. Some tourists were wandering around, looking for a café, as I was, but you had to queue, and when you finally got to the front, you discovered that it closed at seven.

Why had I come to Weimar? To immerse myself in Goethe, of course. There is no escaping him; the only way out is dislike, denial, and that is something I cannot do. In the year I have been living here, his plays have been performed everywhere. I encountered him in the Harz, in quotes and allusions, in the lives of his contemporaries (he intertwined his almost-century with the far shorter lives of Schiller, Herder, Kleist), and in the Staatsbibliothek I come up against the stone massif of his collected works. "Goethe was a plaster Apollo"—I cannot shake off Roland Holst's absurd dictum, if only because his inimitable aristocratic tones made it sound as though the wretched German poet had once, somewhere, managed to lose a cricket match for Holst's side. But even then, it is still nonsense.

Things are different now that spring is here; the house on Frauenplan basks in the sun and I stand at his windows, watching children play by the fountain. Library, antique statues, study, death-bed, memories, letters, manuscripts—I quickly become wrapped up in it all, as I did on my previous visit. Perhaps the most astonishing thing about Goethe's life is that it was so successful, as though it was itself a work of art, one that continues to have an impact. Whether you like it or not, when you wander around that house on your own, reading his writing and thinking about the person who once lived in those rooms, you are drawn in; he is still there.

Before coming to Weimar, I had grabbed a couple of essays about Goethe and Kant by Ortega y Gasset, and I am lying in bed with them now, as a kind of punishment, back at the gas-filled Elephant. The Spaniard, surrounded by this German wall-paper, has become obstinate, and I also picked the wrong place to start. Ortega is complaining about spending ten years in Kant's prison, but he says that the prison was also his home because there is no denying that the "crucial mysteries" of the modern age are revealed in Kant's philosophy. So those ten years were not in fact a punishment, but now, having freed himself, when he concentrates on Kant he feels like someone "visiting the zoo on a public holiday to look at the giraffe." I try to picture Kant as a giraffe, but if Kant is a giraffe, what is Goethe? Ortega calls him the most doubtful of all the classics, a classic *"en segunda potencia,"* because the classic Goethe had himself read all of the classics and had therefore become the very prototype of the heir: someone who lives on the investments of the past, an administra-tor of received wealth. That is a great deal harsher than a "plaster

Apollo" and while Roland Holst left it at those magic words, Ortega treks slowly through an entire range of rocky mountains, weighing up the pros and cons, and at the end of his journey comes to the conclusion that there is no avoiding the master from Weimar. Goethe's contemporaries were already aware of that though, and it is here, in this city that was suddenly drawn back into Germany by the past year's events, that his magnetism enchanted their lives; it is impossible to walk around his house and not feel that force of attraction.

Herder and Schiller, who lived part of their lives in the same city as Goethe, must have had to contend with his powerful shadow as well as his sunlight. If Kant was a giraffe, Goethe must have been a mammoth, but one that had not become extinct, an impossibility. The giraffe may have lived far away in the distant Königsberg, which is now called Kaliningrad, but his writings penetrated deep into the minds of Weimar, sparking difference and debate. While Herder reacted against Kant, Schiller became completely absorbed by him ("Certainly no greater words have ever been spoken by any mortal than these by Kant, which are also the essence of his entire philosophy: Determine yourself from within!"), while the luminary Goethe took from Kant only what he could use.

Attraction, repulsion: Schiller and Goethe had their difficulties, as Schiller's correspondence clearly demonstrates. One day Goethe was his light, the next his eclipse. He wrote to Körner on March 9, 1789: "This person, this Goethe is simply in my way, and he reminds me so often that fate has treated me harshly. How easily *his* genius was borne by his fate . . ." The proximity was evidently hard to bear ("being often around Goethe would make me unhappy"). They express criticism of each other's work and are then suddenly brimming with admiration. It must have been exhilarating and emotional, particularly when you consider what Weimar was like back in those days. Six thousand inhabitants, that was all, 130,000 in the entire dukedom. The palace where Goethe's enlightened friend Karl-August ruled was in the middle of a city whose streets were barely paved. Every evening, the pigs were driven inside the city walls. This was the center of their world, the place where they would spin their threads to the rest of Germany, the city where their statues still live. The duke and Herder stand alone, while Goethe and Schiller are together in front of the theater where so many of their plays were performed. They stand close together, the hand of the old poet resting on the shoulder of the young poet, their other hands sharing a laurel wreath. Poet and minister, poet and natural scientist, poet and poet: the two directors of an intellectual power station that is still in operation.

I find them beside each other again in the ducal vault of the Sachsen-Weimar-Eisenach family, where the two poets have pushed the duke aside. They are lying in the middle of the vault, in their bronze boxes. Two girls have brought along a small bottle of champagne and are toasting the two dead men with plastic glasses—that is not something you see every day. The aristocrats are up against the walls, literally on the sidelines. Of course, Ulbricht and his ilk did not want to discard the duke—he was, after all, enlightened—but he had to be kept in the shadows. What would Goethe have said about that? Perhaps it reveals the true state of affairs, but I suspect that Goethe's sense of hierarchy as a minister and state councillor would have caused him to resist the thought of his duke being sidelined in his own vault. And besides, they were friends their entire lives; as young men they had gone on wild horse rides, and they had grown old together. A good word from Goethe and the duke had helped Schiller, just as he had helped Herder, and he had also allowed Goethe to go to Italy when the inner conflict between the dual identity of poet and minister became too great for that one body.

Goethe and Schiller,
Weimar

The two girls have now walked over to the bronze boxes and are reading poems to each other. It has all become a little too intimate; if they are not careful, the two gentlemen might climb out of their coffins. And I know they are not dead, incidentally, because a few months ago, when the exodus from East Germany began to assume terrifying proportions, the residents of Weimar found their poets in front of the theater one morning with a big sign in their hands: *Wir bleiben hier!* We are staying put!

It is Sunday, and the sixth of May. I have driven to Petzow with a few friends, to a park and country estate near Potsdam. We are lying in the grass beside the lake and someone is reading aloud from Fontane. A polling station has been set up in the castle; this is election day. Fontane described the park where we are lying, and my friends are enjoying this new world they have regained. Berlin has won back a hundred new landscapes. The cage is finally open and in ten years' time no one will be able to imagine the former prison. A D.D.R. citizen who understands this new age is selling home-made cakes and smoked trout. I leave my friends and wander round the park, through waterside meadows full of irises and speedwell. On my wanderings, I happen upon a stone that marks the spot where the owner of the castle murdered an anti-fascist in 1943. That is all it says. I try to imagine what happened, but I cannot. The maples, the full chestnut trees, the sumptuous summer, the little boats on the still water, the bodies stretched out in the grass—everything gives the impression that the evil has been dispelled. The stone is just talking to itself today.

Later that evening, I see the ministers of the four occupying forces commencing their slow peace, and somehow it does not feel real. It is as though they are performing a ballet without an audience, a ceremony of choreographed movements that mimic reality, a pantomime that we recognize because it has already happened in real life.

May 12, 1990

XIV

THESE THINGS MUST HAPPEN IN THE ANIMAL KING-
dom too: a species has outlived its usefulness and is on the brink
of extinction, but its last representatives are unable to behave any
differently from all of their predecessors, and they also look exactly
the same. The courtship display of the final two members of the species will be the same as it was when thousands of them still existed.

Walking down Unter den Linden, on my way to the Museum
der Geschichte, I hear the sound of marching music coming from
a side street. In the distance, I see a crowd clustered in front of the
Neue Wache. I have seen the changing of the guard before, but there
was no music that time. "They only do it once a week, on Wednesday afternoons," explains the policeman who is keeping the road
clear. "And today might be the last time, because they're stopping
it." Just a few days ago, in a book about Prussia by Sebastian Haffner, I came across a reproduction of a painting from 1813 depicting
the same ceremony. The soldiers were wearing tall hats with cock-
ades, short blue uniform jackets, white breeches; the spectators had
top hats, crinolines, parasols. Only the buildings, the Zeughaus and
the Neue Wache, remain the same. As I watch the standard-bearers

coming out of the side street and turning in my direction, one creature with many feet, I remember the words on the back of Haffner's book: "The history of Prussia is an interesting one, even today, especially today, as we also know how it ends. It begins slowly, with a long development, and it comes to a slow end, with a long death. But in between lies a great drama; if you will, a great tragedy—the tragedy of pure *Staatsvernunft*, reason of state."

The tragedy, of course, lay in Prussia's later decay, when people in their weakness and vanity ruined the analytical chess game of that earlier *Vernunft* and muddied the clear scheme. It all started so well; you could almost believe that it had been planned on a computer. One Hohenzollern after another sat down at the chessboard after the Thirty Years War and made his move, and it was as though all of those moves had been agreed in advance, a master game laid out for successive generations. It has become common practice to equate Prussian with German and to dismiss the state's military aspect as dangerous, or ridiculous, preferably both, but that attitude will not get you very far if you are looking for the roots of modern German history. How was it that, out of all those German states, Prussia slowly rose to supremacy after the Peace of Münster? What was different about Prussia? All of the states had absolute rulers; trade and initiative were smothered by a network of borders, taxes,

Neue Wache,
Unter den Linden,
East Berlin,
May 23, 1990

tolls and local regulations almost everywhere; wherever you went, the princes ruled with a caste of military men and civil servants, and money had to be raised to fund that system by the peasants who lived on the land of the aristocracy and had no rights. This fossilization could have continued far longer if the balance in Europe had not begun to shift. In that respect, it was a perfect prediction of what we are experiencing now: without Gorbachev and what he accomplished, the D.D.R. under Honecker could have continued to simmer away for years until only Albanian ashes remained.

So, what was it that made Prussia the exception? A few exceptional men, who did things differently from the other German rulers, who, for example, no longer wished to depend on mercenaries to make up their armies: the army of Frederick William I consisted of more members of the local population than any other European army at that time, and the men were paid from Prussia's own coffers, not from the pockets of foreign powers. This required obsessive economic management and a discipline that was to become exemplary of what some people admire and others despise, according to their inclinations. "I am the King of Prussia's Minister of Finance," said Frederick William I, who was in fact the King of Prussia. The king as the servant of the state is a Prussian concept, and because people are not stupid they could see the contrast with the despotism and profligacy of the other German princes. Of course, the system only worked if the servant was an exceptional one. After his death, Frederick the Great's perfect machine fell into the hands of lesser gods. However, his personal legacy made itself felt for a long time. The power of the lesser gods later became the power of criminals, but for a while they continued to benefit from a legacy of sobriety, discipline, service to their country. By the time some members of this caste realized that they had been deceived, or rather, that they had deceived themselves, it was too late, and there was nothing that any Stauffenberg could do to remedy the situation. Once again, a different regime inherited the obsolete machinery that I am now watching parade in front of me.

I have described it before, so there is no real need to do it again, even though there is music this time, and even though it might be the last time. The aim was, of course, dehumanization, the temporary negation of the individual. And it succeeded, this group truly moves like an object made up of people and, as always, I have an emotional reaction to it and, as always, I despise myself for that reaction, even though I could make better use of my time by attempting to discover where that strange shiver (because that is what it is) actually comes from. I have no interest in the military, so what exactly is happening to me? I look at the others around me. They were just laughing. Some-one said, "*Alles Scheiße*" and the others agreed, but now everyone has fallen silent, as they look at the faces that are not looking at us. Is their silence prompted by the sense of reduction, the fact that it is pos-sible to efface people's identity and transform them into a mechanical component of something else? A couple of black American soldiers in uniform are standing on the other side of the street. They were filming at first, but now actual reality has gained the upper hand over the later possibility of seeing that reality as an image, and the cameras hang at their sides, lenses pointing at the pavement, and I realize that they are seeing something different from what I am seeing. But what?

The marching creature has come to a halt in front of the Neue Wache. It has come to collect and take away the two soldiers who have been standing there motionlessly on guard. And that is the mysterious part: the two who are standing there will soon disap-pear among the others, while the two who are to take their place are still completely invisible. Seduction, a dance, that is what it looks like. There is music, high-pitched, whistling tones that remind me of tropical birds. Then voices, not so much yelling and roar-ing, more like words being dragged over a grater, shredded in the warm midday air. A command, and suddenly the two men among the columns start to move, a strange, shuffling step, a descent, one step, another, then they are standing beside the two others; they circle each other, a moment of idiotic intimacy, a kind of mating, and then one becomes the other, something has been exchanged for something else, no difference can be seen. Then those dreadful steps begin again, and not one of those raised boots will admit that this is the last time. This ritual performs itself; it is detached not only from those men, but also from its own meaning and history. It has served its time. Once it helped to portray a state, and that external image helped to make the state what it was. Now it is extinct, thereby sealing, once again, the fate of that state and, at the same time, the fate of that other, later republic that had adopted the ritual to conceal its inner emptiness, a literal emptiness: a state without a *Volk* is empty. The Piecks, the Ulbrichts and the Honeckers did not understand the lesson of the King of Sanssouci.

Their inheritance is one hundred meters away, a pathetic legacy: the museum that was intended to confirm their glory forever is now used to ridicule them, to jeer them into oblivion. This is happening by way of a special exhibition, *Tschüs S.E.D.* (Bye-bye, S.E.D.), with the banners from the huge demonstrations hung up and draped over the pieces that used to be exhibited there. The effect is rather comical: dummies that were designed to represent members of the armed

Neue Wache,
Unter den Linden,
East Berlin,
May 23, 1990

forces now hold revolutionary placards, splendid agricultural sta-
tistics are half-hidden under ironic maxims or cries of despair, and
as you wander among the familiar phrases and linger in your own
recent past you can still hear the voices of those pioneers, of history
that has been caught up and overtaken by its own pace, so that instead
of looking only six months old it already seems like something from
long, long ago, as though it is almost impossible that you were ever
part of it yourself. The effect of time is a wondrous thing: in a video in
the exhibition space I see images that I saw as new images six months
ago, but the crowd listening on Alexanderplatz is an old crowd. It
looks historical, historic, not because we have seen it so often already,
but because we know we are going to see it so many more times. You
can tell by their expressions that they do not yet know that the state
treaty is about to be signed and that the man with the beard will
be the Minister for Foreign Affairs, and that they are unaware of
the practice that will follow their ideas and their revolution. When
those same banners hung in the museum in West Berlin six months
ago, it felt like a forgery to me: the book of history cannot be written at the same time as the actual history itself. There must be at
least a little distance, or it feels contrived. Here, in the ironic context
of Social Realist art and nationalistic braggadocio and propaganda, it
works, but the room next door, where nothing has changed at all, and
the only form of irony is the absence of any commentary, has an even
more dramatic effect.

The history of the *Arbeiter- und Bauernstaat* from 1946 to
1961 is on display in the different rooms and no one has so much
as knocked askew a hammer or a pair of compasses. I remember
walking around here in December when someone wrote in the
guestbook that this exhibition should always be kept as it was, a
museum within a museum, *camera in camera*. So that advice has
been followed; we are still seeing what the *ancien régime* wanted us
to see, their conception of the enemy, their mighty achievements,

their cult of personality, their heroic leadership. This takes the form of Otto Grotewohl's glasses, keys and wallet, and Wilhelm Pieck's measuring rod and pincers: sacred objects intended to demonstrate their noble working-class origins, the familiar and foolish things that gain extra significance when placed under glass, as though they have been dug up from prehistoric graves. All that is missing is the anonymous skeleton lying alongside. These workers did not want to be among the nameless of history, they wanted to be preserved, and if no one else did it for them, they would do it for themselves: "The government of the D.D.R., in recognition of my outstanding political, cultural and economic contributions to the construction of socialism, asked me to be the first to wear the Order of Karl Marx. After examining the recommendation of the government of the D.D.R., I have decided to accept the Order of Karl Marx on the 135th anniversary of Karl Marx's birth, 5.5.53.Wilhelm Pieck." And there are other things to learn here too, even if only how bad that other Germany, the Western one, was. In the first Bundestag, there were sixty factory and bank directors, 132 senior officials, thirty-five major farmers, five major landowners, nineteen wholesalers, twelve farmers of medium-sized farms, eighteen laborers, sixty-two employees, four tradesmen, thirty intellectuals, twenty housewives and five "others." A double bass with women's tights (and here I am referring to a musical instrument in the exhibition, its hollow belly stuffed with nylon stockings) demonstrates the unscrupulous nature of "speculators," *das Junkerland muß in Bauernhand*, squires' lands into farmers' hands, and there is a large photograph of Ernest Bevin displaying "malicious glee" at the U.S.A.-inspired decision to found a West German separatist state. *Durch das Volk, mit dem Volk, für das Volk:* only the people no longer wanted it. On the day 1,846 people fled via Hungary to the Bundesrepublik, there

---

* By the people, with the people, for the people.

were twenty-eight pictures of Erich Honecker in just one issue of *Neues Deutschland*. Great dreams really cannot fizzle out in a more dismal way, and anyone who feels a sense of *Schadenfreude* has not grasped the dimensions of the misery.

On the other hand, anyone who claims that there is much to regret about the demise of this republic must feel great disdain for humanity. Some West German intellectuals seem to be considerably more excited at the thought of Unity for Germany than they are about the idea of millions of their fellow citizens being liberated from a system imposed on them by force. It seems morbid to summon specters of the past and mock those who have just been liberated because they like to eat capitalist bananas and show inclinations to appreciate things that have seemed perfectly ordinary to us for decades. These shrill purists, who have nothing to offer but their shrillness, believe that the citizens of the D.D.R. must immediately tuck into their new utopia, as if they were not still struggling to digest the previous one. And who are they supposed to be doing it for? For the people in this Germany who always stand on the sidelines, saying that the world stinks and pretending they cannot smell the stench that is still wafting up from their moldering paradise? A betrayed, ragged, rotten utopia is not a pleasant sight. It is riddled with deceit, with a mould that will proliferate in the years to come. We are sure to hear lots more about it. Forty years after fascism, Europe still is not done with it, and the same will happen here, where not one but two pasts need to be taken into account, the past from '33 to '45, and the past from then until now. For some people, the state treaty came too quickly, with almost indecent haste. I do not agree. Slowing the process down would not have solved anything, but only exacerbated the dissonance and conflicts. The problems that exist will not simply go away, and no matter how much bitterness is involved in their resolution, it is better to battle within a framework that is acceptable to the majority, so that the

structure will at least remain standing. When you imagine the confusion, resentment, fury and fear that any hesitant policy would
have resulted in, you can only agree with this government for acting quickly. Electoral motives are sure to be involved, as they are
when the opposition attempts to delay the process, which seems far
more dangerous to me. The "told you so" that Lafontaine already
has written all over his face is not related to the power of prediction
that is part and parcel of statecraft, but to the small change of party
politics, which is going to come in handy as the bitterness in the
West and the fear in the East increase: bitterness about the money
that it is going to cost; fear of the loss of work and security.

The crowds that went out onto the streets last year in Dresden
and Leipzig did not consider any of this. They were giving voice to a
storm. Now that the storm has died down, that crowd looks simply
like what it chose to transform itself into: voters at a polling station, all with their own desires and interests, while the people they
elected look like politicians signing a state treaty. And that is how
we see them: the large, heavy man we already know, who, according to *Der Spiegel*, lives "*in einem Rausch der Eile*," a frenzy of haste,
and that other, smaller man, the one we had never heard of a few
months ago, with the guarded expression and the inward smile. It
is too easy to say that their physiques express something about the
new Germany, but it is tempting to do so. The C.D.U. of the East
is not the C.D.U. of the West; people in the East equate the party
far less with ownership and conservatism. Where there is not so
much ownership, or not yet at least, there is also little to conserve.
In terms of numbers, the East-C.D.U. will of course form a minority in the one party that is soon to come, and the same will apply
to the Eastern socialists. And yet the process will transform those
two large national parties into different parties, because no matter
how great the West's financial and political dominance may be, the
movement from the East to the West remains an unknown quantity

for now—and that too is a reason not to delay actual unification for party-political motives. Not only the Germans, but also the other Europeans want to know where they stand: there are still almost 400,000 Russians stationed in the D.D.R., and they are there for a reason. The glacis that Golo Mann mentioned a few months ago is still intact, as a reminder of the old laws of *Gleichgewicht*, equilibrium, and the waves of attraction and repulsion between Germany and the East that have so often determined the moods of the past. Why should that change overnight?

Behind Brecht's house on Chausseestraße is a small French graveyard. I think that Brecht is buried there, so I wander in through an iron gate in the brick wall. Bucolic—that is the right word, a village churchyard in the Île-de-France: old trees, rickety wooden benches, decaying graves, shadows with the sunlight rippling through them, peace. I walk around, suddenly outside the world, noting the moss on the tombs, the musical names of long-gone Huguenots, lilies, hydrangeas. In the proximity of death, summer is always so much more dense, more vigorous, as though it thrives better here than in the world of the living. But Brecht is not here; he is on the other side of the wall, with Fichte and Hegel and two Dutch Countess Schimmelpennincks, neither of whom reached the age of thirty. I find shade there too, and sun and an immeasurable silence that entirely disregards the city around it. A map on the wall helps visitors to locate the illustrious dead: Brecht occupies the first grave, together with his wife Helene Weigel. A Star of David is daubed on it, and profanities, the usual ones. There is no need for me to be shocked now: I already saw the pictures in the newspaper that morning. Later I ask the guard why they have not been removed, and he says it is because there is going to be a protest at the grave on Saturday. I watch that later on television too: artists with sad faces, no one from the government. It is truly hateful, the words and signs scratched into the black, a message from the realm of evil, anonymous, a reminder that the source of horror will never run dry, not here, not anywhere. And nearby, the graves of Fichte and Hegel with their ladies: quiet graves, unquiet thoughts.

Whatever questions I might want to ask the bushes and the stone, no answer would be forthcoming. Everything has already been said, and everyone has done as they pleased; the thoughts and mindsets of these two men have seeped into brains both fair and foul: Fichte's fiery speeches about the nation-state, Hegel's eternally restless *Weltgeist* dragging anonymous humanity through an ocean of conflicts on the way to a reconciliation of all oppositions, the religious moment of absolute knowledge, when every unspeakable horror is finally legitimized by the sacred aim, which, as in all religions, is an invisible one. "Periods of happiness are blank pages in the history of the world," the mortal human being, and his unimportant fate, caught up in the unfathomable machinery of that ever-elusive world spirit; the individual, surrendering himself to the state, with his name and his soul, and the state, whose right to exist depends on its ability to stand its ground. Then the horrifying encounter between Cortés and Montezuma is no longer some insane coincidence, but a form of rightness. In that kind of system, everything is right, meant to be; the system can accommodate everything. It is simultaneously a form of contempt for others and a consolation, but chiefly for the person who came up with the idea. Alongside this unbearable optimism, Schopenhauer's pessimism is a blessing, if only because it sees evil as meaningless; wickedness is unmasked as itself, not disguised as a necessary phase on the way to something higher. Auschwitz is impossible to stomach in Hegel, just as it is in Christianity. In Schopenhauer, however, it can remain what it is: the manifestation of evil in the world, carried out by humans, originating in the abyss of humans and inflicted upon humans. Any suggestion that the suffering served some purpose is blasphemy.

The grey stone does not respond to my questions. Then Hegel should not have spent his time writing and thinking, I think to myself, but because I am not so good at thinking, and also because I can hear someone raking the path and realize that it sounds like a kind of music, thin, metallic, but not without charm, an inner switch flicks and my mental archive presents me with an image of the philosopher in Frankfurt, playing Rossini on the flute for an hour, probably badly, before tucking into his double meal at the Frankfurter Hof. The world is malevolent, that morning's words have been written, the poodle is asleep, the bachelor in his lonely room is playing the melodies of the Italian composer who liked to eat foie gras with his steak: the story of chance and necessity writes itself and is written.

When I turn around at Hegel's grave to look in Brecht's direction, I see someone standing there, writing, my mirror image. We know there is nothing inside graves, and yet, if that is true, there is no reason to visit them. So there must be something in there after all, but what? Is it their oeuvre, everything they carved into the world until they made it a different place? Suddenly I feel as though all those words are literally lying beneath my feet, a gigantic, inter-woven construction, a mine full of songs and paragraphs, the words of one, so much more accessible, dancing around the gran-ite system of the other, a dual kingdom running rampant beneath the other graves, where Surabaya Johnny rules together with the World Spirit, Mack the Knife dances in Bill's Tanzhaus in Bilbao with *Phänomenologie* in his arms, and a ship with eight sails steals dialectics away to a coast where soldiers are changing the guard for the last time and marching to the beat of the state.

June 2, 1990

XV

Newspapers, voices, notes—these three things have taken over my house. My eighteen months in Berlin are at an end. The household is being dismantled and I feel that I should walk backwards down the three flights of stairs out of some kind of need for symmetry, recreating the moment of arrival, the lack of knowledge. A man receives a grant to work in Berlin, a man wants to write a book, a man is overtaken by events and suddenly finds himself at the center of a vortex. That is how it is here, and that is how it was. My books and clippings disappear into boxes, the voices of radio and television keep on talking to me, I still read the newspapers, but this farewell is a final one. I am leaving, yet I feel that it is not actually possible, that I cannot really do it, that I have become so enmeshed in these events that I can no longer extricate myself, that I must keep watching and writing. What happens in this city in the coming years will continue to interest me, but when you are not there, you no longer belong. You drop out of the ongoing conversation, the options, the constant regrouping of possibilities, memories, expectations. I became part of it, even though I was, and still am, an outsider. I have never forgotten that this is not my country and yet I shared in those events.

History becomes visible at moments of great upheaval, and there have been plenty of those. Travelling and reading in this part of Germany have convinced me, more than ever, of the idea of history as a continuum, with lines branching out, bifurcating, a permanently tangled web of cause, coincidence and intention. And so there is something half-hearted about my farewell; I know that this place will not let me go. The options and projections do not merely extend into the immediate present or the invisible future; the uncertainties also want to take root in the past. In this week's *Die Zeit* (June 15, 1990), Rolf Steiniger speculates about the previous possibilities for unity that there have been since the war, Stalin's proposals, Churchill's ideas, Adenauer's rejections. Fear played a part in all of those opposing movements, and it continues to do so: what kind of country is Germany, what is it going to do, what does it want, what alliances will it enter into, what gravitational pull will it have? Germans' fear of Germans—was that one of the reasons why Adenauer abandoned the other part of the nation to its fate in 1955? That year, in Geneva, Bulganin and Khrushchev informed Eden that they were ready to discuss German unification,

Schloss Sanssouci, Potsdam

and in the November the British once more (Churchill had already given it a shot in 1952) put forward an initiative to start the dialogue with the Soviet Union. The conditions: free elections throughout the whole of Germany and freedom of action at home and abroad for the united Germany. But Adenauer was not interested that time either, just as he had dismissed Stalin's proposal in 1952: a Germany with its own army, united, but neutral. Why did Adenauer not like this idea? His thinking was outlined in a top-secret Foreign Office document: "The bald reason was that Dr. Adenauer had no confidence in the German people. He was terrified that when he disappeared from the scene a future German Government might do a deal with Russia at the German expense. Consequently he felt that the integration of Western Germany with the West was more important than the unification of Germany."

The words are written with the simplicity of a newspaper report, as though the obvious alternative would have been a different Germany, a different history, and yet we cannot imagine that, because it never existed. How would I feel as an East German if I read that piece? That would of course depend on what sort of East German I was, because they come in many different shades. The idea that forty years of a closed system had perhaps been unnecessary would make me melancholy, I think, or bitter, or resentful, as applicable. Or I would put the whole article to one side as just another of the many speculations of the Western press that were now flooding into my world, but not helping me one jot with my real problems: money, job, future, the change in mentality and the resistance to it, the pressure from another society that was penetrating deeper into my life every day. But maybe precisely because of the force with which this new world was advancing upon me, the notion of deceit and betrayal that was lurking inside me would surface at some unpredictable moment, allying itself with the thought that my part of Germany was held in contempt by that other part, with its visible poverty and neglect, and the awareness that my part had not been free since the war and, through reparations and constant occupation, had had to do penance on behalf of that other part, which was now marching in, supreme and prosperous, as though this were some conquered territory, while loudly protesting about the money it was going to cost in the years to come, as though we had not been helping to pay off their debts and guilt for all those years, even though they continued to think, if not say, "It's your own fault."

Soon there will be no Wall; soon this will be one country. But even where that Wall no longer stands, it will still be present. Given its slowness, the gradual interpenetration of the two Germanies will be far less visible than the external signs of unity: the same banknotes, advertisements, road signs, uniforms. The invisible is situated in the mind, in the lost protection offered by isolation. The refusal of the West is just as strong as the aversion of the East, and in a year's time anyone who drives past Magdeburg on their way to Berlin will feel a vague shift in his awareness, the absence of a border, a whisper of former thoughts. He will be driving in a country that is no longer there, and yet which still exists, an invisible state with visible inhabitants, a way of thinking that will not be abolished by decree but eroded by wear and tear.

A few weeks ago, I visited the University of Leipzig. I was there to give a talk of about an hour to a group of students of Dutch. The tutor had warned me: don't expect much of a conversation afterwards. They are sure to have plenty of questions, she said, but they won't dare to say anything—people here aren't used to standing out as individuals and speaking in public. She was right. The school class, because that is what it seemed like, was nice enough. They were mostly young women, and appeared to be well prepared. I could tell that they were listening, but there were no questions, and suddenly I felt like a foreign body, what the Japanese refer to as a *gaijin*, an "outside person." It felt like the dew was still upon them, and if I try to explain what I mean by that, I cannot do any better than describe it as innocence, even though I know that another person might call it naivety. They had all grown up in one world; I had grown up in another. Later that evening, in a café, the stories would come out about membership of the Freie Deutsche Jugend,* about endless lessons in Marxism-Leninism, about the summer course in the Netherlands or Flanders that they, or their tutors, had not been permitted to attend, and no explanation was given. They were still sitting there inside their bell jars, unspoken questions hanging over their heads, anchored in a world whose vocabulary did not apply to me, and that too, I realized, would later exclude the others, the people from the West. These women, still so much like little girls, had grown up in a walled garden, and anyone who did not speak the language of that garden was a stranger.

What did they want to do with their lives? They did not know, or they did not want to know, because perhaps it would still not be possible, even now. Everything was so uncertain. No one knew what was going to happen, not them, not their parents, not their teachers. It was possible to travel abroad now, but you needed money to do that, and how did you get money when there was no work? One of the women I saw as girls actually had two children of her own. She wanted to do a doctorate on German-language emigrant literature in the Netherlands, but she would need to spend some time in the Netherlands, and how did you do that? She had been to Berlin once since the Wall fell. And how did you feel? Furious. She had stood beside a gap in the Wall, in those first few days, back in November, and had seen "in a flash" that the prison had not been built of bricks, but of people.

Anyone who wants to become acquainted with this world should read Uwe Johnson's *Begleitumstände: Frankfurter Vorlesungen.*

---

* Freie Deutsche Jugend (F.D.J.)—Free German Youth. See also Glossary.

Understanding this country involves travelling back in time along lines of written words, over and over again: they draw you into the past in order to clarify the present. This is the dual function of literature: subversion during and testimony afterwards. The lucidity of the rebel reveals the stupid sophistication of the system. Stupid sophistication—is that even possible? Yes, it is. It occurs when a system uses political sophistication to allow its intellectual stupidity to penetrate into every corner of the state, when it constantly knows where it needs to focus its attention, and that is always on those who do not participate. This causes the totalitarian state to suffer. The opposing view is a void it cannot tolerate; the subversive thought is what is lacking from its totality, a gap it must fill with its power, because where the state is open, it is vulnerable.

New images are now mixing with the old ones: on television I see the wooden shed at Checkpoint Charlie, which I have passed by so often, slowly rising into the air on a tall crane. Levitation, a spiritualist séance—for a moment it seems as though it is being taken up into heaven. There is something peculiar about the sight of a building hanging in the air; you suddenly see what a foolish structure it always was. The onlookers gaze at the resulting empty space like children watching a conjuring trick: now you see it, now you don't. There is a lot of magic going on these days; the whole city is populated by magicians. Walls and towers disappear, vanish into thin air; what once existed is now a *fata morgana*. People walk through the Wall as though it is made of air; what is there is not there.

I know that I must say farewell to this melting land, but I cannot do so yet. There is too much unfinished business; words and images are still entangled in my thoughts. Johann Georg Hamann saw in history "ciphers, hidden signs, hieroglyphs of God." I do not know whether they belong to God, but after all those months I feel enmeshed in those signs; they are scars on a living organism, as in

Dresden, as in Potsdam. Germany is unfinished. It is ancient, but it is still being made, and that ambiguity makes it fascinating. Herder says that nations develop at different rates, like people. If you subscribe to that idea, you could say that France and England are fully formed, adult: we know them. But do we know Germany? Does Germany know itself? Does this country know what it wants to be when it is big? And Gombrowicz whispers about "another, probably more hidden and less legitimate, aim of man . . . his need for the Incomplete . . . Imperfection . . . Inferiority . . . Youth . . ."—and now, in my last week here, that thought keeps coming back to me. Even after all these centuries, there is still no definition of Germany; it remains an enigma. In his latest book, *Die Schere*, Ernst Jünger reflects upon that word: "enigma" was a word shared by the Greeks and Romans for a puzzle, a secret, the unfathomable. It is Kant's *An sich*, the essence that cannot be known; it is, in Luther's translation, "*das dunkle Wort*," the dark word. Germany as a dark word, as a spiritual mystery behind a veil of power and material success, as a country that you attempt to read, ancient, and yet the youngest of all European states.

I remember seeing a picture of Dresden: a man standing in front of a sculpture, staring as though he hoped to unravel its mystery. The day was grey, rainy, with those strange flashes of fateful sunshine that distort everything. The sculpture was the head of a hero on a pediment, out of context, on the ground near the Schloss. As I said, things unfinished: pediments on the ground, checkpoints in the air, walls lying flat. Everything flows. The man stood with his back to me, hands clasped; you could see that he was thinking. His shadow lay beside him like a small pet, and the two of them had a great deal to think about, as did I. I had just seen the ruins of the Frauenkirche with, in their midst, a blackened statue of Luther holding an open book that could only be the Bible he had translated. He stood there in front of some sort of construction trailer,

Hermann Maternstraße,
East Berlin, May 1990

young, thinner than usual, as though this still visible war had caused him to lose a few pounds. A scorched wreath lay at his feet and, in the background, a golden angel danced on one leg above a dome that looked like a peeled tropical fruit. I thought about the connection between that man and the ruins, about his anti-Semitism, about how his mighty Bible translation had forged the German dialects into a single language, providing the impetus for Germany as a nation, about how impossible my wandering, unfinished thoughts would be to prove, how frivolous, because everything in history is connected to everything else and the earlier darkness must often bear the later guilt. But those ruins were not frivolous; the black of the air pollution made it seem as though all of the broken, cracked walls, columns, spandrels, capitals, arches and stones were covered with lava, as though this harm had come not from above, rained down by a destructive, vengeful enemy, but had boiled up from a burning underworld.

Nowhere can architectural details be seen as clearly as in ruins, where ornamentation that was designed for an entire structure now exists only for itself. The drama of a ruin is determined by the beauty of its disconnected elements. And maybe these are Hamann's divine hieroglyphs: architraves and archivolts, mouldings and cornices,

Dresden, May 1990

stripped of their function, protruding from the debris, maybe foolish, maybe magnificent. As so often happens, my thoughts found
an echo later that day: I visited a second-hand bookshop, where
I found a book about the First World War, *Das Antlitz des Welt-
krieges*, edited by Ernst Jünger in 1930. Luther, Jünger, Hamann,

Herder, nothing to do with one another, everything to do with one another; German figures from the endless series of spirits that can be summoned up when you reflect upon that country at night. "*Im Kriege selber ist das Letzte nicht der Krieg*" (In war itself, war is not the ultimate purpose), it says in the front of Jünger's book, but he did not write this oracular statement himself; it comes from Schiller's *Die Piccolomini*. It sets the tone, though, the mystical veil that characterizes so much of the work of Jünger the shaman-samurai, shrouding its lucidity. The man who could write so clearly about enigmas is himself one. Delphic profundity, the architecture of a beetle's carapace, designer of a portrayal of humankind in which freedom and obedience are supposedly identical, a terrible Faust, who works on paper to cobble together his "Typus" as a utopian robot, while people of flesh and blood walked all around him, people for whom freedom had long been equated with obedience. Great writer and frequenter of collaborators, hermit and symbol of contradiction—I never know quite what to make of him. When I mention his name to a group of philosophers and young academics one evening in Berlin, one of the young men stares at me, raises his hands like a priest and says, "*Vade retro, Satanas,*" and yet that young exorcist leaves at the end of the evening with the new Jünger biography under his arm. The book I have bought is in Gothic script, and that too has certain connotations for a non-German, connotations that are not easy for Germans to feel, particularly when, as in this book, the chapter headings are in Gothic capital letters, which is not unlike deciphering runes: "𝔉𝔄𝔥ℜ𝔗 𝔷𝔘ℜ 𝔉ℜ𝔒ℜ𝔗," "𝔇𝔈ℜ 𝔏𝔈𝔗𝔷𝔗𝔈 𝔄ℜ𝔗," "𝔗ℜ𝔒𝔐𝔐𝔈𝔏=𝔉𝔈𝔘𝔈," "𝔊𝔗𝔒𝔊𝔊=𝔗ℜ𝔘𝔓𝔓𝔈ℜ." In the photographs accompanying the words I see neither "princes of the trenches with hard, determined faces," nor the "purer, bolder warriorhood" that was forged by fire. As usual, I see nothing but pictures of atrocities, intensified by the outdated photographic technology, which makes the atrocity somehow seem

more absurd (everyone is already dead anyway), reducing the antiquated, bullet-riddled tanks, the dead horses, the men in the mud,
the living creatures in the rubble, the bayonets in the snow, the
nameless columns of men in the stunned landscape, to an aesthetic
category from which all the suffering and humiliation have melted
away and heroes have become victims, robbed even of their deaths.

Maybe only someone who was still suffused with the spirit of
the Middle Ages and knightly ideals (or their nineteenth-century
echo) and who also had an ice-cold, modern eye for our mutation
under the totalitarian rule of technology could capture and describe
the contradictions of that era in this way. But precisely because his
writing is so effective, the image I see as I am reading is a horseman
of a frozen apocalypse, on a pale horse, of course, riding over an
endless battlefield of anonymous corpses, painted by Francis Bacon,
untouched by his own fate or that of others, a blind prophet, literally
so—because if I do not think that, all I see is an older gentleman
dressed in civvies in wartime Paris, someone who reads Psalm 90
after breakfast and browses in second-hand bookshops, who stud-
ies butterfly wings and in one single page of his diary leaps from
the aesthetics of a bombing to the fourth act of *Don Juan*, meditates
about scissors as a unity of opposites, becomes lost in contemplation
of the tiger lily on the table in front of him, muses about the strength
that can break flowers and other paradoxes of the wall of time, and
then goes off again to visit wealthy ladies, or writers we might perhaps call traitors because they sided with the enemy under Pétain
while the Vichy police were transporting their Jewish compatriots
to that country about which that same elderly and maybe somewhat
eccentric gentleman—who has the uniform of that country hanging
in a wardrobe at home, but is now running his hands over twenty
volumes of Saint-Simon with aesthetic delight—had written at the
end of his own book: "For the power of the secret Germany is great
and the concerns of the world recognized this far sooner following

the Great War than the Germans did themselves." And that is still true, and yet it is no longer true.

What awaits me now is a temporary cessation of entanglements, questions, paradoxes. *Ostgeld* flows into *Westgeld*, the border evaporates, one national anthem dissolves into the other, the embassies in East Berlin shrivel away, elections in six months' time, the words "East" and "West" revert to their former meanings, the entire map of the country is a single color, the chemical wedding of a male citizen of Cologne and a female citizen from Weimar, the platonic union of these two individuals as citizens of the only Germany that now exists, two citizens rocked in the arms of Europe, from which no country can now break free without injuring itself.

I decide to celebrate my farewell in the melancholy gardens of Sanssouci and drive there over the Glienicker Brücke, Smiley's bridge. It is weather for spies: squalls of rain, followed by vanilla-colored sunlight. A squad of Russians comes towards me, a long line of men carrying spades. They look like they have been walking for days, but that cannot be true, as they are not carrying any kit. I have to wait as they cross the road and I get a good look at them, because it happens so slowly. There is something ancient about the passing crowd, faces from all regions, Kyrgyz, Uzbeks, Russians, the great masses of the East. What is going through their minds? Their oversized caps perch on their heads; some of them smile in the general direction of my car, but I cannot see what they are thinking. They have partly withdrawn from Hungary and Czechoslovakia already, but they will be staying here. There are no houses for them at home, no work; the changes can already be seen here in a world that is pulling away from their own. What sort of memories and opinions will they take with them when they return home, and how will those thoughts become deformed and return to us as a far greater challenge than German Unity?

I park my car and go for a walk in the gardens of Frederick the Great. The rain drums on my umbrella, the distances between the buildings are immense, I am made to feel small, a homunculus among the luxuriant rhododendrons, a sketched figure beneath the classical arches, sheltering in the symmetrical forest of columns. Gloomy weather, clairvoyant afternoon, a clarity that allows you to see everything: the green twig emerging from the bark of the lime tree, the ragged Corinthian capitals of the ruin, the tattered, beheaded angel on the steps, the pointless spiral staircase of the Belvedere ending in mid-air, the dead field mouse in the mud still staking some claim. With the obligatory slippers on my feet,

Belvedere, Schloss Sanssouci, Potsdam

I glide across the polished floor of the ballroom in the Neues Palais, but I cannot keep pace with the Rococo. I stalk past the Jagdkammer and Unteres Damenschlafzimmer and think about the young prince, whom his father ordered to be taken, under strict guard, along the still-existing Reichsstraße I to Küstrin (Kostrzyn), where he was made to watch the execution of his friend Hans von Katte, who had assisted him during his failed escape attempt. Outside, it continues to rain. A Moor looks out over nature that has been deformed and clipped into shape, raising his triple lamp to the leaden sky. Beside him stands a dismantled woman, naked, headless, her hands just rusty iron spikes, a submissive posture, mound of Venus sooty from the invisible dirt in the air. The great king would not recognize his palace. Past trees he would have seen when they were just saplings, I walk to the orangery, the golden pavilion. The daisies shine in the grass like some kind of mould, and in the distance I can hear trains and crows. My German year is at an end. I shall say farewell to my friends and leave without leaving, because of the memories I am taking with me and leaving behind and, when I return, everything will be different, yet still the same, and changed forever.

June 30, 1990

PART II

BERLIN SUITE

The final photograph in Part I of this book shows the Belvedere in the gardens of Sanssouci, in Potsdam, and the last sentence ended with the words: "and, when I return, everything will be different, yet still the same, and changed forever." It was in itself not a difficult prediction to make. The Wall would be gone, but the familiar buildings would still remain, and the two parts of the city would, I believed, slowly move towards each other, along with the people who lived there. Old newspapers would disappear and new ones would take their place, West Berlin would become busier and busier, and in the East the signs of capitalism would start making gradual inroads. I recently went back to visit the Belvedere. It was no longer the open, wounded ruin it had been since the war, dismantled, violated, weeds among the pillars. Its decay was wrapped up like one of Christo's buildings, the desecration invisible. The signs of war will disappear from this building; it will no longer serve as a memento. On the contrary: if it ever resurfaces from beneath those black rags, it will gleam, a model of classical architectural style, a showpiece. Yet it will also look a little dead, like an actress with a facelift.

What kind of city had I returned to? I still did not know. This was in fact a double return: the first in February, the second in April. In the intervening period, the doubt had intensified; it was becoming increasingly difficult to say anything about the situation. I myself remained more or less the same, even though no one steps into the same river twice. The setting was also the same: same city, same house, same wooden lion on the handrail in the dark hallway, same smell of tobacco and German food in the stairwell. My Chilean friend had taken some of his books and paintings away to the other side of the earth, but there was still enough Spanish there to keep a reader occupied for a year, and the strange furniture of exile also remained. It snowed on my first return, and the chestnut tree in the courtyard still reached close to my windows, and I could see how cold the tree felt. The neighbors with the children in the flat opposite had disappeared and the new ones were invisible. The old woman beneath me, who was the oldest resident and had known the house before the war ("you simply can't imagine what the bombings were like"), had become increasingly confused over the past few months, and then she had died. I wondered if anyone in the world still thought about her sometimes. Big cities allow people to disappear without a trace, but I can still picture her big shoes, her stiff gait, her closed expression. But no one ever mentioned her. A company with the word "Europe" in its name had moved in on her floor. The people I sometimes saw coming out of there looked as though they had stepped straight out of an advertisement.

I went on scouting expeditions in the snow. I remember one time encountering a surviving piece of Wall with metal rods sticking out of it, a dead, snow-covered passageway, the rods like grasping, black tentacles, but nothing happened. I stood there on that narrow piece of land that would soon be ordinary again, part of a much larger piece of land, with no more than traces, imprints of the two missing walls in the soil, and I realized that there was nothing to say. Any thoughts about that concrete memory had been thought to death; like the Wall itself, they had met their end. It felt much stranger in those places where the Wall no longer was, at Checkpoint Charlie, for instance. But you could no longer say "*at* Checkpoint Charlie" either, because now it existed only in photographs. Describing a place in terms of what is no longer there can be difficult. The Wall that is no longer there exists in duplicate, because you have to imagine it in the place where it once actually was. Or maybe not, but it happens automatically. You cannot walk through a wound unharmed, and that wound is everywhere. As are the scars. Many of the checkpoint buildings are still standing, empty, pointless. They have to go, or someone needs to find a use for them. The currency exchange office at Invalidenstraße has become a Beate Uhse sex shop, which is sure to go down well. Slowly the big clean-up will begin, but that is outside, in the city. The inner clean-up will have to wait for people who have not yet been born, for the new inhabitants, or for the unthinking, but there are few of those. It seems as though everyone has the Wall in their mind; sooner or later it comes up in every conversation. Are people becoming used to it? Not really. You can now hop onto the S-Bahn to the East without having to get off at Bahnhof Friedrichstraße; you just carry on through. The train windows sketch the city for you: the gap where the Wall once stood, the drabness, the Stalinist architecture, the other. No, you cannot get used to that, and you cannot blow it up either; it is going to remain intact. Soon, rents for the unpainted houses will rise, and growing numbers of unemployed people will be living in those colorless buildings. And that too is a Wall of a kind.

And what about the West, where the privileged people live? They are unhappy, sometimes even malicious; I will come back to them later. And they keep themselves to themselves. In fact, it feels as though, after the initial euphoria, the Wall has returned. If you have no business being in the other part, East or West, you stay at home. Too expensive for one, too shabby for the other: "The people in the East have a sergeant-major mentality. There's no talking to them." "The people in the West are arrogant. They want to colonize us." "They put up with that system for forty years. What does that say about them? One person in six was a member of the Stasi. Can you imagine that mentality? That's all we need!" "Money, money, money, it's all those *Wessis** think about. They think we're all beggars. They were just lucky. Coming over here for a nice little tour in their great big Mercedes, seeing if they can find an old house of theirs still standing."

"Don't you think it's all changed?" friends ask me. You don't want to say so, but you think that perhaps they are the ones who have changed; you are amazed at their bitterness. They go on and on about rising crime rates, but I come from a city with its own problems, so I am not impressed. The long lines of Poles outside the cheap supermarkets and electronics shops on Kantstraße that they were complaining about so much last year have not returned, in spite of the new visa freedom. Most of the Trabants are staying in their dens or their owners have bought Western cars. The petrol is a better quality, so the stench has gone. The West of the city is once again its former, park-like self. House prices are rising daily and in every respect this is the most peaceful metropolis I know; even the May Day riots were less violent this year than tradition dictates. Anything else? Just people living, and waiting. They are waiting for better roads and a decision about whether Berlin will be the capital city, waiting for a balanced budget and for new buildings on Potsdamer Platz, for the Mielke trial and for new immigrants,

---

* East and West Germans referred to each other as Ossis and Wessis. See p.221.

for work and for revelations, for investments and bankruptcies. The entire city is sitting in the waiting room of history, and while everything that happens here is very real, there is still a sense of unreality about the streets and squares, as though this world might not be real, as though something completely different might yet happen and nobody knows what, but whatever it is, it will have something to do with the idea of history. This city cannot escape history and perhaps that is the issue here, or one of the issues.

History should be something that has already happened, not something that is happening now. Anyone who believes he is making history cannot keep his mind focused on reality, but a city that is saturated with signs of the past, with planned statues and chance bullet holes, with damaged columns alongside intact ones, a city that reads like one large memory in stone, a city that is reminded every day of its role from before and even before that, is not free to move in the present. History is invisible because it happens so slowly; only very rarely does it allow itself to be hurried along. One such moment was that day in November 1989, but the consequences of that day are moving with the slow deliberation of a chess move, and the city's inhabitants are the people who will have to make the next move, and they will also have to wait for the results—and there is more evidence of waiting than doing. They while away their time in the waiting room by talking, complaining, arguing, blaming, investigating, remembering, condemning, asking. The pages in this history book are as heavy as the lead in Kiefer's books: you can turn over only one page a year at most.

But do you really think, you peculiar Outsider, that the Berliners you can see sitting in the weak spring sunshine on a bench behind Schloss Charlottenburg, or their distant fellow citizens who are looking with a mixture of embarrassment and bewilderment at the pale and pimply faces of the Hare Krishnas bouncing up and down on Alexanderplatz to the east, are that bothered about the idea of history?

"*Jein*," I would have to answer, like a true Berliner: both *ja* and *nein*, because how can you not think about history at such a time? Historic: the word pops out of politicians' mouths on a regular basis ("If we miss out on this historic opportunity . . .") and strides through the editorials and television commentaries. Monuments still testify to history: the days of your own lifetime can turn to stone and take the form of a ruin, a half-demolished Wall, a facade full of bullet holes or a colossal statue of a grieving mother with a fallen son in her arms. And there is another way in which almost everyone here is affected by history—even the youngest citizens of the former D.D.R. were members of the F.D.J. If you go further back in time, you encounter all kinds of different combinations: people who, under Hitler, were on the wrong side and after him were nothing, people who were on the wrong side twice, people who were heroes during the Nazi era, and then joined the Stasi, and all shades in between, from fanaticism to indifference. You meet them and you do not know who they were; they carry their invisible pasts with them in this transitory present. This much is certain: twice in the lifetimes of some of these people, once in the lifetime of nearly all of them, something was over, finished, history took a turn, made a move or a feint that made it seem as though they could start afresh, all over again, which of course is never really true. But that is at least how it seemed. German National Socialism was destroyed in 1945; East German Communism went bankrupt in 1989. Democracies are organized differently. They may have a beginning but, all being well, they have no end, and this explains some of that strange feeling of temporariness and unreality that is hanging over Berlin and East Germany. In a sense, they have landed in utopia, because that was their reason for going out onto the streets: freedom, democracy, the right to have a say, everything they did not have. But now that they have it, it does not look like a utopia, except for the fact that, as with any utopia, there is no end in sight. If all goes well, this history will not be "over" in their lifetimes, not complete, and that brings it into conflict with our human dimensions. Utopias belong in paradise, where, as we all know, it is impossible to live. Now that utopia has to happen here, it is actually proving to be something of a disappointment.

I listen in on conversations and make notes. Nothing in the following comments is invented:

The Polish professor: "What they haven't understood here in West Germany is that capitalism has not conquered socialism, but that capitalism will be socialized from the East. There's a slower movement going from East to West and it's much more difficult to see. Incidentally, did you realize that Kohl, despite his recent defeat, is actually still in power thanks to the *Länder* of the former D.D.R.?"

The well-known feminist: "I don't care about the taxes, just as long as they rebuild the Wall. They're different people over there, nothing to do with us. It was so different, the way they grew up. This is never going to work, not in our lifetimes."

The journalist: "You should keep an eye open, see how many pairs of green trousers you spot in East Berlin. They may well be wearing Italian jackets, but they're wearing them with green trousers. Army issue. They can't wear the jackets, but they don't want to throw out the trousers. And if you notice that they seem to be walking a little oddly in their Adidas trainers, that's the same thing: they've been wearing army boots all their lives."

The property owner: "We didn't ever expect this to happen. Our family still owned a building in Erfurt. It was part of an inheritance for me and my sister. It was all managed very well. We had to pay a bill of 1028 Marks, but then it was ours. The estate duty had already been paid. It's estimated at almost a million. There are about fifty people living there. I should get them all to line up and submit to an inspection. No, not really. Only joking."

The feminist: "If at least they'd liberated themselves, the way we feminists did . . . But no, even that had to come from Russia."

The student from the East: "My dad's brother left for the other side early on, when you still could. My dad didn't—he wanted to stay. We had a small family business and he tried to keep it going. Once a year, my uncle would come to visit us in his big Opel. And he always laughed at us because of all the things we didn't have. I hated it when he visited."

The bookseller from the East: "I don't need to tell you all the things that weren't allowed. But there were also loads of things that *were* allowed. Just look at the lists of titles published by Volk und Welt, or Reclam. And now everything's allowed, but nothing's possible, because my shop's been bought up by a chain. Everything I know, everything I've learned, it's all become useless. You don't need to have read Updike or Goethe to sell books about sex or travel guides. And the only alternative is the door."

The student of Dutch from Leipzig: "Before, I wasn't allowed to go to the Netherlands, and now I can't go to the Netherlands, because it's too expensive. Of course I'm happy the *Wende* happened, but it still hurts when you hear people over there saying we've got no initiative. We've got plenty of initiative, but where's that going to get you? My dad's been laid off—he'll never get another job. And it's the same everywhere. People are frightened."

The translator from the West: "All they know how to do is complain. It has to happen right now, it has to happen today. We didn't get things handed to us on a plate after the war either. We couldn't just head off to Majorca. They act as though we fought that war on our own. Like it was nothing to do with them. The fascists all lived in the West. And you should hear what they have to say about the Poles and Vietnamese. They're giving all of Germany a bad name."

The Hungarian writer: "My seven-year-old daughter was on a school trip with children from East and West Berlin. I asked her how it went. It was awful, she said. There were all these *Scheiß-Ossis* there. *Scheiß-Ossis*? Oh, they were just so stupid. Stupid? Why's that? They all looked so pathetic, in their weird clothes. And what did your teachers say? Oh, our teachers never talk to their teachers."

The photographer from Haiti: "Racism exists wherever you go, but I had a good life here in Berlin for thirty-three years. That's over now, my friend. I don't dare go to the East anymore, not in the daytime, and definitely not at night. People have been stabbed and thrown off the train. Dead, I mean. There were a lot of Mozambicans and Angolans living there, solidarity between the nations—you know, all that stuff. They were always invited to march past the tribune with everyone else on May Day. But they treated them like slaves even before, and now they've got to leave. There's no work. They were all part of the old regime, of course. Not their fault, but that's how people see it now. *Ausländer raus*, good riddance."

In the *Tageszeitung* (West edition), I read something about the Museum der bedingungslosen Kapitulation, the Museum of the Unconditional Surrender. I had never heard of it, but it sounds promising. I ask a few friends, but no, they have never been there. Where is it? Fritz-Schmenkel-Straße. Oh, in the East. I decide to pay the museum a visit, pass through the visibly invisible border-line, change at Alexanderplatz. I want to stop myself from repeating yet again that it is different, but yes, it is different. The same city, only ten minutes away, and completely different. Someone looks at your raincoat, categorises you. You are from *drüben*, over there. So that much is established. And what do you find yourself doing? Projecting the latest survey, with its fear and negative expectations, on the waiting crowd, thinking you know at least some of the thoughts in those heads. You buy a newspaper that costs half the price of the other newspapers and hop on the S-Bahn to Erkner.

This is a city full of trains. You see the big Moscow–Frankfurt express and would like to change trains, but heading in the other direction. *The Polish professor*: "I was late, and I had to go through the Russian sleeping compartment to reach my seat in the German section. You can't imagine the stink! They all bring food with them, because they don't have enough money to buy any. And there's luggage piled up in the gangway, cardboard boxes. Honestly, it was like the Third World. You could barely get through."

I get off in Karlshorst, which used to be an exclusive residential area. The Haus der Kultur has become Restaurant Centre Ville, and there are large Cyrillic letters above the Spielbank on the corner. Fritz-Schmenkel-Straße is a quiet street. Villas, trees, the discreet charm of the bourgeoisie. There is something strange about it though, and before I can tell myself that it is because of all the Russians wandering around, something else occurs to me: "It's like a ghetto." Or something along those lines, anyway, but it is a strange kind of inversion, because the people inside this ghetto are Russian officers, walking alone or in pairs, people whose clothing separates them from the rest of the world, like Chassidic Jews in Antwerp and New York with their ringlets and their long black coats. I am in a Russian enclave. Even the children walking past are speaking Russian. I see a big white Zim or Zis with a woman in the back and a soldier at the wheel, words I cannot read, more officers with diplomatic bags. Soon they will leave these calm and comfortable avenues, depart from the houses of their former friend and, before that, their former enemy. Pages are turning in the place where they are heading, too, and they do not know what will be written on those pages. But for now they are still here, unloved, a closed community in the country that is paying eight billion for their departure.

At the end of the road is the museum commemorating their arrival, forty-six years ago. Streaming red banners and, on the other side of the trimmed lawn, trucks, a tank, a *Stalinorgel*. I remember that word from back then, "Stalin's organ," a multiple-rocket launcher. A bronze plaque announces the full name of the building: Museum der bedingungslosen Kapitulation des faschistischen Deutschland im Großen Vaterländischen Krieg 1941–1945 (Museum of the Unconditional Surrender of Fascist Germany in the Great Patriotic War of 1941–1945). I head inside. There is no one around. Later, I see a young Russian soldier. He smiles a greeting and we say hello. The wheels of time start turning again: leaflets about perestroika and glasnost lying on a low table, while a gigantic Lenin stands at the end of the room, hands in pockets. He is looking over my head and far into the distance, in the direction I came from. There is always something portentous about Soviet statues; kitsch does not cover it. It is more the suggestion of something that you yourself are not: you are not the peasant with the child in his arms, not the hero with the sword at the enemy's gates, not the owner of that square jaw, those enormous hands, that obvious will to die for the fatherland. They are idols representing virtues that are too demanding, platonic ghosts of bronze and granite.

On the walls and in the display cabinets, polemics and pamphlets by Marx and by Engels, newspapers from the time of Lenin's exile in Switzerland, a visit to Rosa Luxemburg, a letter to Gorky, a portrait of his sister: an iconographic Via Dolorosa whose meaning is still in flux, words and images that can never be erased and which look so different today, even though they have remained the same. I hurtle through time, no pact between Hitler and Stalin to halt me in my tracks, a pact signed by the same von Ribbentrop whom I will later see lying on his back, pale and dignified in pinstripe, with an atavistic noose around his neck, a brand-new rope. That pact never existed; in this *museion* all Germans are forever fascists. I walk directly to the room of the Surrender. I am alone, and I can hear that loneliness. My footsteps on the polished parquet. The furniture from Hitler's Reichskanzlei. The empty carafes with their long necks. The silent chairs. The flags, chandeliers, blank sheets of white paper in front of every seat at the green baize tablecloth, the precise arrangement of the tables.

There are photographs here, too. Zhukov, Tedder, Spaatz, de Lattre de Tassigny, who will lose his battle eight years later at Dien Bien Phu: marshal, air chief marshal, general, another general, they all entered this room, 8 May, 24:00 hours. I look at a photograph of the German delegation on the airfield; they have just climbed out of the small Dakota. This is Keitel's last May but one, but of course he does not know that. He is leading the group—tall, boots, a certain coded beauty, Iron Cross around his neck; behind him, von Friedeburg, Stumpff: field marshal, general admiral, senior general, land, sea, air. They are summoned inside, Keitel with his field marshal's baton, the other two with their decorations. They are told to go and sit "at the table that had been designated for them, which was close to the door." By 00:43 hours (Moscow time), it is all over. Germany has surrendered unconditionally; the Second World War is over in this part of the world. The declaration is drawn up and signed in English, Russian and German. According to point 6, only the English and Russian versions are "authentic"; the German one does not count.

The rest of the museum commemorates the war, which was a war between the Russian people and the fascists. The signs are usually in Russian, occasionally in German. This is a strange panopticon. Aluminium-colored statues of heroes, a display cabinet featuring artificial snow around dented and perforated German helmets, with more than thirty Iron Crosses scattered around those five or six helmets, rusting away in the snow of crumbled plaster. Residents of Moscow listening to the radio on the day war breaks out, photos of German brutality, mass executions, mass graves, a girl hanged, with snapped neck and blonde hair, and beside her a young partisan, neck already in the noose, cap still on his head, face as though his hands are still tucked into his pockets, an actor from a play by Brecht.

Other staircases, other floors. Weapons, medals, certificates. A female soldier who "downed" thirty "fascists" single-handedly. A jar of ashes from Buchenwald. An ampoule of poison. The topographic map that Hitler used to follow the movements of his troops. Another map showing how the Russian units closed the ring around Berlin. In a corridor downstairs, the hangings in Nuremberg: Göring, who escaped that particular death, one eye obscenely half-open; Keitel, the man with the field marshal's baton, his face covered in blood; and beside it the charred corpse of a sinister, roasted grasshopper, the scorched, blackened head raised in a scream, the moustache and hair singed away. I cannot read the caption. I have never seen the photograph before and yet I know that it is Hitler.

Soviet tanks in front of the Brandenburger Tor, unknown artist, Museum der beding-ungslosen Kapitulation

Twenty million Russians died in that war, civilians and soldiers, 102,000 soldiers during the battle for Berlin alone. The building designed to commemorate the war lies at the heart of the former Germany, but for whom was it intended? Can it remain here? Like this? With all that it reveals and all that it conceals? Without Katyn and Molotov–Ribbentrop? Designed for only one German state at a time when there were two? On October 10, 1949, the head of the Russian military administration handed over the management of the museum to the first prime minister of the German Democratic Republic, Otto Grotewohl, but what is going to happen to it now that republic no longer exists and history is being rewritten in Moscow, too? Perhaps, as the *Tageszeitung* columnist believes, it should stay just as it is, to commemorate the real dead and the sacrifices, to reveal the real crime, and forever freeze the unreal ideological lie as evidence that good can be used in the service of evil.

In the hallway, Gorbachev and Bush shake unreal hands on a boat, while in another photograph the Wall opens up forever— random postscripts following a grim hiatus. Outside, I find the German spring, people walking by, the world slowed down to a present tense. If you do not agree with the tempo, you can shoot dead the chairman of the Treuhand.* Or throw a tomato at the chancellor— that is pretty harmless. The chancellor stands in the midst of *"Wir sind das Volk"*—and *das Volk* throws an egg at his glasses. So now the chancellor has it in for *das Volk*. The waiting room is packed. The clock will not tick any faster, but the people who are waiting are in such a hurry.

May 1991

---

* At the time of reunification in 1990, the Treuhandanstalt oversaw the privatisation of formerly state-owned property.

DEAD AEROPLANES AND
EAGLES EVERYWHERE

FIRST IMAGE. I WALK INTO A LARGE ROOM. IN THE room is an aeroplane that will never fly again. I peer in through the windows. Inside, there is an empty snakeskin, dead twigs. Aeroplanes cannot live and therefore they cannot die. So what is it about this plane that makes me think it has lived, died, been buried and dug up again? It is slightly decayed, in the way that living matter rots. Sometimes you see a photograph of an exhumed soldier, a tattered piece of uniform, still a little hair on the eyeless skull. It is a little like that. The dead aeroplane is twisted in a way that contradicts the technical perfection of a real plane, but also that of a real plane wreck: this is not how planes meet their end. I look at the twisted lead, the softness, flexibility, vulnerability of that material. Then I notice another aeroplane. This has only one window, a square hole around where the cockpit must have been. The nose is pointed, like a supersonic jet, but the scratches and dents make the front resemble an animal's head, transforming that square, glass-less window into a mournful eye. The head belongs to an extinct species of bird. More dead twigs where the turbines should be, rust-brown, withered blossoms. Nature, but desiccated, dead. Books on the wings, with weeds growing out of them. Those weeds are dead too: twigs of yellowish brown.

Second image. The sky is grey and northern; this is a northern city. I am in a park. Cars parked on the roads, on the pavements, anarchic, gluttonous, as though a large mass of people have upped and left their possessions behind. Clouds sail past, high overhead, threatening; a storm is coming. In the park, a hill with trees, gentle grassy slopes. I am in no hurry. I know where I am going: to a statue of an idol that stands high above everything else, with the face of a man I recognize. As the trees begin, gentle steps lead upwards. I climb and I watch the statue above me becoming increasingly vertical. Naturally, as it grows larger, I grow smaller. It stands on a circular base that is the size of a small village green. I climb other steps, up to the first gallery. Naked figures of men are carved from the granite. They stare and they think; you can see how hard they are thinking. "Ruminating" is perhaps a better word. A tautology in stone. In spite of the granite, their bodies are just like bodies: muscles, curves, strength. Their age is an average of all ages, they are not permitted to have names, they have removed their clothes to think. They are there to magnify the glory of the bald man above them, but they could never have been bald themselves. Not old, not bald, not fat; their masculine bodies are the distant German echoes of a Greek ideal. I climb higher, growing ever smaller, but I will never be able to reach the feet of that large statue. The man's legs are supported by a peculiar bulwark of stone, as though he is wearing an anachronistic suit of armour. Of course he has a sword (which he never used), and two eagles perch close to his legs, their wings like protective shields, their heads twisted to look around, like those birds at the zoo that seem to have two heads: one at the front and one at the back. Their expressions are fierce, their beaks like hooks. Granite, but you can imagine the color of those harsh eyes. Primal anger: that is how a woman will describe it when she speaks to one of those eagles later, a different one, the same. I take another walk around the statue. Standing directly behind it, I see the stone mantle as a wall of scales; the back of the head looks as though it might belong to a statue of the Buddha. That is something no one has ever said about this man before. Back at the front of the statue, his cheeks are plump, but not with the fullness of the Enlightened One. Moustache, double chin, uniform collar, power. He stands beneath a leaden sky, looking out at the city that did not love him, but his gaze touches no one. In the distance, a sudden shriek like a tempest rising, the scream of a large crowd. Mass shiver, mass pleasure, a competition. The sound races around the treetops and then fades away.

Third image. A woman, her face harsh, contorted. She is in an empty, white-lit space. I do not know what time of day it is; perhaps that kind of measure does not apply where she is. Dream time. Beside her, a cage with an eagle in it. This one has turned its head

Anselm Kiefer, Mohn und Gedächtnis, *1989, Nationalgalerie im Hamburger Bahnhof, Berlin*

away from everything, a dead silhouette on a dead branch. But she is talking to the eagle. I can hear her clearly; her space is directly opposite mine. It would seem that she wishes to tempt the eagle, to seduce it, in a special German variation on Leda and the swan. She reminds the eagle of the look of love he gave her that morning with the primal anger of his eyes. She cuts open his cage with her wire cutters. She offers herself, not actually for mating, although that is what this most closely resembles, but for a much more intense form of communication: as human sacrifice, as prey. I know who she is (I have been in this space for some time): Anita von Schastorf, daughter of a Prussian Junker who supposedly participated in the assassination attempt on Hitler. A father she barely knew, but whom she idealizes, and whose diary she is publishing, having excised the more unsavoury confessions, as a young historian has just accused her of doing. He has a different, infinitely less flattering image of her father, and she berated him furiously, but now she is alone with her eagle, no longer screaming, but seductive. She says she is very naked under her clothes. A bird can have no idea, she says, of "how wretched it feels to be so naked and helpless, without one's plumage," and she repeats her offer: blood, intestines, sinews, fat, skin, glands. This most German of all creatures can have all that her feeble human body has to offer; it is all for his beak and for his claws. He does not move and then it goes dark and when the light returns he is sitting on her half-naked body, wings outspread, but she is not the one who is being eaten, because she is still sitting there after another spell of darkness, now covered in blood, hysterical, feathers and large bird bones around her, wailing, "*Wald* . . . *Wald* . . . *Wald* . . . *Wald* . . ." as though the whole thing were not already dark enough.

Fourth image. I have returned to the northern city on the water. It is lighter this time, another day, and the storm clouds have passed.

A rectangular monument stands on a broad street, with soldiers depicted on it. *"Deutschland muss leben, und wenn wir sterben müssen,"* say the words: "Germany must live, though we must die." That strange formulation means that the survival of Germany is worth the death of those stone men who are marching, rigid and motionless, in a con-tinuous line around their rectangle. This procession can never arrive, can never stop walking, has no beginning and no end. The carving is in relief; their right sides exist only as an idea, buried in the stone, the familiar form of the helmet overlapping the next man's helmeted head, over and over again. As there is no beginning and no end and every man has a man in front and a man behind, they must all continue walking like this forever, on their way to death.

Fifth image. Now I am back where I began. I walk past the dead aeroplanes to a library made of lead. The books on the shelves are so big that I would never be able to pick them up. What could be written inside them? They are old, sagging, falling apart; they lean against one another for support. Obligatory thoughts of the library of Alexandria and of Borges, but books from the former once served as fuel for the city's hammams for six months, while the second brings to mind something that is definitely not made of lead, an internal, mental library where the books are always available to read, but which itself remains invisible. The books here seem more like the volumes in a land registry office, catalogues of the living and the dead, something along those lines. I once visited the Spanish national archive at the castle of Simancas; it was a chilling experience. A few scholars in deathly silence, among kilometers of folios, parchments, a never-ending battalion of leather-bound spines. Somewhere in the midst of all that, I took down a volume: the seventeenth-century land register of the city of Cuenca. My next thought was inevitable: that all of Spain was described in that archive, every centimeter of land, every event, every missive, as though the country and its history were reproduced there, but in paper. I suspect something similar is happening here, but without a method. There must be leaden names inside those books, but they are the names of chance, just as the long ribbons of film stills dangling from the warped leaden video recorders on the top shelves show only random people, strangers, contemporaries, people who were or who are, and whose names will slumber on in these leaden colossi, unseen, because no one can read them. "Euphrates and Tigris" is written on those bookcases, and it seems as though the books want more from me than I can see, as if my fleeting presence must be held up to the light of world history, but anyone who claims that has forgotten that my own origins are in that land between two rivers and that, no matter how anonymous I am, the history of my world lives inside me more vividly than in those closed leaden books.

Sixth image. The room with the woman and the eagle, but two hours earlier. Someone just shouted "DEUTSCHLAND," and it reminded me of another sound, the sound of the crowd in the northern city. This one voice shouts like an entire crowd. It is a little frightening, and the word it shouts only increases that effect. This is not a

Monument in Hamburg, detail, 1991

crowd, and yet those fifteen people, standing at different heights, but close together and with their faces turned in the same direction, have the effect of a tribe, a small *Volk*. "*Wir sind der Chor*," they chorus. They are speaking to the photographer, but I and the people around me hear it too, and of course what we are meant to hear in those words is: "*Wir sind das Volk*." *Volk*? What does that mean? This collection of bickering, backbiting, spying, infighting chorus members, at the moment, that one moment, when they are all photographed together? Is that a *Volk*? A random group of people who have arrived together at a certain point in time must be *das Volk*, that one ineluctable *Volk* with the capital letter, the group that everyone (a photographer is, after all, everyone) looks at, that we, those who do not belong to that *Volk*, look at? The photographer, a lightning-fast historian, does his best, and so he should, because they are keeping him under constant surveillance. He has to take them at that one, unrepeatable moment, catch them exactly as they look right then, capture (that is what photographers call it) the group before it breaks apart into separate individuals. But the photographer does something wrong; a hat is blocking a face, someone is missing, the whole *Volk* is not included, and so it takes revenge on the photographer by devouring him. His clothes remain there on the floor, neatly folded, his trainers on top of the pile. The female photographer who comes after him will not fare any better; this crowd is dangerous.

Final image. Once again, I am back at the aeroplanes, at the leaden library. I walk down a staircase and enter a large room full of paintings. If I had to name one color first, it would be black, the scorched, singed black of things that have burned. Only later do I realize that many of the young women there are wearing the same black: black and the next color along, ash grey, the grey of crushed stones, the light brown of desert sand, the cold snake of dead wood, dried-up leaves, dirty snow. *Lilith, Jerusalem, Entfaltung der Sefiroth, Die-Rheintöchter*: weighty names have been assigned to these scenes. They are images of melancholy: the curled-up snake inside the aeroplane, a lonely ladder to an empty sky, two black angel wings without an angel, landscapes from which a dangerous kind of light has driven away the people, a saturnine world of dead matter, loss and absence, train tracks that end in destruction, like in Theresienstadt, stones whose written names conjure up the world of the Kabbalah, as though, at the end of our passage through all of those dead worlds, it might somehow be possible to escape the filth of history, a redemption. Azila, Jezira, Asijjah: as temptation, as hope, these words wander among the lead and the dead dresses with no people inside, dresses of women, children, maybe even dolls, stained, pressed between the twisted, wrinkled lead, like the fern that was once green, like the loose propeller, like the shocking mass of dead hair on the portrait of the woman, which already is almost invisible.

"*C'est la vie et la mort*," I hear someone say behind me, and of course I have to turn to look. The young man who just spoke those words is looking expectantly at the equally young woman to whom he addressed them. She cannot even turn her head to look back at him, as they are standing too close and the peak of her black cap is too big; she might even decapitate him. It is sticking out like some kind of weapon.

"*C'est ni la vie ni la mort*," she says, and I think she is right. It is neither life nor death. She stands there very still in her pointed silver shoes and looks for a while and then she says, "*C'est la souffrance*." Again, I agree with her. It is the suffering that comes before cleansing, before catharsis, before the longing to be released from a contaminated era, from the blasphemous narrative of history. When I turn to walk out of the oppressive room, I see a guard stop her at the next door. He points at the duck's bill of her cap, but she laughs and turns the thing around so that the huge peak now hangs down the back of her neck like a starched veil. Somehow or other that simple reversal lends a sense of liberation to the afternoon, and I feel lighter as I head outside, freed from those images.

But where have I been, and when? Perhaps that is enough puzzles for now.

Where do Prussian maidens devour German eagles? That would be in Botho Strauss's *Schlusschor*, which I see at the Deutsches Theater, in what used to be called East Berlin. And that is also where the chorus that does not sing sings, and where someone shouts, "Deutschland," just as Anselm Kiefer's *Die Rheintöchter* at the Nationalgalerie immediately evokes thoughts of Germany, just as the soldiers in their eternal rectangle are wearing German helmets, just as the giant stone man in the northern city of Hamburg was the founder of the Germany of 1871, just as the eagles at his feet are the same eagles as the eagle on the naked woman's shoulder, which is of course also the same eagle that I see later that same week (I saw all these images in one week) on a wall in Charlottenburg, the black filth of air pollution dripping like blood from its beak.

But aren't you mixing up your images? You talk about reality in one image and then move on to the next one and start talking about art that is a reflection, depiction, imagination, sublimation of reality. That is true, but I have seen these images—eagle, chorus, leaden books—with my actual eyes, in an actual space, as I have seen the soldiers of the 76th Hanseatic regiment on that rectangular monument in Hamburg, and the statue of Bismarck. Who determines the hierarchy of such images? The imaginary is just as much part of this world, even though I am well aware that the eagle was stuffed and that no one really ate it, just as I know that those books are made of solid lead and do not contain one single name, whatever I might claim, just as those aeroplanes are not decaying, but were simply made that way, just as the dead ferns have been glued into the lead, and the chorus removes its make-up after the performance. Art feeds on reality and, all being well, returns to reality. German art, German reality, you cannot escape it here. Heavy, charged, murky, romantic, sometimes taking a diversion through the slums of kitsch, but even then it is a reflection of reality: the kitsch of the Bismarck towers from the *Gründerzeit*, the kitsch of the cathedrals of light and torch processions of half a century later, the kitsch of the silver eagle that I found so terrifying as a child when I saw it dancing above the procession of grey men marching into The Hague.

German friends are unimpressed by the way I become entangled in such profundities. You go out looking for things, they say, but that is only partially true. Bismarck in Hamburg was unavoidable, as was the monument with the marching soldiers. Such things are just standing there in streets and parks, I say, maybe I am simply quicker to spot them. So did you see Hrdlicka's counter-memorial near the marching soldiers, they ask, the sculptures that he did not complete, because he fell out with the city council? Yes, I saw that too, a dialectical monument, intended to contradict the other one. For Hrdlicka, war is not about marching soldiers, but about victims, women and children in bombings, corpses of soldiers in trenches, about executions, torture, resistance. The city had kindly provided a sign to say that the monument is still under construction, but it is open, it refers only to itself, it is unfinished, it has not yet had its say, it hangs around the other monument like a lament, around those marching men with their closed faces who all appear to be thinking the same thought.

"And Bismarck? What about him?" I would say that any politician who is convinced that it is not he who is making history but that he, like everyone else, must wait to see how it will unfold is attempting a correction to Bismarck's grandiose monument (which, of course, he did not erect himself). The portrait that Golo Mann paints of Bismarck—Faust *and* Mephisto, pious *and* cynical, monarchist *and* despiser of princes, melancholic, power politician, great orator, contemptuous of every form of ideology—is at any rate more nuanced than the image my German friends seem to have of him.

"Alright, then, but Kiefer?" Do I not realize that he is totally passé? He may well be, but why should I care? I can see perfectly well that his art is as heavy as the lead he uses to make it, but isn't it the country itself that has for centuries pressed this weight, this didactic heaviness of heart, onto its artists? They talk about *Bildungsbürgertum*, the educated classes, about Kiefer in his role as *praeceptor Germaniae*, as a self-proclaimed prophet who has not really digested the images he borrows from Jewish mysticism but merely uses them as cosmetic set pieces, just as during an earlier, provocative period he appropriated German myth for his own purposes. That may well be, but I am never very concerned with how a work of art comes about or what the barometer of the art world says, what other people think of it and what hidden motives and political or financial manipulation they suspect; all that matters is the actual object I am standing in front of, capturing me within its apocalyptic force field, as someone behind me says, "*C'est la souffrance.*"

There is clearly no talking to me. I am obviously determined to note the German in all that is German, but can I at least see that Strauss is no more than a sensationalist who weaves political profundity without any clarity into his plays, who has produced only empty words and innuendo on the subject of unification? And did I not hear the booing during that insanely kitschy scene with the eagle? Yes, I heard it, and maybe I even understood it, because it is a scene that belongs in a Spielberg film, not on the stage, and I cannot imagine an English play in which a lion is invited to have its way with the leading lady, and yet I also saw some magnificent scenes that night, and thoughts about the performance keep running through my mind. And, possibly even worse, I keep seeing eagles everywhere I look: Prussian ones and Hessian ones, the eagle of Weimar, which is once again the present-day eagle, tamed ones, crowned ones, post eagles and police eagles, until someone shows me the most beautiful eagle of all, the one with the straight, horizontal wings that I remember from my childhood, the one from the flags, only now it is no longer dancing through the streets, it is hanging in stone above the entrance to the tax office near my house. It has been allowed to stay, but the swastika has been removed from the ring in its claws, and in its place there is a number 48, the number of the building. I will keep it to myself that this lends the number 48 a kabbalistic significance that comes somewhere close to redemption.

June 1991

Village within the Wall

Before the Wall, after the Wall, that is how time is divided now, even if you wish it were not so. You do not feel it every day—sometimes it is just a twinge—but then it hits you again, often on Sundays. It is inconceivable now, but this city once was captive, and what little greenery there was always ended in a Wall that you could not miss. You wanted to get out, but wherever you went, the others were there too; you could never escape.

"Everyone knows about that."

"Yes, but I'm going to say it anyway."

We often used to visit Lübars, a small village with a church, a pump, a village pub, the illusion of countryside, as though it was somehow possible to get out of the city. Girls rode horses over the cobbles of the village square. You walked past the farm with the geese and chickens, where they sold herbs and pickled gherkins, and at the fork where Blankenfelder Chaussee meets Schildower Weg you chose the latter, because it was unsurfaced, just a path.

A gently undulating landscape, with lonely lime trees dotted here and there. Like everyone else, we had developed techniques for avoiding oncoming walkers, for ignoring them, so that it felt as though we were almost alone. The path veered left after a while, and in the distance was the drab shadow of the Wall. Sometimes the hazy light made it look almost beautiful, an ancient monument. We usually left the path there and walked on through the grass to a small river that I only later realized was the Tegeler Fließ, and we would stand there for a while. And that was it. The water was brownish, but clear and rather deep. The strong current carried all sorts of things along with it: twigs, leaves, straw-colored reeds. Right in the middle of the river stood a post with a sign that said the border ran through that exact point, and that attempting to cross to the opposite bank, which was so close, was forbidden and danger-ous. The land on the other bank looked the same as the land on our side. More reeds, and crows, and lime trees, no-man's land as a mir-ror image, and the mirror was empty. Still in the distance, the tall lights, the real barrier, the concrete. Naked, no writing on it. Then we would turn around, go right, up a little hill, and where Schil-dower Weg headed towards the forbidden world—and was therefore a dead end—we would come to a new tarmac path that ran along-side a narrow strip of bushes. Beyond that was a steel fence; if you stood there, the men in the nearby tower turned their binoculars on you. You could almost feel your face being comically magnified, no longer entirely belonging to you, as it was drawn upwards, as if somehow it was up there in the tower too, in that square room with the large windows, where those men were sitting, bored. I could smell their boots and heard without hearing what they were saying about the women on our side riding past on horses. But maybe their boots did not smell and maybe they were not looking. Sometimes a silly little car in army colors drove along the narrow road that went from tower to tower. That is how it was. A steel wall, a fifty-meter strip of sand, a road, a tower. After that, Wall, landscape, church. Blankenfelde, maybe the men even lived there.

On Sunday, I was back in Lübars. I took bus 222 and got off at the last stop. The grave of the local landowner was still there in the green grass around the church. He has been lying in the grave-yard since 1899, through two world wars, without anyone waking him up. There are very few walkers, and the path is wet and muddy. Crows, rotting leaves, a pheasant taking flight in the undergrowth. The post is still in the middle of the river, but the board has gone. The water is flowing quickly, but where is it going in such a hurry? Leaves, twigs—I stare at them, and then, just as we used to, we head uphill, but where the tarmac path ran along the wall of steel there is no longer a path. I can see the traces of a harrow in the soft earth: path has become field. The tower no longer exists and I look through the absent steel at an absent tower with absent men, an absent Wall. Where the silly little car once drove, walkers now head to Blanken-felde. After the war, the Dutch poet J. C. Bloem wrote, *"En niet één van de ongeborenen zal de vrijheid ooit zo beseffen"* ("and not one of the unborn will ever comprehend freedom in this way"). Standing here, I feel the impact of his words. My path has become a field and the forbidden road is now my path. I walk across a space where men would once have had to shoot me and I feel a shiver that soon no one will feel. History erases its traces and that is how it becomes history. (Invisible traces, visible reality.)

February 1993

Rheinsberg: An Intermezzo

RHEINSBERG?

My German friends nod. Of course, Rheinsberg, the word, the name, flows naturally from their lips; perhaps they even feel a little sympathy for this curious foreigner and his questions. Rheinsberg! And immediately that word is surrounded by other, more familiar sounds: Frederick the Great, Tucholsky, von Katte, Fontane . . . He hears the mild reproach in their voices, but does not know quite how to connect all those familiar names to the word he has never heard before.

Of course, he is guilty as charged. What is this peculiar, dark gap in his knowledge of their country? How is it that they have never caught him out before? And now they are coming at him from all sides: Frederick, the great King of the Prussians, and Voltaire, to whom the young, enlightened prince sent countless letters from Rheinsberg, his summer residence in the Mark Brandenburg, about which Theodor Fontane would later write such wonderful travel accounts. And Claire of course, the unconventional Claire from Tucholsky's classic *Rheinsberg: Ein Bilderbuch für Verliebte* (his "picture book for lovers"), with her odd, confusing language, strolling and romancing with her Wolfgang in the woods around the castle; the young crown prince looking out over those same woods from his tower room as he writes his *Anti-Machiavel* ("What! You've never read it? But I hope you've read the letters to Voltaire. You have, haven't you?"). And then there is the other prince, Frederick's brother Heinrich, who would so much rather have been called Henri. He lived in Rheinsberg for fifty years, but my German friends seem ready to forgive the curious foreigner for not knowing anything about this, and he senses that there is a degree of irony in their laughter.

An air of mystery surrounds this forgotten Prussian noble—suggestions, suspicions, contradictions, as though vague rumors are still drifting out of history, rumors of loneliness, fraternal hatred, courage, of a small, ugly man who loved big, beautiful men, of French poems, conversations, speeches that floated away into the archetypically German landscapes of Brandenburg, of the childless marriages of this prince and his brother, and of wives who dissolved into thin air, with only their silent ghosts remaining in insignificant paintings.

Now they are handing him books, maps, leaflets. Whatever he might have imagined, it was not this. "Rhein" perhaps suggested the idea of the river that lies much closer to his own home, of knights' castles high on pine-covered hills, of the sweet and baneful song of the Lorelei. What he sees in the photographs looks like two neighboring mansions with red-tiled roofs. They are connected by a colonnade and lie at right angles to the water. At the point where they almost touch the water, they each have a squat, round tower with a conical cherry-colored roof. The buildings themselves are the color of vanilla ice cream, which reflects so beautifully in the dark, pond-like water. In other photographs taken from the water he can see that the buildings are not actually as close to the lake as he thought; there is plenty of room to insert charming, contemplative figures, a garland of flowers, an elegant hand, folds of plaster that part to reveal an attractive, emblematic knee, a cool round shoulder. These statues have French passports; perhaps they are feeling homesick for summer in France, far away from these Brandenburg forests where the darkness descends so dangerously early in winter. But it is summer in the photographs: beeches, limes, oaks in full regalia, a victorious army.

On the day he finally goes to visit, that same army has changed unrecognisably, its festive finery lying in faded shreds on the wet ground. The silence of lengthy anticipation reigns, as if a fatal battle might begin at any moment. The arboreal regiments stand there naked and unprotected, masters of their own memory, silent men who give nothing away.

But he is not there yet. He and his friend the philosopher are heading out of the big city on the Autobahn to Hamburg. Both of them can still remember the border crossing points from before 1989 and are amazed at how thoroughly history can wipe out its traces when it wants to. There is nothing to see, just great grey cloud formations that appear to be moving out in every direction, but now and then there is a sudden break in the darkness, and the landscape lights up with a strange glow of copper or zinc.

Forests, fields, distant church towers, the foreign traveler remembers how mysterious he found it all, the villages you were not allowed to visit with your transit visa, forbidden territory where people led hidden lives. He reads the once inaccessible names on the map in his lap and it seems as though they all have an extra, coded significance: Krähenberge, Karwe, Ludwigsaue, Papstthum, Roofensee, and he notices his eye straying eastwards, taking in the one hundred kilometers to Poland, to the east, in a single movement, which is more distant, more exotic for him, as he comes from the coast. They stop in Lindow, have something to eat at the Hotel Klosterblick, gaze out over the water, which looks cold and wintery, and decide that they would like to stay there or come back just to read and let the wind blow the world away from their minds. An old monastery wall, a few graves. What was it that his friend had said as they drove over the now invisible border? "The German that the border guards used to speak ... sometimes it was almost as baffling as if a Papuan in New Guinea had suddenly started speaking German to you." Here, on these graves, the language is still as it was; it has not been deformed: *"Gleich dem Wanderer am schwülen Tage drückte dich Erblassten oft die Last des Lebens am Stabe. Noch deine letzten Stunden waren dir ein bitterer Kelch, aber du gingst dem Frieden Gottes entgegen."** Names, years, but the dead have taken their secrets with them and are giving nothing away.

There is just one, abandoned car in the car park; this is not a day for visitors. Wood, park, castle, but he feels that he is approaching the house in the wrong way, as though it does not yet wish to be seen, or only from a distance. Woods and parkland: how do they compare? Poodle and sheepdog? Or is it more like sheepdog and wolf? Parks are nature tamed, instinct trained: you may grow so far and no further, grass like a military buzz cut, shrubs standing in a line, gardeners as hairdressers and beauty specialists; as he crosses Fontane-Allee, he sees a team of young gardeners gathering fallen leaves as though they were a treasured harvest. The eighteenth century did not tolerate rampant growth or acknowledge ungovernable forces; it demanded submission: meticulous squares of pruned roses, vegetal geometry, bowers and pavilions with doors that opened outwards, and through which, in accordance with the

---

* As the walker suffers on a sultry day, the burden of life often weighed heavily on your staff, oh pallid one. Your final hours too were a bitter cup, but now you have departed for God's peace.

rigid laws of perspective, a prince might observe a young count approaching in the distance, rehearsing his opening gambit in French. Connections, relationships, both literal and figurative, the enlightenment of the *Encyclopédie* as opposed to the darkness of possible chaos, always lying in wait—this is what the two friends discuss as they walk along the reed-fringed bank, before moving on to the correlation between reality and art, because as they walk from the regimented park into the dark mass of the Boberow-Wald, the bare trees suddenly become Caspar David Friedrich's threateningly naked oaks, clawing at the iron sky with their arthritic, grasping fingers. All is still, one of those charged silences that summon snow or heavy rain, with the busy chugging of a small tractor as a counterpoint. Old-fashioned words come to mind, reed fringes, lily pads, all accompanied by the dull sound of an axe; this place does not want to join the present day.

A sign points to Poetensteig, the poets' path, and slowly they climb a gentle slope to the obelisk perched up there like an admonishing finger turned to stone. This symbol has something to say. And if monuments remain standing for long enough, they always get their way. One brother was king, the other three were not. This monument, even over two hundred years later, is a stone letter from brother to brother, written from the third to the first because of the injustices done to the second. The fact that the first and the second were already dead by then is irrelevant; this is about justice, about a score that must be settled.

It was only after the death of the king who was his brother that Prince Heinrich, who inherited Rheinsberg from him and lived there for fifty years, was able to write him this letter in stone, a coded revenge intended for future generations, who, as is their wont, generally walk past with unseeing eyes. Is this because the winds of time have blown away part of the code or because ignorance or indifference has obscured the message? Who can say?

What is the process by which such things occur? The hierarchical life at the court of the Soldier King and his four sons, straitjacketed by Prussian ritual, may seem as alien as a scene from Noh theater, but dramatic atavisms can help us to travel back in time. In one corner, we have the iron father who equates himself with the state that he is still working to expand, who hated the extravagance and ostentation of his own father and unrelentingly imposed his own ideals of duty, frugality and discipline on a new caste of military men and officials, proclaiming, "I am ruining the authority of the Junkers: I shall achieve my aim and establish my sovereignty as a rock of bronze." In the other corner, there is the king's son, the successor who in his turn will one day have to embody the state, but who attempts to escape father, fate and state by fleeing to Poland with a friend.

The father's revenge was like something out of the Old Testament, a warning written in blood on the Prussian soil of a fortress courtyard, a lesson the future king would never forget: one dark November morning, the prince with the poet's soul, whose heart was drawn to the light of France, was made to witness the beheading of his dearest friend, Hans von Katte.

The story has been told a thousand times, but that makes it no less true, and it must have had the effect of electroshock treatment: that same eighteen-year-old prince with whom we sympathise on that sad morning would one day, when he became king, treat his second and third brothers in just the same way as his father had treated him. Following a defeat, the second brother, August Wilhelm, was lambasted as a coward in front of the entire general staff, and humiliatingly relieved of his command. He died a year later, dishonored, at Oranienburg. The third brother, Heinrich, in spite of his bravery and his skills as a general, was required to ask permission before every journey, which was usually denied. The result was a lifelong relationship that pulsed with conflicting emotions of attraction and repulsion, and an undertone of hatred, which shimmers through in the bitter letters and hovers around this monument, an echo of forgotten lives. The obelisk is not dedicated to the dead ruler, but to the second brother, the very man he disowned, and to other Prussian war heroes whose merits Heinrich felt the great king had not sufficiently acknowledged. The prince immortalized their names in bronze letters inside twenty-eight medallions.

Fontane lists all of them, with their heroic deeds: von Hülsen, von Wedell, Leopold Fürst von Anhalt-Dessau, von Seydlitz, von Kleist, up to and including the other son, the fourth one, Ferdinand.

Schloss Rheinsberg

But by an irony of history, the writer's words now have to take the place of the bronze, because, during a very different war, the Korean War, all of the monuments in the D.D.R. were looted. The bronze letters with which Heinrich had intended to honor the neglected heroes of the Seven Years War were made to perpetuate Kim Il-Sung's despicable regime, something that might have raised a bitter smile from the young author of the *Anti-Machiavel.*

Somewhat bewildered, the two travelers gaze at the empty medallions, at the humanless suits of armor and helmets symbolising the spoils of war, at the wreathed medallion of the maligned general whose German glory is lauded in French: "*A l'éternelle mémoire d'Auguste Guillaume, Prince de Prusse, second fils du roi Frédéric Guillaume.*"

Across the silent water lies the castle where the lonely Hohenzollern spent his final years in a routine that ran like clockwork, as though he had himself become an integral part of time: reading, writing bad poetry, painting watercolors, taking dinner, supper, walking, conversing. First it was his brother who had thwarted his French dreams, now it was a revolution that he secretly admired, but which prevented him from going to live in the country where he felt so at home and where, during two extended visits, he had finally been able to celebrate his triumphs, in spite of his height of just one meter fifty, his squint and his pockmarked face. But if he could not go to France, then France would have to come to him, and so the bad poetry was written in French, and French actors were enticed to those distant, eastern provinces: Suin de Boutemars, Maria Louise Thérèse Toussaint (daughter of the exiled writer), a Demoiselle Aurore, who had to make do without a surname, and a Monsieur Blainville, who had to go without a first name.

I try to imagine those hours in Rheinsberg, the voices, poses, roles, plays, but, of all the arts, acting is perhaps the most transitory. With their half names, these actors were hurled into a limited eternity as footnotes to a Prussian prince, who has himself been forgotten. No one kept a record of which plays were performed in the small theater, which was later destroyed. These second- and third-rate actors must have flitted around provincial eighteenth-century Rheinsberg like rare French birds of paradise, *rarae aves*; someone ought to write a play about *them*. Blainville was the prince's favourite. Rumour has it that he committed suicide when the clique of courtiers conspired to make his lofty patron end their relationship, which may have extended beyond the merely professional, but no one can say for certain, because that too remains hidden in those distant, insinuating whispers that have also remained attached to other, better-preserved names: von Tauentzien, von Kaphengst, guarded, suggestive words that echo even now, valets, pages, standard bearers whose names are lost to the mists of time, members of a household that revolved like a small solar system around this little prince, a prince who, sabre raised, had once decided a battle by leading his much larger men through a river, who had been received by Catherine the Great with such respect, and who, in the final years of his brother's reign, had conducted vital negotiations related to the division of Poland, always such a bone of contention for Germany and Russia.

Now another king had come, one who no longer needed his advice, and so the years went by, filled with readings, dinners, obligatory visits and theatrical performances, and the princely sun slowly began to dim. Others would inherit the castle, which would fall into disrepair and, under a regime the eighteenth-century court could never have imagined, become an institute for diabetics, and get buried beneath new layers of history, which would seem so much more exciting, solely by dint of being new. And then everything would change all over again and, whether for nostalgia or profit, the past would be disinterred, the stucco touched up, the portraits, those that were still around, rehung, the Rococo gilding reapplied.

It is time for the travelers to do what they came here for, but not before tumbling into the trap of a brilliant anachronism: to buy a ticket for the castle of the Prussian princes you have to visit Tucholsky, because the ticket office for the tour is at the Tucholsky Memorial, which is inside the castle. For a moment, they wonder what the sons of the soldier king would have thought of a resident Jewish writer whose words "*Soldaten sind Mörder*"* triggered a legal case two centuries after their own time, but they are true members of the postmodern era of historic apathy and so they meekly line up in the deserted stairwell for the tour, together with a pale and awe-struck husband and wife who are dressed for tea with the prince.

At three o'clock precisely (Prussian virtues), the guide appears, a friendly lady of indeterminate age, who speaks encouragingly to her four guests, as though they are about to climb a mountain. Over time, guides assume the characteristics of owners, and so it seems as though not only the castle, but also its former inhabitants and, in fact, all of that past time, now gone for good, have become her personal property. The princes and their entourage are gently reduced to the status of children, their peculiarities become entertainment, with a knowing wink at the guests (all adults together), who allow themselves to be dragged along, just a little too quickly, past what remains of that bygone splendor: the portrait of an exiled French marquise; the paintings of the princes' neglected wives, whose lives will never be set down on paper; the charming young men in close-fitting uniforms; the painted marble that still looks cheap even after two centuries; the little study where he wrote his letters to the great philosopher; the many mirrors, which make the travelers' own modern faces look strangely old-fashioned; the foolish frills and trills of the Rococo ornamentation; the new, gleaming gold around Pesne's ceiling painting with its radiant, naked bodies whirling

---

* Soldiers are murderers

Schloss Rheinsberg

around in an allegory of light and dark, night and day; the library (*merde, mon Prince, où sont les livres!?*), where one of the travelers notes down the names of the great thinkers (Descartes, Tacitus, Lucretius, Buffon, Leibniz, Epicurus, Cicero, Molière) painted on the ceiling, and the awe-struck couple look at him as though he is mad—and all that time they can look out through curtainless windows at the water, the park, the wood and the obelisk in the distance. The vanguards of night are already clinging to the windows. Another hour and a half and everything will be dark, and then the princes will come, the counts, the adjutants and the old generals, the favourites, the actresses and the marquises, to recapture their lost territory. The red silk ropes designed to keep the visitors in their place will be removed, and the memory will be banished of all those vulgar interlopers who paid money to secure access and pry into their bygone lives and steal the secrets that they hid so well.

The first stray notes of music quiver from the Spiegelsaal as the twentieth-century parvenus stumble dozily down the wooden stairs. They linger briefly over Tucholsky's typewriter, but the contrast is too extreme; Tucholsky belongs to their own vicious, rebellious century and, for now, they are still enveloped in that other, earlier time when everything seemed so much more simple and yet was not.

1997

RETURN TO BERLIN

IT WAS IN MAY, AND IT WAS IN LOS ANGELES. THE president of Loyola Marymount University, the Reverend Thomas P. O'Malley of the Society of Jesus, had invited me to the ceremonial unveiling of a section of the Berlin Wall, a gift to the university from the city of Berlin. Various people were going to speak, including the consul general of Germany, Hans-Alard von Rohr. It was a sunny day, the heat from the nearby desert tempered by the ocean. I felt a little strange as I drove there along the endless freeways. Merely the word "freeway," with all its associations, made the thought of the Wall and the memories it evokes seem grotesque. The two cities are part of my own personal history: I have lived in both Berlin and Los Angeles, and it says something about the mysterious make-up of our brains that two such incompatible concepts can coexist within the limited space of our skulls, although perhaps not without an element of hostility.

It was a peculiar ceremony. How could it not be? The *rector magnificus* was a cheerful, round Irishman, who looked as though he enjoyed a drop or two, and who had not, as is customary nowadays, disguised himself as a civilian, and so he still looked as priests did in my youth, which at least meant you immediately knew you were dealing with a man of God. The consul general had all the stature that his name and title implied, and an additional fifty centimeters on top of that; it was not hard to imagine him in a movie. There was also a rather endearing woman from the American Customs Service, who glowed as she told us about all the bureaucratic hurdles she had had to overcome to get this painted piece of concrete into the port and, of course, a Dutch professor from the Department of Political Science, who had come up with the whole scheme. The historic object itself stood there like a little orphan girl without an orphanage, shy and perhaps a little unhappy. It was doing its best, but it no longer represented any real threat. There was a declaration of love on it to someone called Kristin, which was surrounded by the kind of painting you can see in every gallery throughout the first, second and third worlds nowadays: cheerful, childish colors in a design that was not entirely without structure. The students, standing in a large circle around the Wall and wearing clothes in the same color palette as the art, listened attentively to the sacrosanct stream of words flowing over the green lawn: Oppression and Freedom, Conflict and History, platonic ideas dressed in capital letters, their Sunday best, abstractions that, in this context, appeared to have as much connection to that block of concrete as the two sparrows that briefly perched on it, with all the innocence of creatures that are their own eternal repetition and live outside of human history. I felt those young minds around me trying with all their might to think something, but I doubted that they would succeed.

And what about me? When I closed my eyes, the weather changed. It became winter, because it was winter when I saw that Wall for the first time, the winter of 1963. Now, in order to picture that day again, I had to imagine that the consul and the rector and the students were not there. I had to deny the existence of the green leaves on the tree above us. I had to make it become icy cold, summon up the biting snow of Central Europe and, using only the power of my mind, seamlessly reinsert the lonely concrete between other broken fragments. Only then would I once again be standing before a Wall, only then would I be twenty-nine again, cold again, frozen into place within history as history, and not in this curious, ironic, postmodern offshoot which—and here is the irony—is just as much a part of history, one of Hegel's blank pages. You could almost die laughing.

But I was not in the mood for laughter. What had I thought about it back then, at the time? I thought it sounded like the kind of situation that might have existed in Greek antiquity, or indeed any other an-tiquity: a city divided in two by a wall. Wrapped in legends and stories, an almost obsolete proverb, a comedy by Tirso de Molina, found in a corner of the library of Salamanca, an adaptation of Molière, an opera by Salieri, and later, of course, a couple of hours of highbrow video froth, an anecdote with symbols popping up all over like mushrooms, cultural heritage. But the kind of antiquities we usually encounter are no more than a few thousand years old, as old as we ourselves have grown throughout the interlocking series of civilizations to which we still belong. Perhaps that is why, in spite of the nuclear arsenal that is as much a part of the world as the ozone layer, an air of antiquity clings desperately to everything we do, an archaic atmosphere that no journeys to Mars or Jupiter will ever dispel. And that is how it looked: all you had to do was stand in front of that Wall and squeeze your eyes half-shut, and you could see the clumsy bustling of medieval foot soldiers guarding a city wall in the Land of the Others. The same species that is able to cover thousands of kilometers in a day, that can visit planets at home and split atoms like a piece of old rope, can also build a wall, two or three meters high, a wall that can never be crossed. An

Egyptian or a Babylonian would not have been able to climb over it either, a person from the Middle Ages would have had to surrender his weapons at the gate, an Athenian might have drowned in the River Spree, while this Dutchman banged his head on the Wall and woke up decades later, on the other side of the earth, to see a priest and a diplomat removing a cloth from a piece of concrete with childish drawings on it, a remnant that must always remain there as a reminder of something that is not easy to sum up, and never will be summed up, if only because history has a head like Janus', looking in two directions, at the past and, paradoxically, at the future. I believe it was Schlegel who said that historians are prophets who face backwards; that is both true and untrue. Through some inimitable alchemical manoeuvre, yesterday's future has transformed the threat and force inherent in that chunk of concrete into an innocuous sight for tourists; this monument is pulling the wool over my eyes even as I stand there in front of it. My fear, or my fury, or my abhorrence, has become invalid. I have to summon up images of men and guns, of watchtowers and searchlights, in order to feel any sense of the reality, images that the other bystanders do not have in their inner archives. And yet, I was always an outsider as far as that Wall was concerned, so how would the insiders fare in this place?

Berlin, 1997

How could you bear the denial of your past in a monument that was intended to perpetuate it? How would you feel about this minimisation of something that was always so much more than the concrete of which it was made, a symbol, on permanent display, which for you was not just a symbol, but a daily reality that dominated your life, in many cases, until death?

Two weeks ago, back in Berlin, I had the opportunity to think about this again. I wanted to pay another visit to the Hotel Esplanade, because I have sentimental memories of the place, but I could not find it. I came up out of the S-Bahn on Potsdamer Platz and found myself in pandemonium. I was standing on what seemed to be a temporary bridge, which shook from the weight of the heavy lorries, and I did not know where to look first. Far below, swarms of laborers were working away on the foundations of the Tower of Babel or maybe even a giant tunnel to Moscow; anything was possible here. I looked at the chaos of yellow and white helmets, leaned over the railing, saw men down there *in profundis* installing reinforced concrete, and gazed back up at the forest of cranes, their lights waving, transporting black slabs of marble through the air and slowly lowering them, all to the accompaniment of the ancient sound of iron on stone. I attempted to follow the labyrinthine movements of the hundreds of people beneath me and wondered who was choreographing this

Potsdamer Platz, 1997

movement, how all of those men knew so precisely what they had to do, how anyone could find the way through all those pipes, cables, tubes. These men were driving all kinds of things into the soil, but it felt more as though a gigantic city was in the process of rising up out of the earth, as though a city wanted to exist here and was creating a path for itself using natural force. I felt a sense of euphoria at all that activity, but also, I will admit, something more like a shiver of disquiet, because of the implications, because of the power that was in evidence here, which seemed such a contrast to Germany's recent lamentations, as though that had all been some kind of masquerade, a theatrical gimmick to lull the rest of the world to sleep. If what I was witnessing here was not some kind of phantasm, a Potemkin village, then it must simply be exactly what my eyes could see: a vision of future power. Here, with the thunderous force of the pile driver, a page was being turned. No fewer than three pasts were being buried in this place; history was being dug into the soil of this magical landscape of orgiastic labor at the rate of a million images per second: trams, fashions, armies, bunkers, barriers, walls, the People's Police, all of them disappearing beneath the foundations of the temples to the new powers. Once again, I was standing in this square in the midst of something that meant a lot more than what could

Construction of the new Reichstag dome, 1997

actually be seen at that moment. Somewhere in a corner were a few miserable pieces of Wall, like scenery pushed aside after a failed performance. What had it been? An operetta? Wagner in modern dress? A play by Heiner Müller? Or just reality after all, its lingering shadow trying to connect with the other lonely piece that I had seen in California in May?

Again I shivered, but this time it was the cold. In the distance I saw the wooden frame of the new dome of the Reichstag, a Renaissance theater model, and suddenly there it was, the dwarfed Hotel Esplanade, looking a little foolish among all that violence, and at the same instant the memory within me also shrank. What did it look like here back then? How could the hotel suddenly be so small? There it stood, strangely boxed in, surrounded by the oval, gleaming, rising force of Sony. I tried to imagine future Mercedes and B.M.W.s slinking into the car parks, nouveaux riches from Warsaw to Novosibirsk entertaining themselves behind the windows of new apartments, following the rituals of the new age, pampered by Filipino maids and with the gentle buzz of Dow Jones, D.A.X. and Nikkei in the background. It was just as difficult as picturing my own bygone reality, in which, for several winters, I had spent days on end in that building with a long-gone lover. She was a singer and her recordings had been made there, in that empty, hollowed-out building. Her producer came from Cologne and had been in the Luftwaffe. In a way, he is back in the air now, because his feet no longer walk this earth. From the hotel windows, there was a view in every direction, and the producer had once pointed in one of those directions, towards the Führerhauptquartier, where he had had to deliver a message as a courier from Bordeaux. As he was about to slip the sealed envelope into the letterbox, he had felt a hand on his shoulder and, turning, he found himself face to face with Hitler. "*Diese Augen, nein, das kannst du dir nicht vorstellen.*" No, I could not imagine those eyes; I was too occupied with what was happening in the empty, snow-covered square below, the mobile etching of men and dogs among those strange, angular pieces of metal that were reminiscent of an early Mondrian, the beach at Domburg.

But it was also exciting inside the building. I spent hours with its only resident, Otto Redlin. This was in the early 1970s, and Otto was already seventy-six, so I suppose he too is no longer around. The hotel had 418 rooms, but now it looks so small that I cannot imagine how that was ever possible. *"Ich bin der älteste Bundesangestellte,"* he always used to say: I am the oldest federal employee. His wife was dead and he lived, as I can still remember, in Room 31. I have a photograph of him sitting at one of the empty tables, which were neatly laid with tablecloths, in an empty salon. Sofas, lots of chairs and barstools that no one sat on anymore. We had lit the chandeliers for the photograph, and they reflected back at us, multiplied in a huge mirror in which I am just about visible behind what looks like a monstrous Chinese vase. Downstairs somewhere, there was a wooden platform that tourists could stand on and see all the way to Vladivostok. Not far away was the ruin of the Bayerischer Hof which had recently been demolished. I made a note in my diary back then: ". . . a few laborers are working on the demolition, golden Germanic mosaics thunder down into the mud. I wipe one of them clean with a little rainwater and read: *Deutsche Frauen, Deutsche Treue, Deutscher Wein, Deutscher Sang Sollen In Der Welt Behalten Ihren Alten Schönen Klang.*˙ Not in this place, not anymore, I think. The things on the ground were once attached to something, but now are attached to nothing. Lonely toilet bowls, baths without taps, taps without baths, glasses from which no Breslauer, Nordhäuser or Cottbuser will ever flow again, everything, boots, dirndls, waiters, menus, ashtrays, trumpets, all crushed,

---

* May the ancient and beautiful melodies of German women, German constancy, German wine and German song resonate throughout the world.

pulverized and taken up into Heaven, gone forever. The small and rather modest café next door has two menus in the window, per-haps in remembrance. '1940' is written at the top, followed by a list of what some Messerschmitt pilot or holder of the Knight's Cross, killed in action long ago, might have eaten on that day: *Geschmortes Kalbsherz, Westmoreland, mit Spinat und Schwenkkartoffeln (100 Gramm Fleischmarke und 10 Gramm Fettmarke, 1 Mark 65)*. Did he drink the 1938 Niersteiner Spiegelberg with his meal, as sug-gested? The café itself is closed, the chairs are covered with dust and arranged as though the last customers have just left for the front, but maybe," I wrote at the time, "they will return and everything will begin all over again."

Now, thirty years later, I no longer think that. I have been here too often and for too long, and know that whatever might begin anew in this place, it can never be the same. And yet, even now, the date on that menu, the unfortunate year of 1940, is forcing me back to my own past. I do not want to linger on this for too long, but even though my life began seven years before that date, I am unable to explain myself to myself without thinking of 1940, if only because the start of the war—which will be over and done with only when everyone who remembers something about it is dead—seems to have erased the first seven years of my life, aided by something I discovered only recently.

I am going to have to take a couple of different detours at the same time now, which is impossible in real life, but possible on paper, which is probably the reason I became a writer.

The first of these detours has to do with being a writer. There is a famous controversy between the novelist Proust and the critic and essayist Sainte-Beuve, which boils down to the latter believing that we should know as much as possible about a writer's life—his atti-tudes and opinions, his character, his relation to and relationships with women, money, politics—while Proust thought it should all be about the books, and only the books, and never about the biography. Proust also believed that writers and poets never truly express themselves in conversation, so that too is meaningless in comparison with what an author *writes*, because then he is drawing on a completely different, much deeper layer of his personality, one that is often hidden even from himself, through which he wanders like an explorer, returning with treasures that should not be wasted on a superficial conversation. This implies a degree of mystery and maybe also isolation, which Proust, who spent much of his life wearing the mask of the worldly sophisticate and who, judging by his magnificent dialogue, must in fact have been a masterful conversationalist, saw as a prerequisite for a life of writing. Now I cannot compare myself to Proust, but in this respect I am most definitely a Proustian: in the shameless showcase culture we live in—perhaps less so in Germany than in the Netherlands or in America—it seems that private life has to be played out in public. Writers become their own public performance and are required to remain in character. We know their personas better than their books, because their writing can never capture them as well as an interviewer does. The hidden core of their being is no longer mysteriously transformed into the wondrous and sacred lies of fiction, but flows unfermented from the glass screen into a thousand living rooms of people who would never, and will never, read their books. The point of this entire detour is to say that I think we can speak about ourselves only in moderation. And yet, in the more elevated form of conversation that is a speech, I cannot escape doing so.

And this brings me to the second detour, which is about my peculiar lack of memory. Nabokov was able to command his memory to speak—*Speak, Memory* is after all an imperative, or at least an entreaty expressed in the imperative form—but such a command has not the slightest effect on me: my memory simply will not respond. Augustine talked about memory palaces through which we might wander and find all sorts of treasures; for me, that palace remains closed. I cannot even enter the building. One of the key moments in Proust's great novel occurs when he dips a certain cake in his tea. At that same moment, to remain with Augustine's analogy, the door of a room in the palace flies open. Nabokov writes in his last great novel, *Ada*, that he is against the idea of the *mémoire involontaire*, the involuntary memory: the doors of the palace must be forced open; remembering is an act and we need to work to achieve it. But that suggestion does not work for me either: scraps, shadows, fragments are all that I can make out through the dirty and broken windows of my palazzo, which also appears to be situated in a part of the world where it is always twilight.

In my simplicity, I have always believed and maintained that this is a result of the thunderous clap of the first day of war, its deafening effect extending both forwards and backwards, creating a hole into which children's books, friends, teachers have been sucked, namelessly. However, I recently discovered that perhaps the Heinkels and the Stukas of those early days and the sight of Rotterdam burning on the distant horizon were not the only causes. At the end of October, an exhibition about my life and work opened in The Hague, the city where I was born. This also involved, much against my will, a search for my past, undertaken by a very thorough investigator, who soon discovered that during the years of crisis before the war—I was born in '33—we moved within the city no fewer than seven times. My mother, who is still alive—she is eighty-seven—denied this vehemently, but she had to give in when she saw the copies of the official registration documents. This was followed by the war years, chaos, my parents' divorce, evacuation, the winter of starvation, my father's death in a British bombing raid: that, in short, is how to lock the doors of a palace. Later, when I gained a degree of control over my life, I added a new wing to which I have access—life, and therefore writing, would have been impossible otherwise—but the main building remains closed. I will never, like Borges, be able to say which books I read as a child in my father's library or, like Proust, be able to write about my long conversations with my grandmother or, like Nabokov, hilariously reveal the eccentricities of my Swiss-French governess. This is not only because my father had no library, because both of my grandmothers died before I had a chance to know them, or because the woman who could have been described as a governess only if you were being exceptionally charitable had run off with my father in the middle of the war, but also, and primarily, because something had been wiped out, radically and permanently, by a destructive external force, leaving me with nothing.

I am not saying this because I wish to elicit even an ounce of sympathy, as I have no need for sympathy. It gave me the opportunity to invent a life for myself by travelling and by thinking. More than that, it left me with a fascination with the past, with disappearance, with transience, with memories and ruins, with antiquity, with everything that can be summarized under the heading of "history." And I have related this history—because even those personal stories that make up only a very small part of history are still entitled to be called history—in order to explain, not so much to you as to myself, why this city has fascinated me inordinately for such a long time. I feel that here, on an infinitely larger scale, and with horrifying consequences for the fates of so many people, somehow the same has happened as happened to me, that the ruins and the gaps I encountered here that first time had something to tell me that I did not yet truly understand. That something was, at first, nothing. All of those gaps, those lacunae, those absences wanted to speak to me about nothingness, about destruction, which in both German (*Vernichtung*) and Dutch (*vernietiging*) is founded on the notion of turning something into nothing, the negative, negation, *nicht, niet*, not, a city become nothing. This emptiness and absence resulted from the actions of a man who, back in the 1920s, wrote a book that loudly and clearly proclaimed a program: the *Vernichtung* of a *Volk*. Of all the *Berliner Lektionen* I have read—and this is not about aesthetics, but about historical essence—I found Daniel Libeskind's the most effective and the most affecting, if I may use those two words, which do not always belong together. He constructed his thoughts and his museum around the site of that nothing, the something missing, the present absence. A place for building nothing is something that only art can create, but the power of the constructed nothing resides precisely in what is not there—and what is not there is what *was* there. What was once present is commemorated in the intangible absence. This is something we can speak of only hesitantly, because it is all so mysterious.

Frederick I of Prussia,
Charlottenburger Tor,
West Berlin

During my first visit to Berlin, I was not yet capable of thinking in this way. Reality had continued to write that man's book, and it resembled an orgy of destruction, the morning after the dance of death. You could still taste the war and it seemed like a continuation of what I had seen and heard as a child. Yet at the same time a new element had been added, a crack that ran through the world and which was more visible here than anywhere else, like a heart attack turned to stone, as though once again Berlin had the task of demonstrating something to the world, the logical conclusion of Yalta, which was itself the logical conclusion of the desire for destruction that had begun in this place. I made my journey with two older friends who had both been in Dachau, which added to the apocalyptic effect of those first experiences, along with the nuclear threat—which now seems to have been so carelessly forgotten—that was hanging over our heads like a plague cloud.

No, the 1950s and early '60s were perhaps not the best time to be young. I had seen Budapest in 1956, so I already knew what impotence and betrayal were. Now I was seeing, in its German form, the practice of that doctrine to which so many of my friends still clung, full of hope. So I was immersed in a chaos of emotions and experiences that was fortunately eased by hard-boiled concentration-camp humor, and the amazing ways my travelling companions had found to deal with their memories. Perhaps it will never again happen that two such different social and political philosophies are put into practice in one language, not merely in the forms they have always assumed—pamphlet, essay, newspaper article—but also in the wording of laws, regulations, verdicts, government policy statements, orders to shoot, warnings, editorials in the party newspaper, secret reports. The shared, inherited language became a divided language, another language developed out of the same language, the language became bilingual, exposing its fundamental ambiguity, a lesson for later ages. The philosophy that enabled people to resist one dictatorship, risking their lives, mercilessly steered them towards another dictatorship. The heroes of one age became the culprits of another, and in order to justify themselves they invented a plausibility that was valid nowhere else. Two countries that could not physically distance themselves from each other entrenched themselves, and it would later require huge mental exertion to recapture every intellectual millimeter they had ceded.

I could perhaps sense all of this back then, but not yet contemplate it; I was too busy thinking about the rest of the world. My first travels, when I was about eighteen, took me to the North, to countries of great brightness, but also of doubt and melancholy, that monstrous alliance of clarity and angst that dominates the films of Ingmar Bergman and which preoccupied me at the time. But my own terrain was the South, the Mediterranean, Provence, the theatricality of Italy, the dazzling radiance of the Spanish plateau, where the light conjures up *fata morganas* that allow the imagination to run riot, and which seemed capable of driving away the darkness of those post-war years. The Netherlands was then, like Germany, a place without color; I remember those years as predominantly grey. On my way back from that first hitchhiking trip to the far North, I had traveled through Germany for the first time. The scraps that my faulty memory throws me reveal broken roads, whole neighborhoods collapsed, the wanton, unimaginative uniformity of reconstruction, and when I focus more sharply I can see and hear shunting locomotives and a deserted railway yard at night, as I bid a dramatic farewell to someone, while a voice from a loudspeaker makes incomprehensible announcements in that language that I have not yet become accustomed to, a language that refuses to resemble itself, that does not want to be the same language as the language of the poems of Goethe and Rilke that I studied at school.

My first novel was published in the Netherlands not long after that, probably far too soon. Its illusionism was far removed from the razor-sharp realism that was the norm in those post-war years. But in that book I had said all that I had to say. I was suddenly a writer because I had had a book published, but I had become one in the same way as a swan is born, or a bat, without expressing any explicit desire. Swans and bats have an easier life in that respect— they already have the Kantian a priori in their wings—but I had no other option than to set off travelling again with the aim of gaining the knowledge required by this peculiar career that had chosen me, a career that I tried to shake off in my new novel by having the main character, who was of course a writer, commit suicide, even if only, I think in retrospect, so that I would not have to do it myself. And so I travelled, the surviving doppelgänger of my own self, to Bolivia and Mali, to Colombia and Iran and all those countries in the so-called Third World, where I found a deformed mirror image of my own world, in military dictatorships and pseudo-democracies and all those other variants that, in one way or another, belonged to the same family as the vast schism that divided Europe and Germany. That schism found its perfect metaphorical expression in the fission of the atomic bomb, devised by the iconography of science to keep fear alive and so confirm the systems that made all of us, each with our own slogans and lies, our own scholastic rhetoric and exorcism, merely bit-part players in an absurdist theater, players who thought they were just actors, until the year when the violent fiction exploded and the cards of appearance and reality were reshuffled, and our maps changed along with them. *Faites vos jeux! Rien ne va plus!* One of the legs of the card table upon which the great game was played stood in Berlin, where I was living at the time, because the D.A.A.D. had invited me to spend a year there.

That year was 1989, and I experienced everything that happened that year not just as a casual visitor, but as a resident of Berlin. I may not have been a German, but I was certainly a European, and it was not just a country that was being welded back together again, but, all being well, an entire continent. Once, in 1962, when Germany was again responsible for 45% of Europe's annual production, I had seen Adenauer and de Gaulle standing on a balcony in Stuttgart, a strange couple, older than the century itself. De Gaulle had raised those peculiar long arms in the air and cried out his heavily accented declaration of Franco–German friendship, *"EZ LEBBE DOIZLANT! EZ LEBBE DIE DOITZFRANZÖZISCHE VROINDZAVT!"* He had started work on that great construction from the Atlantic to the Urals—Willy Brandt would kneel in Warsaw on one of the stops on the journey, and later Mitterrand and Kohl would stand hand in hand on the battlefield of Verdun in an attempt to bury the war for good. But old fears are not so easily buried, not in Moscow, not in Paris, and not in London, let alone in those other, smaller countries that lie in the shadow of that one big empire in the middle. History may perform a few lightning-fast pirouettes and pull a *fait accompli* out of its hat, but the ancient specter of the *Gleichgewicht* continues to trouble the age-old family of Europe. The historical imperative is accepted as though by a class of obedient Marxists sitting at their school desks, but the old distrust shimmers in the memoirs of both Mitterrand and Thatcher. England, France, Germany and Russia sit in their theater boxes like jealous old actresses and keep an eye on one another: Who is flapping her fan too much? Who is spending too much time with whom? Who has been given the most flowers? Who is going to play the lead? Why is she being so nice to that insignificant supporting player? Why was I not invited? Intrigue and suspicion in Theatre Europa. Behind a semblance of absence, the memory of nations is an ancient, viscous mass, and one question was on everyone's mind at the time, and by everyone I perhaps mean the Germans themselves most of all: What kind of country are we becoming? Students at my readings would ask, "Aren't you frightened of us?" No, I wasn't, but I was concerned that they thought I should be, as though they still did not trust their own country.

The historical imperative is a religious idea that I am unable to believe in. There are always too many imponderables, too many irrationalities, fanatics, starry-eyed idealists, rabid dogs darting out of their kennels. They operate within a specific territory, but no one can be certain of anything in a world that, intellectually and materially, is no longer in synch, where the power of destruction is already almost within the reach of individuals, and the death of as many other people as possible has become one of the cheapest commodities. At the end of a *saeculum horribilis*, the prevailing mood is one of disquiet, not unlike the mood at the end of the first millennium, as described in the writings of the Benedictine monk Raoul Glauber, a tale of plague and famine and cannibalism that makes the paintings of Hieronymus Bosch look like happy fantasies. When you read his words, you feel inclined to think that we have made progress over the past one thousand years, and that, of course, is true. And yet, there is poison gas hidden in Iraq, throats cut in Algeria, mass slaughter in Rwanda and in Europe (so much closer to home), and landmines in Cambodia. None of this seems like a world that has learned its lesson from the wars that began on this continent in this century and which, as Václav Havel recently calculated for us, have cost over two hundred million lives. It is these absent ones who haunt the space around us. Their names, at least the ones we know, are on monuments from Sicily to Stavanger, from Athens to Kaliningrad, but the world seems able to live with their absence. Maybe this is the only way, but it also means that the world could probably manage just as well without us too.

Once again, no, twice again, to Berlin. After 1989, I went away and came back again. I added to my notes on Berlin, and travelled through East and West, which made my notes more like notes on

Germany, rather than just Berlin. I read about the history, which meant reading lots of things I had not known about before, and made new friends, which is not so easy at my age. In short, I felt comfortable in Berlin and I frequently returned in the following years. And yet there were still things that surprised me. I may not believe in the historical imperative, but I do believe in a vague notion of the relative density of countries and a certain natural way of the world. It seemed "natural," for example, that Germany should once again become one country—just as it seemed natural that this would require a great deal of effort. It seemed equally natural that Berlin would become the capital city of that one country, and that the united Germany, which had developed into a modern European democracy over the past fifty years and which, as evidenced by the never-ending stream of publications, had focused on its ill-fated past by means of increas-ingly intense commemoration, would now take up its place among the other countries of Europe. But in Germany itself I heard different voices, voices that ridiculed the new German citizens, who of course had something to say in response, and voices that attempted to resist the relative density of their own country by refusing to send soldiers on European and other peace missions. This reluctance elicited the following comment from one of my more bitter compatriots: "It's always the same with

East Berlin, 1990

them—when you don't invite them, they come anyway, but when you ask them to take part, they don't turn up."

Meanwhile, in Germany I was held responsible for tomato growing in the Netherlands, for the behavior of our Dutch football fans, who clearly represent the most intelligent element of every nation, and for every survey in which yet more half-baked sociologists secured their positions for the next few years by asking a bunch of teenagers what they thought about Germans, while in my own country—which has never entirely come to terms with its colonial past—I was suddenly nominated as an expert on Germany. That meant that I was required to debate on television whenever something happened in Germany that also happens in other European countries, but which has a different impact there, because of the country's difficult past and also because of the laziness of the media.

It was a Dutch friend—Willem Leonard Brugsma—who took me to Germany for the first time. Brugsma was arrested by the Gestapo as a young member of the Resistance in Paris, and was interned in Natzweiler and in Dachau for a number of years. He died a few weeks ago, and at his funeral I recalled memories of the past, of that emotionally charged first trip to Germany, which had been so astounding for me because he harbored no resentment. The same man who could tell horrific tales about his time in the camps, a big man who weighed only forty-five kilos when he was liberated, was a passionate advocate of German Unity, not, as people sometimes cynically say, in order to render Germany harmless by tying it to Europe, but because he believed that one Germany belonged in one Europe. I am mentioning this now because such voices appear to be increasingly rare in Germany. Lately, all we seem to have heard from that country are sounds of infinite fatigue, lamentation and defeatist complaint emanating from the depths of the sacred piggy bank.

Suddenly it is no longer about ideas, but only about money; not about one of the greatest adventures in European history, but about fear of the neighbors who have been buying things on credit from the grocer; not about the Europe of Erasmus and Voltaire, of Tolstoy and Thomas Mann, of Rembrandt and Botticelli, of Hegel and Hume. No, it is about much greater faceless figures, like 3 point 0, 3 point 1, and the satanic 3 point 2, which the politicians hide behind, since for reasons of their own they do not want

Potsdamer Platz, 1997

Europe, or not yet, or not ever. Any child can understand, and certainly in this city *every* child understands, that there have to be criteria, but taking the whole idea of Europe, a subject about which many of the same people have waxed lyrical for years, and reducing it to abstractions following a decimal point, has meant employing the demagogy of common sense to bury the citizens' enthusiasm under ashes. Ash is not a vital principle, but it fits very well with the lamentation I just mentioned. This has always been a dangerous continent. It has long been after its own blood, because of land, because of dynasties, because of religion and because of colonies. All by itself, it came up with both of the ideologies that made this century the most disastrous in history, a twin ideological catastrophe from which America rescued us not once, but twice. Perhaps we should not count on a third time. I know that the Europe of the single currency is a massive, extremely complex political and economic maneuver that scares many people. I also know that political unification is limping behind like an unhappy child, hampered by multiple languages, ineradicable national ambitions and a parliament that is pampered, impotent and often invisible. But that is precisely the challenge. Once, for better or for worse, this continent discovered the rest of the world. If the Europeans back then had spent as much time ruminating as these Europeans now seem to require, everyone would have stayed at home. But then there never would have been a piece of the Wall standing in Los Angeles either.

December 1997

PART III

SEPTEMBER. BERLIN TWENTY YEARS AGO, BERLIN ten years ago, Berlin now. The first time, I was invited by the D.A.A.D.; the second time, I invited myself; the third time, it was the government of Nordrhein-Westfalen. During that first visit, I had started my notes on Berlin in all innocence: a writer lives in a foreign city and makes notes about what he experiences, what he sees and reads. A concert by Mauricio Kagel, a walk in Charlottenburg, a visit to Lübars, which was just inside the Wall. All of it normal, except Berlin was no normal city, and for anyone living there in that eventful year of 1989 it will never be normal again. I will never be rid of it, that double line of separation, the line running between two political systems, the line between two eras. Long before 1989, I had seen the bare, snowy space of Potsdamer Platz from the windows of the Hotel Esplanade, with the obscene bulge of the Führerbunker in the distance and, so much closer, the geometric lines of the chevaux-de-frise, dark pieces of metal, angled upwards, designed to thwart any escape attempt.

Potsdamer Platz,
Sony Centre, detail

That is not something you would wish to discuss again. It is in the past, just as the photographs of the same square in 1929, full of old-fashioned cars and crowds rushing or strolling past, were already part of the past back then. Later, during my first return, I saw the foundations of what were obviously going to be enormous buildings being rammed into the sandy ground, which looked like some immense mass grave. And now that the buildings are there, you have to crane your neck to take in their entire height, Babylonian temples, which have crushed the past beneath them. I look for the Hotel Esplanade, but when I finally find it I recognize nothing. A section of the former Kaisersaal is preserved behind glass, but it is like the double death of butterflies pinned inside a display case; they should have perished long ago, but they are still here, although they will never fly again. I wander among the big buildings for a while, a homunculus in a giant architectural model, but this is not a model; it is real. Do I miss anything? The Berlin of the past? No. I am simply unable to delete the past from my system in such places; the only option would be to go and live there again. In that sense, my three months in Westphalia are perfect practice. I shall surrender myself to the city once again, a visitor from a small European country in the capital of a large European country that

Der Löwenkämpfer *by Albert Wolff, 1861, in front of Das Alte Museum, Berlin Mitte*

shares some of its past with the small country. I can read the drama of my first farewell in my own book. I wanted to know what would become of Germany "when it is big." As I read those lines again, I detect a sense of pathos, but that sensation is never entirely absent in the vicinity of the Reichstag and the Brandenburger Tor. Such buildings are out of keeping with the introspection of Bach or the intellectuality of Schönberg; if they could sing, they would produce a different kind of music, heavy and dramatic. Wagner is the most German of all composers, the generals around the Grosser Stern could be taken for heroes from an opera, given the poses they are striking, and for someone who comes from a small city with narrow streets and quiet canals, the open spaces and wide avenues of Berlin, with their imposing buildings and statues flanked by heraldic lions and eagles, seem like an expression of power. Memories of Prussia, film images of parades, never entirely forgotten, of heroic music drifting on the wind . . . and then that other pathos of the two living Russian statues planting the flag of victory, and therefore defeat, on the Reichstag: damage and destruction, division and reunification, a Wall and an airlift, a city pushed to and fro like a chess piece on the board of history. Try acting normally after all of that. But there lies the miracle: the Germans have managed to do so. Germany has succeeded, as far as such a thing is possible, in coming to terms with one past through grief and understanding, by realizing that it will never entirely disappear. Not only that, the country has also internalized, again as far as it is possible, that other past and, without wiping it out (you can never do that to a past), has transformed it, through accountability, habituation, wear and tear, into a present that looks like today.

But am I right about Wagner and Schönberg? With Schinkel, wouldn't you be more likely to think of . . . actually, which composer would you choose if you wanted to express his architecture as music? What music did Goethe listen to? I can't come up with an answer. The gigantic Greek columns of his museum beside the Dom call for lofty triumph, Apollonian radiance, but less than half an hour later, near the Nikolaikirche, I come across a statue of a horse and a dragon engaged in a furious fight, and that takes me back to Wagner.

How have I not noticed this statue before, even though it is not far from Zum Nussbaum, a pub I used to visit back then when I came to the East? There is nothing else for it: I shall have to get to know Berlin all over again. I begin with the humblest of lessons: I disguise myself as a tourist from Phoenix, Arizona, and I go on a boat tour. It is a glorious day in October, not yet the grey tundra weather that will reign in a month or so, and you can still sit outside, on the top deck. It is not busy, the wind is tugging a little at the words coming from the loudspeakers, at the names and the dates, but that is fine by me. I am happy to let the city glide past. Almost everything I see comes with a memory attached, but I do not want to think about that now. I want to see the city as a stranger, as someone who has never been here before.

I find the Bundeskanzleramt modest, and actually rather beautiful. Is this where the government of the third-largest economic power in the world has its seat? Is this the place that somewhat reluctantly sends soldiers, who once appeared to have returned home for good, to hostile deserts on the other side of the world, because it does not want to let down its allies? Power has a gentle face here; somewhere behind all those windows sits a person who does not believe that German savings should be handed out to all of those other Europeans who have been living on credit on such a grand scale, a person who embraces old-fashioned values and will not be forced by friend or foe to push up inflation until the dollar becomes so cheap that America can pay off its immense debts to China and the whole game can begin all over again. The world as a roulette table is not an attractive image; protectionism is not an option, nor is the state as the owner of the means of production, or Lafontaine as a reincarnation of Marx. These are confusing times. The people are grumbling, quietly for now, but their complaints may soon become louder. There is a constant stream of foreign guests here, the man from Russia and the man from China. This building may not be the center of the world, but it is an intersection that no one can avoid. The Obama who lives here is a woman, but her opposition is in the government with her. The cacophony of the media is rising; everyone knows what should be done; tables, figures, prognoses are carried into the building and back out again; press conferences, spokespeople, editorials . . . Everything whirls around this building that was not even built twenty years ago, when that other whirlwind raced through this city.

But the water of the Spree does not care. That is how rivers are, like the birds rocking on the waves made by the boat. Agitation is for humans. Seen like this, from the boat, the building rejects the drama, as though it is itself a river. It has no agitation of its own; it soothes the past, like a long, pink sedative pill. As I pass beneath the Moltkebrücke, I feel myself returning to the nineteenth century. Winged mythical creatures in reddish stone guard their lost era with anachronistic zeal. Claws, vicious beaks . . . they are prepared for the worst, but their might is deflected by the innocent restraint of this building, which refuses to express the power that resides within. Griffins have no place in the twenty-first century, and neither do the swords and trumpets of the helmeted beings along the bridge, or the hexagonal, atavistic crown above the eagle with its overlong tongue, forked and curling, on the other bridge beside Bahnhof Friedrichstraße. The iron of this giant bird is rusty. Through my binoculars I can just about make out the wings spread on either side of the chest, which carries the Prussian coat of arms (which itself features another bird and another crest). Beneath it are the orb and scepter, the symbols of royal power. Absurdly, someone has hung a modern bicycle chain around the bird's leg, as though hoping to park the empire on the bridge until better times came along. The voice on the boat babbles on. To the right is the station where I had to pass through the border checkpoint so many times, and later I see the ruins of the Palast der Republik. Now that it is no longer there, it seems as though it was much larger than I actually remember. The stairwells are still standing, on this autumn day, towers of steps surrounded by cranes and bulldozers, the demolished church of a forgotten religion, ridiculed by the mighty shadow of the Dom behind, with its triumphant golden cap. There is something unutterably sad about buildings that have not yet been entirely demolished. Rusty iron bars protrude from the bare concrete of the walls; rubble lies on the steps that no one will ever walk on again. I can see the distant quadriga of the Brandenburger Tor between two of the towering stairwells. Sometimes I think this city does it on purpose—the constant intermingling of now and then, and the associated layers of memory—and when I look in the other direction I see the television tower on Alexanderplatz with that strange glass bulge at the top and the absurd red-and-white level-crossing barrier pointing into the sky. What thoughts might run through the mind of someone who once got married in this dismantled building? Someone who once governed here? Before long, the stairwells will have vanished too, and their memories will be destroyed in the demolition, and whatever remains will later be buried beneath that other form of nostalgia that wants to rebuild the Schloss of an earlier era, which has disappeared and is gone for good.

I wrote the above in autumn last year, but 2008 was not 1988. The torrent and the momentum of those days have given way to the gentle flow of democracy, to the blank pages that Hegel wanted to tear from the book of history. Of course, history continues to be made here, but suddenly I realize that I am an outsider, much more so than I was back then. The unification of Germany, like the long-ago war and the occupation of my country, was part of my own history.

Weidendammer Brücke, Berlin Mitte

The dramatic events of 1989, so much more recent, also had a significant emotional impact on anyone who experienced them, as did the struggle of the years immediately afterwards, and the mutual attraction and repulsion that the two Germanies continue to show. However, the practice of democracy, with its ritual mating dances, the courtship behavior of the politicians, the masquerades of giving and taking, the posturing of talk shows and parliamentary debates, that was something you could watch with fascination, but always from the outside. You have your own country, your own home, in those distant lowlands, your own government and your own parliament that people here know little about and understand even less. Your interest is that of a stranger. And indeed, it is as a stranger that I have watched that chorus of the goddesses of fate who control much

*Demolition of Palast
der Republik, Berlin
Mitte, October 2008*

of public debate in Germany. Their television news representative is Marietta Slomka, who, with her Snow Queen demeanour, really knows how to get a minister hot and bothered. Eyes like icicles, set with frightening symmetry in that deep-freeze face, a face clasped within a helmet of blonde hair. Her diction is gentle, but extremely effective, and she dissects politicians' answers with the precision of a surgical instrument. It is a pleasure to watch, especially when she brings her conversation to an end and turns to her more masculine counterpart, looking like an Egyptian hieroglyph, a cross-section of a woman who now consists of one single dimension, a Wayang shadow puppet. The other three are mistresses of the talk show, who gather the mighty of the republic around them in order to play them off against one another. Left and right, union and employer, banker and minister: these are almost always high-quality debates to which the *Volk* also contributes, in the form of articulate, carefully selected victims or other interested parties, reminding the politicians of their promises or confronting them with their dilemmas. Anne Will, Maybrit Illner, Sandra Maischberger—sometimes they have to swish the cane to keep order in their lively class of the high and mighty, all of whom are aiming to break the world record for talking, backed up by their own conviction that they are in the right. What I am watching is the parlour game of the *polis*, a game that people long to play when playing it is forbidden. This is the luxury of freedom. Politics as entertainment. The philosopher Giorgio Agamben speaks somewhat enigmatically in his *Kindheit und Geschichte* about the poverty of experience, distinguishing between *Erfahrung* and *Erlebnis*, the two words that capture different concepts of "experience" in German: "The modern individual returns home in the evening, completely exhausted by a jumble of *Erlebnisse*—entertaining or boring, unusual or everyday, terrible or pleasant—without a single one of these events becoming an *Erfahrung*." The talk show is simply an extension of such a day, a drama that takes the form of a battle, and therefore an event, even though, fundamentally, it is not one. Is that bad? Is Heidegger's banality of the everyday a disaster or a formula to live by? If peace is boredom, why do we yearn for it when it is absent? Is true experience something that can only come from outside? I live here now in the settings of my earlier excitement and, together with the city, I become normalized, an urban nomad, a passer-by, a consumer. I find a sentence related to this experience in Agamben too: "They are like those characters in the comic strips of our childhood who can continue running in mid-air until they become aware of it: when they notice, when they experience it, they tumble helplessly into the abyss."

In the café on Stuttgarter Platz where I go in the morning for my coffee and newspapers, I watch my contemporaries doing the same thing. They read the reports from places where there is no avoiding fate and history: Afghanistan, Gaza, Iraq, Darfur, Kosovo. I cannot work out what they are thinking. When we go back outside into the gloomy autumn weather, we are not thinking about bombs and attacks. The abyss into which we have helplessly tumbled cannot be read on our faces. Or have we discovered the secret of being spared from banality by suffering it? Agamben is referring to Walter Benjamin when he states that what we experience are only *Erlebnisse*, experiences in the sense of brief events and sensations, rather than accumulated wisdom. Benjamin's example involves the *"Armut der Erfahrung,"* the poverty of experience—and specifically deals with soldiers returning home after the First World War: "A generation that had travelled to school on horse-drawn trams stood under an open sky in a landscape where nothing had remained unchanged but the clouds and, beneath them, in a force field of destructive currents and explosions, the tiny, fragile human body." One might think that these were in fact existential experiences, and as I read I feel myself becoming entangled in a semantic game, as the philosopher puts forward as evidence the fact that this era is unable to come up with any new proverbs, because they have been replaced by slogans. But how long does it take for a proverb to become a proverb?

I have barely got here before I have to return, and it is for the sake of a paradox, as where I am heading is all about the place where I am. The Cobra Museum in Amstelveen is staging an exhibition of work by the Leipziger Schule, which it has invited me to open. So I shall travel to Amsterdam in order to go to Leipzig. And of course my speech in Amsterdam begins with a memory:

> It was back in the days of the D.D.R. I was living in Berlin and I went with the Dutch ambassador on a short trip to Leipzig, in what we called East Germany back then. Our aim was to meet up with some students of Dutch. Before I was about to speak to them, the female professor, who committed suicide after the *Wende*, told me not to expect any questions from them, because, as she put it, the students were not used to asking questions. Twenty years later, that seems like a strange thing to have said, but it is exactly what happened. Even so, we still ended up having a chat in a lovely old pub afterwards. The students had read a great deal, were rather well informed about our literature, and when, after the *Wende*, I returned to the same place, the climate had already changed.
>
> Why am I telling this story? To give an impression of the atmosphere that existed at the time, an atmosphere we can scarcely imagine nowadays. It has already become history, you can read about it, but you can no longer feel it, just as you can no longer feel the sense of threat that hit you when you had to cross the border at Checkpoint Charlie or Bahnhof Friedrichstraße, or when you tried to imagine the lives of the

people who lived there, and who were unable to leave, unless they happened to be, say, a writer or an artist and were on such good terms with the regime that they were trusted to return.

History, past, twenty years ago, the age of an adult who never experienced any of that. I actually find it a little embarrassing that I am still talking about it.

The people who taught the painters and photographers whose works are exhibited here lived inside that system; some of them were even ideologically entwined with it. I remember seeing large scenes of the peasants' revolt by Werner Tübke, who, along with Arno Rink and Bernhard Heisig, was one of the greats of those days. They are still the teachers of many of the younger people whose paintings hang on these walls, who have themselves become the teachers of younger artists. I found Tübke's enormous frescos strange, yet impressive. They had no connection to what was happening on our side of the curtain, but they were certainly big, so much larger than life, with an incredible amount to see, and all of it was most definitely painted. This was art created to serve a view of history and so, by definition, art that shielded itself from art that served another ideology or even no ideology at all.

And what do we see in this exhibition? Painters, first and foremost. What they have in common is their connection to Leipzig. Sometimes they had the same teachers at the famous institution where they trained or, like Neo Rauch himself, still work as tutors.

What they do not share is a style. So I would not go so far as to use the term "school." The word "school" refers instead to their common origin; the style and subject matter of the work exhibited here is so heterogeneous that it seems as though the Leipziger Hochschule must have had twenty different exits, and the students, painters and photographers all found their own way out. That does not bother me, because it means that there is plenty to look at. Subdued contemplation, exuberance and expressive pleasure in painting, realistic documentary-style photography, alongside extravagant, staged photography and, as in the case of the stylistically very different Neo Rauch and Matthias Weischer, an almost wanton love of the preposterous, which strays far from Socialist Realism without ever renouncing the lessons of painting as a craft—on the contrary. It is remarkable that the work varies considerably even within the oeuvres of individual artists. At first sight, Weischer's insanely crowded *Innenräume*, with their absurd logic and surreal notions, appear to have little to do with his gouaches of cars, which, with their photographic precision, look more like advertising brochures. Rauch's paintings from 1993 might, as far as I am concerned, be by an entirely different artist from the painter of the 2005 work *Kommen wir zum Nächsten*, that very same Rauch. This piece is a painting by one single artist, but the dreams of several different people seem to be depicted on the canvas and, as is always the case with dreams, these images present us with puzzles. What is that young man, dressed in the classic costume of German Romanticism, downcast eyes, sad expression, doing in what appears to be a contemporary setting? He is sitting, anachronistically, on a plastic garden chair, and, at the point where his knee-breeches and silk stockings should meet, some kind of unpleasant black stream or slick of oil is swirling out. The young man's right hand is tucked into a large, modern-looking briefcase beside him on the ground, while his left hand is resting on some papers that are lying beside a thick, unlit candle on the tomato-colored, slightly shiny tablecloth, which might be made of plastic or linoleum. A woman is leaning forward, with both fists on the table, and looking at the young man, who has not noticed her. Behind them is some kind of craftsman in a stained apron and with a rope binding his wrists. Two other craftsmen are holding large beams of wood and standing on a sort of scaffold that is decorated with green garlands, beside a device that could be a guillotine, but probably is not. Is that everything? No, far from it. Two houses, with trees behind, a blue sky with a few light clouds and perhaps a flock of birds, all lined up and ready to serve, but there is also something that is far more difficult to describe: glistening, fatty growths or clots that have no name and possibly no function, but which exude a threat of the unknown simply because of their presence, so detached and autonomous among these absurd, but familiar images. A peculiar, broken sea-green object in the foreground on the left plays the same role. Its function is unclear, as is that of the oily, bilious green blob of unknown origin that is lying on the table.

If I have gone into too much detail here—and yet at the same time nothing like enough detail—it is because this painting expresses something of the long way these artists have come, as do a number of other paintings in this exhibition, even though, once again, their styles are so different. While their masters were bound to an ideology that would have viewed opacity as a personal luxury, here doctrine has given way to ecstasy, chaos and the problematic issue of freedom, which everyone solves in a different way. And so a bunker can be photographed in an unnatural, apocalyptic light, as in Erasmus Schröter's mannerist photography, which appears to be as far removed from Rauch as Henriette Grahnert's subtle *Netzwerkprobleme*, or Christian Brandl's delicate, traditionally painted symbolism. As an outsider, one can only guess at the ideological battles and disputes that have been

fought in Leipzig over the past thirty years; I have only been
able to touch upon the range and variety of the art that has
been made there.

Hans-Werner Schmidt, director of the Museum der
Bildenden Künste Leipzig, writes about this subject in his
introduction to a book I read about the Essl Collection. One
day in 2000, he received an invitation to view an exhibition
by a group that called itself LIGA. He explains that he went
to see the exhibition without any real expectations, just to get
out of the house for a while. But he goes on to say that he will
not forget that afternoon any time soon.

What he encountered were canvases painted with
enormous self-confidence, works of an entirely different
calibre than he had expected. What really struck him was
the difference between this art and the art of the period
immediately following the fall of the Wall. There were still
late echoes of Cobra and Joseph Beuys, but also, as he phrases
it, memories of "the art of verismo and late Expressionism,"
somber in nature, dark in palette. LIGA was light, fabricated,
focused on the city and its architecture, and had in a sense
bid farewell to the teachers at the Hochschule für Grafik
und Buchkunst. Three years later, Schmidt organized a new
exhibition at his own museum, "*sieben mal malerei.*" The rest
is history: that evening, gallery owners from all over the world
came in droves, the phenomenon of the Leipziger Schule was
born and, to cut the story short, because otherwise it will
become far too long for this occasion, a new School needs a
mastermind to collect its output and the new artists found this
person in Karlheinz Essl. Essl's background is in construction,
but he is also a passionate collector, who attempted to interest
a Viennese museum in his collection before the painters
had achieved the fame that they now enjoy, or suffer—both

enjoyment and suffering being possible. Vienna refused—not everyone sees the light—and so Essl built his own museum in Klosterneuburg, ten kilometers or so from the capital. The Cobra Museum was able to draw on this collection and those of Leipzig galleries to create this exhibition, providing a glimpse into a world that, not so long ago, was closed to us, and which has produced new names that will soon become well known here too, if they are not already, names such as Tim Eitel, Tobias Lehner, wild Wunderkind Sebastian Gögel and photographer Matthias Hoch, who has two superb architectural photos of Amsterdam in this exhibition, which form a wonderful counterpart to Ulf Puder's paintings of architecture, which are also full of light and free of people. The perfect hanging of these works in the bright, open spaces of the Cobra Museum succeeds in uniting pieces that perhaps do not in essence belong together, and the effect is as it should be: a wonderful surprise from Leipzig.

October 2008

POST. A STRONG, ORNATE BAROQUE HAND THAT I recognize. Prof. em. Franz Rudolf Knubel has sent me some kind of exhibition catalogue. The narrow, elongated book does not have a title so much as a note written in small letters, preceded by dots ". . . *zur kleinsten Schar* / . . . with a chosen few," followed by the words "In memoriam Mildred Harnack-Fish." At the front of the book is a portrait of a woman with strong features, looking out at the viewer. Her hair, carefully combed close to her head, gleams; her eyes are watchful; this is a woman who exudes seriousness. Inside the catalogue, I find poems, photographs. It was published by the Gedenkstätte Deutscher Widerstand, the German Resistance Memorial Center, and when I start reading I understand why.

This woman whose face I have just seen for the first time was born in Milwaukee, Wisconsin, in 1902. She studied literature at the University of Wisconsin, where she met Arvid Harnack, whom she married in the summer of 1926. After moving to Germany with him, she taught at the University of Berlin until she was dismissed from her teaching position in 1932. She then taught evening classes and, together with a number of her students, participated in a discussion group led by her husband, which focused on social and political issues. Until 1942, she still had contact with the American embassy, which gave her access to speeches by Roosevelt, news of the Spanish Civil War and also commentaries on Hitler's policies, which were not available in Germany. She passed this material on to a small group

Mildred Harnack, ca. 1930

of people who were critical of the Nazi regime, so supporting her husband's underground movement. There is a photograph of the two of them sitting together in the peaceful countryside: a smiling Mildred wearing a fur collar, Arvid with a pipe in his mouth, more thoughtful, a flash of sunshine among the dark pines. I never read far enough in Agamben's book to understand exactly what he means by experience and the absence of experience, but I feel myself drawn into these two lives in a way that appears to contradict his words: "No one would recognize an authority whose only legitimization was founded on *Erfahrung* . . . This does not mean that *Erfahrungen* no longer exist nowadays. However, they occur outside of the human being."

I must be on the wrong track somehow. When is an experience something that takes place without a person? At the end of 1941, Mildred Harnack was awarded her doctorate by the University of

Giessen. On September 7, 1942, she was arrested with her husband in Preila on the Kurische Nehrung, the Curonian Spit, a mysterious name for a place. The Reichskriegsgericht sentenced her to six years in prison on 19 December, but Hitler did not accept that sentence. He wanted a new trial, which duly occurred, culminating on January 16, 1943, in a death sentence. A month passed before Mildred Harnack was beheaded at Berlin-Plötzensee. During that month, she worked on her translation of Goethe's poem "*Vermächtnis*," and she continued to do so until the final hours before her execution. Her last words were: "*. . . und ich habe Deutschland so geliebt*": and I loved Germany so very much.

> *Kein Wesen kann zu nichts zerfallen!*
> *Das Ew'ge regt sich fort in allen,*
> *Am Sein erhalte dich beglückt!*
> *Das Sein ist ewig; denn Gesetze*
> *Bewahren die lebend'gen Schätze*
> *Aus welchen sich das All geschmückt.*

And in Mildred Harnack's translation:

> No being can to nothing fall.
> The Everlasting lives in all.
> Sustain yourself in joy with life.
> Life is eternal; there are laws
> To keep the living treasure's cause
> With which the worlds are rife.

What kind of moment might that be, as an American woman waits in a German cell to be executed and continues to work on her translation of the most classic of all German poets? The banality of everyday life is so infinitely distant here, an intellectual abstraction that evaporates when confronted with the weight of history and the fate of the people within it. But haven't there always, throughout all the centuries of history, been such moments of intense experience within the ocean of banality where most people's lives take place? And how does that, and how does Walter Benjamin's own fate, relate to his notion of the poverty of experience in the modern era?

In his letter, Franz Rudolf Knubel writes not only about the how, but also about the where, providing details of the location of the prison: "*Plötzensee liegt im Norden Charlottenburgs am Saatwinkler Damm am Hüttigpfad.*" The photograph in the catalogue shows the innocence of the red brick and the guilt of the black bars. A Berlin building like so many others, probably not built for the purpose it served during the war. Above the two windows are arches of upright vertical bricks amidst the horizontal bricks of the wall. The surroundings are neutral, but take on the color of what has been done there. Three thousand people were executed in this place. A metal bar in the execution room still has hooks for hanging people, and a scaffold with a guillotine once stood there. After these events, the gaze of posterity could never again be neutral, just as it is impossible to read Goethe's poem and Mildred Harnack's translation without thinking about how and when that translation was created. Knubel's homage to Mildred Harnack, because that is what it is, involved visiting the places that were connected to her and searching for her traces—but he has to admit that he rarely finds them. It is, in his words, "*ein nicht gelingendes Unterfangen,*" an undertaking that will not succeed, a hopeless cause, as the pale innocence of some of the photographs demonstrates: addresses where she once lived, houses that prove nothing because they could have been anyone's house, front doors, pavements, garden fences. Here, the banality of our lives becomes visible, but not the lives themselves, not anymore; that happens only in the places where the tragedy occurred, in that brick room behind those bars, where a woman who has just turned forty looks her executioner in the eye. The old professor took large sheets of paper to the place of execution and, kneeling on the hard ground, rubbed charcoal over paper on the concrete floor. The surface was uneven, irregular, and the traced image consisted of streaks, stripes, grainy marks, which now form the cover of the catalogue. He writes about this:

> "A red cordon divides the room. Above the windows, the bar with the hooks. Beneath that, a wreath and dried flowers on the window ledges. I step over the barrier and take out my 70 x 100 sheets of paper and box of pencils. I go down on my knees and calmly carry out the work I have planned as an act of remembrance: tracing marks from the rough concrete floor, which has so many scars. In the front third of the divided area is a narrow drain with seven iron bars, not much bigger than a sheet of A4. Close to this drain stood the killing machine: the guillotine. The whole process is incredibly peaceful: I observe myself, I listen to myself, as I transfer the traces of the iron grate onto the paper, check the result, repeat it on a smaller sheet of hand-made paper. I immediately see that the second attempt was superfluous . . . I changed my materials once, but there was no need. As it is, this work can only be read if it is called 'Spiritual Exercises in the Incomprehensible.'"

The advantage of the big city: when people become too much for you there are always animals and plants to provide instant healing, the balm of creatures without any visible guilt or history, whose only goal is to perpetuate themselves into eternity. Wolf and owl were already wolf and owl a thousand years ago. If any evolution occurs, it takes place over tens of thousands of years: a slightly longer claw, a shift in the color of the plumage, three more thorns on a twig, that kind of thing. Around the time of the *Wende*, I often used to go to the zoo in the East. The animals did not belong to the Party, nor to the opposition; they did not denounce one another; all that happened was that lion and eagle attempted to convince the visitors of their endless, immutable nature. You might look into their eyes for a minute or an hour and, as usual, not see any sign of communication there; the only statement consists of the creatures themselves and the way they look at us without any form of encounter. I can spend hours there, just marveling at the fact that everyone has eyes: fox, deer, snake, crocodile, elephant, grasshopper, seal, monkey, all of our travelling companions in their prescribed uniforms, fur, hair, scales, shells, feathers, spines, and every single one of them is equipped with eyes. If you look into those eyes for long enough you start to think about how you can never see beyond pupil and retina, the point where the strange, unapproachable other begins. I find that a calming thought. I saunter past the cows, feel the autumn leaves tumbling down on me, hear the metrical feet beneath me penning an ode to the panther and the heron, sense the gradual healing flowing through me. I am ready to face humanity once again.

Plants generally do not say very much, even though, given the right wind conditions, they can of course whisper and sigh. A famous line of poetry was written in my language by the Flemish priest-poet Guido Gezelle, a sort of Olivier Messiaen of poetry: "*Mij spreekt de blomme een tale*": to me, a flower can speak. One afternoon in 1989, as I wandered around the Nikolai-Viertel, I happened upon a pub called Zum Nussbaum. Nussbaum means "nut tree," as does Nooteboom, so it was probably the name that tempted me inside that first time. Inside, it was a little like an old Amsterdam bar: small, brown, a few gleaming wooden tables, a sense of cosiness. Although it was in the East, it reminded me of home: dimly lit, quiet people, a gentle buzz, cold outside, mounds of snow on the icy streets, a vicious wind from Siberia rubbing the Spree up the wrong way, but inside it was warm, and the *Glühwein* made you glow. It used to be a rather exclusive place: you had to go through all those checks at Bahnhof Friedrichstraße to get there, so there was something adventurous about it. For a brief while, you were in another world, even though you felt as though you were sitting in someone's living room. You stood out as someone who had come to have a look around, which meant you were too visible, a feeling that no longer exists today.

And today it is autumnal; it might even start drizzling. I have had a drink, one of those beers we do not have in Holland, tall, tapering glasses that you are allowed to take an hour over: meditation beer. Maybe that explains why, once I had finished my beer, I could not quite remember what I had been expecting from that day. I had already read all about the crisis in the newspaper; I had seen Angela Merkel guarding Germany like a mother hen and refusing to allow Gordon Brown to tempt her into throwing baskets full of money into the wind. Even though, just a few months later, we would be unable to imagine that he had not been there forever, Obama had yet to be elected, but we were not allowed to vote, suicide attacks in Afghanistan and car bombs dominated the front pages, the world was a panopticon of unbearable atrocities—perhaps that was why, when I saw the 48 bus coming, with its sign saying, "Botanischer Garten," I got on without hesitation and climbed up to one of the box seats to watch Berlin gliding past, all sorts of districts that I did not know, shops selling exotic food, snatches of the Third World among the big grey buildings. I wanted to preserve something of that day, so I made a few helpless notes in my notebook: "Hauptstraße, Dominicusstraße, Günlük Taze Ve Halâl Et, Rathaus Friedenau, Kaisereiche, U-Bahn Schreiberplatz, Losgehen um anzukommen, Halte Kielerstraße, Malik." I do not understand half of my notes when I look at them now—it looks like a secret code for spies. But no one wants to rifle through my papers, and no one arrests me. I listen to the quiet conversations on the bus and to the whining voice of a woman behind me as she divulges her love life to her mobile phone, an excerpt from a novel, written without the refinement of art. I am a man wrapped up in words. One person's freedom is another's captivity, and when I get off at the botanical garden her failed marriage is hanging all over me like cobwebs and, still in that state, I enter the realm of multi-colored silence and walk along a hedge of angel's trumpet and tall, pink stalks of gamba grass. Copper sunlight, the threat of rain. I pick up a big tanned leaf that would like to tell me something about the autumn; it is as purple as a bishop, lined with a system of golden veins. Why is the decay of plants beautiful while the decay of humans usually is not? Everywhere, the green is starting to assume the colors of death. Lonely leaves fall in slow, floating circles like suicide parachutists, as though they still have one last secret mission to perform on the way down. I marvel at a tree fern that has not yet decided what it would rather be: a fern-like tree or a tree-like fern, poet or novelist. Soon I am standing before the powerful leaves of the *Peltiphyllum peltatum*, which hang contemplatively over shining, black water. Their silence is breathtaking, and yet if I stand still for long enough I can hear what they are saying: it comes down to the fact that they know they are there; it is a thought about presence in the here and now. Paths, tracks, the occasional illusion of wilderness, then the first drops that force me into the big glasshouses where the exiles from the tropics reside. If they are feeling homesick for the savannah or the rainforest, they do not show it. I write down their precious names, which I will soon forget, and think how strange it is that they themselves do not know what they are called, even though some of these plants are such good matches for their wild names: hairy festoons, rolled-up leather sheets for which a new variation on green has been invented, twelve curved daggers poised around a blood-red heart, cacti in all the forms of the Euclidean catalogue. How amazing to be a cactus, if only for a night and a day, a silent and meditative creature covered with all those needles that send out only one message: I Am Thinking. Do Not Disturb. Leave Me In Peace.

I read in the newspapers that Tempelhof is being closed down. Images of the Airlift* and the associated stories come to mind. I once wrote a story† featuring a short scene that takes place at that airport, and I can still picture the long hall, the neon strips high up around the edges of the ceiling, the glider hanging beneath them. It is a day of final flights, imminent dismantling. A man is holding a placard: *"Wir dürfen uns das nicht gefallen lassen, es gibt hier nichts zu feiern"*: We should not stand for this—there is nothing to celebrate. His expression says he knows he has already lost. The flights on which I departed from or arrived at Tempelhof always involved small aeroplanes, which, along with the peculiar design of that long hall, which I had not seen at any other airport, made the experience of flying feel rather old-fashioned, as though you were playing a part in some 1950s spy movie. But there was something else about that airport, something that has to do with a deeper layer of my past. Whenever I see and hear an aeroplane taking off on television, the noise takes me back to the first day of the war. On the tenth of May, 1940, I was woken by the sound of bombs and anti-aircraft guns, by planes diving and then accelerating away. It was daybreak and the planes were bombing the military airfield at

---

* In response to the Berlin Blockade (June 24, 1948–May 12, 1949), during which the Soviet Union blocked the railway, road and canal routes into those areas of the city under Allied control, the Western Allies organized the Berlin Airlift, delivering necessities such as food and fuel in more than 200,000 flights over the course of eleven months.

† *Lost Paradise*, translated by Susan Massotty (London: Harvill Secker; New York: Grove Press, 2007).

Ypenburg, not far from our home in The Hague. I do not remember now whether they were Heinkels or Junkers, but the noise I can hear now is unmistakably the same as back then, the sound of the pre-jet era. For me, it is associated with the red sky over Rotterdam in the distance, with parachutists slowly floating down to the green meadows below. Now I would like to hear that sound once again for real. I read something about the *Rosinenbomber* and a *Zeitreise*, a journey in time—apparently they are planning one last flight in the old planes that were used in the Airlift—but that is no good to me. The past I am in search of is even older. On the square in front of the entrance to Tempelhof is the head of an enormous eagle, black and gleaming, its beak pointing downwards like a sharpened dagger, but when I go inside everything appears deceptively normal. There are still people at the check-in desks; the floors are polished to a gleam; an aeroplane engine is displayed like a monument or a stray work of art by Beuys, sparkplugs and electrical wiring sticking out in every direction like a Gorgon's hair; stewardesses stand at the Air Service Berlin desk in their cappuccino-colored uniforms; and the light-blue hands of the clock on the big dark wall indicate the time, time that is connected to scenes of arrival and farewell, and

Tempelhof airport,
October 2008

*Poster: Journey through time
with the Rosinenbomber,
October 2008*

which therefore always has a different significance at airports than
on a church clock.

I walk around the building, along an extremely bare and simple gallery that once looked so modern that totalitarian ideologies
found it easy to appropriate its sober, geometric forms, which were
inspired, I feel, not only by Adolf Loos, but also by Cistercian architecture. Outside, I walk towards Tempelhofer Damm in the hope
that I will be able to stand behind the fence and watch the aeroplane of my childhood taking off. As I walk, I realize how large
Tempelhof actually was, a huge space carved out of the center of
a metropolis. I find some stairs that bring me closer to the metal
fences. I am not the only one there; a group of plane spotters stands
beside me, glued to the iron net. Together, we watch the prehistoric
machine speed past us and into the air, with that little jump that
always comes as a surprise, as though it is briefly mocking gravity.
When I look around, I realize that I cannot share the memory of

that sound, which I am hearing again after almost seventy years, with anyone here, simply because the people around me are too young. When you listen with the ear of memory, what you hear is the same, yet different; that is what it comes down to. A historical event needs only to have occurred sufficiently long ago to become deformed. Then it assumes the characteristics of the mythical, the legend, or the fairy tale. One day, someone in this world, or another, will read about a city which, during some distant, misty prehistoric era, unthinkably long ago, was once saved by birds.

October 2008

EIN PUNKT IST, WAS KEINE TEILE HAT. EEN PUNT IS WAT geen deel heeft. Why do I find this sentence easier to understand in English? "A point is that which has no part." Perhaps there is some interference from the Dutch: *deel hebben aan.* But would it not be better to say that a point consists entirely of itself? I am on dangerous ground here, having ventured out to an exhibition about math, a failed student, perversely drawn to the traps and snares of his earlier defeat. If there is anything I regret, it is missing out on the mysteries of mathematics. I was, to stick with the terminology, a zero, and to hide from that unavoidable truth I took refuge in my imagination. During tests that cannot really have been all that difficult, I invented theorems that I thought were perfectly plausible myself, but which actually made no sense at all. I would arrive at sound results, but they were valid only for me, within some made-up system of mathematics where everyone was drunk or belonged in an institution. My teachers had given up on me. I did not really mind at the time, but I do now. Between my chaos and the order of mathematics, there was a barrier of unwillingness that the teachers could not break through. I do not want to apportion blame, but sometimes I think that if someone had taken the trouble to come and find me within the maze of my adolescent stupidity and lead me out into the big, bright garden of figures, formulae and logic, I would not be seized by the unholy terror that seizes me even now when I am reading certain books, ones that I understand until the author suddenly starts spouting magic formulae that everyone can read except me. This is part of the reason why I never took my final school examinations. My past, short though it was at the time, consisted of chaos, and I was on the run.

For years, my greatest nightmare was having to do a math exam and failing hopelessly. In 1998, when I received an honorary doctorate from the Catholic University of Brussels, I said that I viewed that day as my last day at school, and I hoped my nightmare would never return. And that is what happened; the illusions disappeared. This is in itself a miracle of autosuggestion, but my regret remains. And so it is with a certain hesitation that I enter the Deutsches Technikmuseum, the museum of technology, where they are putting on an exhibition called "*Mathema.*" My old desire to share in that world of transparent mysteries, from which I cut myself off so long ago, is apparently still there. There is a plane hanging on the front of the building that will never fly anywhere again, and as I enter the museum I fall straight into the arms of a quote from Einstein: *Das, wobei unsere Berechnungen versagen, nennen wir Zufall.** Einstein is soon demanding attention again: someone has written on the wall that, in light of his special theory of relativity, we should imagine the world in four dimensions, with the three dimensions of space and the one dimension of time forming an indivisible whole. The underlying principle is the notion that there is no absolute time,

---

* What our calculations fail to solve, we refer to as chance.

which is a pleasant thought. Dalí must have been thinking something along those lines when he melted his watch, and anyone who spends a lot time travelling the world will often have seen time condensing, racing backwards, and acting as though it does not exist, which may in fact be true. That notion gives me a strange sense of freedom: time as a fluid element in which you can swim around, even against the current if necessary. I once wrote that time is the system that ensures everything does not happen simultaneously, and even though there is an odd tautological kink in that thought, I am comfortable with it.

It is quiet inside the exhibition and I walk undisturbed around the wondrous world of hyperbolic geometry. I feel myself curving along with this space; I tick inaudibly somewhere in the world as a watch and, when no one is watching, I allow myself to be enticed into flying through a virtual city with a pair of wings on my shoulders. In short, I join in with the game the exhibition has devised for me; I surrender to it. I learn that the interwoven ornamentation of the Alhambra, just like the patterns on a Gucci bag, falls under the heading of "Patterns with Translational Symmetry" and that Gerhard Richter used a random generator to determine the colors for his big new window in Cologne Cathedral.

How different my Berlin days now are from that chaotic time when I saw Modrow racing down the corridors of Schloss Bellevue and Krenz at the Dom, desperately and against his own better judgment, attempting to turn the tide of the *Weltgeist*. Order and calm reign here. Instead of the chaos and turbulence of everyday history, this is Pythagoras' theory of harmony, the golden mean, the story about the butterfly that causes a hurricane with its fluttering. That is, of course, also agitation, but it is logically explicable, which helps. Kant said that mathematics is the foundation of all exact knowledge, but elsewhere I have read that it is sometimes better to allow oneself to be guided by chance when working on certain scientific problems if you cannot solve them by other means. My life was not a scientific problem, and so did not need to be solved, but when I look back, I see that it depended on variable series of random events, each of which may have had a certain inescapable logic of its own—you are, after all, born at the moment and in the place where your mother happens to be—but which was still dependent on the fact that my father once happened to see my mother walking past and found her attractive. And that made me a Dutchman from the twentieth century, but probably has nothing to do with my not becoming a mathematician.

FRANKFURT. ANSELM KIEFER IS RECEIVING AN award, the Friedenspreis des Deutschen Buchhandels. The Paulskirche is full of familiar faces. People know one another; the public face of Germany is sitting here. It is a church without a church, a pulpit now standing where once the altar was. I know that spot; I once stood there myself. You have to climb some steps to get there, and then you feel strange, as though it is not entirely right to be standing there. If that sounds dramatic, it is not intended to, but still there is that brief, peculiar sensation of loneliness; no one is standing beside you. No matter how often you do such things, that feeling never entirely goes away. The gentle murmuring of voices, then the usual speeches, the praise, and finally the prizewinner himself. When he starts to speak, the room falls silent. He is in black, an ascetic figure, and perhaps it is because of the church-like atmosphere, but what he most closely resembles is a Benedictine monk.

The award is not without controversy; Kiefer's preoccupation with the German past, with its Teutonic aspects, has not been universally appreciated, particularly at first. Werner Spies addresses this in his eulogy, and says that he had his own doubts at the time, that what was in fact a quest was perceived as identification, at a time when no one wanted to hear about the past. The artist went in search of it, and what he brought back, accentuated, emphasized in his work was viewed as empathetic nostalgia, a longing for the wrong era. The man in the pulpit also refers to this issue. He starts talking about his own past, about his youth, and one word leaps out. When I read the speech later, it is printed separately, on a line of its own:

Langeweile.

Boredom. The source of so many things. A childhood without television, without the internet, without the cinema and without the theater. Emptiness, tedium. Then poetry. Poems as buoys in an ocean of emptiness: "I think in images. Poems help me to do so. They are like buoys in the sea. I swim to them, from one to the next; between them, without them, I am lost." As he speaks, I consider the peculiarity of the situation. I imagine what it would have been like to hear one of the great painters of the past give a speech: Zurbarán, Delacroix, de Chirico.

More so than writers, painters have always disappeared behind their images, and suddenly that becomes a puzzling notion. I can picture one of Kiefer's monumental paintings behind him as he stands there, assuming the pose of a speaker and resembling other speakers in such situations, speakers who do not have an image of lead and straw behind them, of a rust-colored landscape of sand and clay and dried paint, lead-blue, ash-grey, coal-black, accompanied by words that refer to history, and I do not know why it should be that particular painting, but it is a seascape that I see there. The slender figure in the pulpit is dwarfed by the width of the painting that my imagination is projecting behind him, white foaming waves of cracked paint, great sweeps of movement and, within them, the sinister forms of submarines, orange, and in the ominous sky above them, words over the horizon, like a natural phenomenon, as though there are always words floating in the sky, words that only the artist sees: "*Seeschlachten alle 317 Jahren oder deren Vielfachen*": Sea battles every 317 years or multiples thereof.

Puzzling: the word is no coincidence. The man in black who is standing up there conforms with the environment in which he now finds himself, but his art does not. That art derives from the knowledge that beneath the semblance of order that is civilization, an indomitable chaos always resides. In this of all places, within the civilized conformity of the world of editors-in-chief, ministers and ambassadors in this church-like space, that is an additional irony. I once wrote the following words: "When do paintings rid themselves of their painter? When does the same material become a different thought?" Does "Guernica" still belong to Picasso, and if so, for how long? When I look at Hieronymus Bosch's "Haywain" in the Prado, does it still have anything to do with the painter who created that painting, or have later gazes, throughout the long centuries when that object of wood and paint remained its material self, transformed it into something completely different, as Borges essentially contends in his famous story "Pierre Menard, Author of the Quijote," which is about a man who, centuries later, writes the same book as Cervantes, word for word, and yet still a book that was completely different? Will future eyes take Kiefer's paintings from their creator and make them so autonomous that the painter himself would no longer recognize them? Only great art makes us contemplate such questions. The painter himself has only his circumscribed life, the concerns that have fuelled him, a fascination with the history of his country and the pits and precipices within it, and his own confrontation with this history, which people have not thanked him for because the *"Unfähigkeit zum Trauern,"* the inability to mourn, prompted the desire to cover up, hide, deny that shameful past. What remains is the whispering in his library, the poetry of Bachmann and Celan, the notion that a mythological image can be stronger than science, which is constantly changing, and that what is lacking in an artwork must seek an alliance with what is lacking in history and in nature, which are also incomplete. All of this has inevitably penetrated Kiefer's paintings, his gigantic books of lead, his library without words, written by all of the words that he has ever read and recorded as he swam from buoy to buoy: words of poets, of the Sephiroth, the echoes of Chassidic legends, a legacy guarded against disappearance, visible and invisible, the painter as a scribe, who became what he read, and created what he was.

As I leave the hall after the event, a friendly man offers me a pamphlet, a protest against this award ceremony. I take it and I thank him. Sometimes democracy makes it clear that there are things that remain invisible, even to the well-meaning.

October 2008

BERLIN, AN AUTUMNAL AFTERNOON, A SUDDEN URGE. I want to go back to Falkplatz, to see what has become of the trees I once planted, along with some other people, twenty years ago. I still remember the peeling paint on the buildings, the expressions of the people on the balconies; they probably thought we were mad. I attempt to remember something of the atmosphere of that day, but with little success. The presence of the People's Police created a strange sense of sudden goodwill on all sides. We were dreamers, but there is no shame in that. So what is it like now? There are plants, bushes. The ones that we planted? Some of the trees look too tall; they must have already been there. In the background, there is a sports center that I recognize. I had had a sort of vision too, that "in fifty or a hundred years' time, I would like to shelter under the mighty crowns of this forest in waiting," and had hoped the planters would not be disappointed. Have they been disappointed? I do not know.

It has not turned into a forest, and maybe I am the only one who can still remember that day. But there are a few small trees. Maybe the same ones, maybe different. They are swaying gently in the wind, as trees do on an autumn day, and they are not revealing what they think.

NOVEMBER 2008. THE FREIE UNIVERSITÄT BERLIN IS awarding me an honorary doctorate in philosophy and the arts, and the war child of back then cannot ignore his memories because, along with everything that happened to him here later, they have defined his relationship with this country. I am honored, but I hesitate for a long time about what to say on the day and whether it is a good idea to start talking about the past again, as I have recently done in my story about Tempelhof, but I also know that ultimately I am that past, and so that can be the starting point of my story, which begins with the same abruptness as the event, which has always remained unforgettable for me. A war is only over when the last person who lived through it is no longer around. This is the story I tell:

The first Germans I ever saw in my life came from the skies. The next ones came from the water, in the disarray that is typical of death. Only after that did they come over the land, in long, grey lines. I was six years old and standing beside my father, holding his hand, just as I had been sitting beside him on our balcony on that early May morning in 1940 when the parachutists fell from the sky. My father, who later died in that war during an English raid, had put an armchair on the balcony so that he could look out over the meadows behind our house. Am I telling you this so that I can start talking about the war again? To "rub it in," as they say in English? No. I am telling you because it is an unavoidable part of my story, because stories have to have a beginning, and because my age will not allow me to forget the beginning. I did not suffer, I make no claims to suffering, I do not even know if I am right to say that my writing may have begun on that day, because if that were the case everyone would have become a writer that day. No, my only justification for telling this story again is because I think my life as a writer has been determined by the idea of memory, by that special form of memory that we call the past, or better still history, history that for me is not an abstraction, but a form of existence, a story written by the world and written by each of us at the same time, which often means that we are inventing our own history in the midst of the inevitable events that are presented to us by the world. I had not made up the war; my memories of it, and the way in which I tell them, repeat them, formulate them, invent them or maybe even lie, belong to me, a story that, as you grow from one age to the next, constantly requires new words.

Reincarnation does not take place after our lives, but during, I once wrote in *Zelfportret van een ander* (Self-portrait of an Other),* in one of those moments of possible

---

* *Self-portrait of an Other*, translated by David Colmer, with drawings by Max Neumann (Chicago/London/Calcutta: Seagull Books, 2012).

clairvoyance when you already know something before you know it, one of the inalienable privileges of poetry.

What kind of person would I have been if I had not remembered that first day? The Stukas and Heinkels, the incredible noise that I believe wiped from my memory everything that preceded that day, depriving me of that basic material that other writers, such as Proust and Nabokov, utilized to such great effect, with the result that I have no recollections of those first years to draw on—it is as though I was not born until that day, as a fully formed six-year-old, an impossibility and therefore a miracle, but I cannot shake the feeling associated with that miracle. I look in amazement at the photographs that prove I existed as a three-year-old and that I really did receive my first Holy Communion, but my inner archive refuses to confirm the truth, for that is what it must be. And it is that feeling that tempts me to think I may in fact have invented my life, complete with the actual fabrications that are part of that life and which we call novels and stories, a double layer of fiction that is inextricably entwined with the actual person of the Dutch citizen who is now standing before you. Does that citizen want something from that war? No. I was not a victim, not a perpetrator, I was a child. But the historical fact of that war wanted something from me.

The soldiers who fell from the sky were parachutists. The ones from the water had driven into the water, car and all, and were dredged up later—a first sight of death. Water dripping from long grey leather uniform coats. The six-year-old will not forget that, or the apocalyptic noise of the V2s fired from a site near our house on their way to England, an early precursor of space travel.

Rhyme is a concept from poetry, but it has, probably by analogy, another meaning for me: events that reflect other events, sometimes also forms of historical justice, confirmations of a prophetic inkling, an almost metaphysical relief that history is not only changing course, but making a radical about-face and seeking its opposite, while retaining all of the intervening time—because eliminating it is impossible; history is made up of time and of people—and yet making it apocryphal. In 1956, I stood in a smoldering Budapest and watched Russian tanks, and in 1989 I stood in Berlin and watched the Wall fall. That is what I mean by rhyme: when history finds a connection with itself, without the intervening period of crime and destruction, which is also history, itself being destroyed. Three old men in Yalta, splitting Europe in two with their wicked spell and then the moment when another spell cancels out the first spell, and the consequences that both of these spells have had for Germany and for Europe. That too is rhyme. There is an expression for this in English: full circle. If you live long enough to see it happen, there is a sense of satisfaction in knowing that evil often wins, but not always. In 1957, I was on a bus from Miami to New York. We were driving through the southern states, whites in the front, blacks in the back, separate restrooms and restaurants along the route. I remember a deep feeling of shame. As I write these words, it appears possible that a man who once would have had to sit at the back of the bus is going to be the next American president, and that too is rhyme. History, an amalgam of fate and chance, the story of everything that was the case.

War is chaos that later looks deceptively like order. My youth was a chaos in search of the clarity that, for me, could be found only in writing. This is something that takes a long time to discover. Chaos creates outsiders. Outsiders have to invent their own worlds in order to survive, the chaos of the self among the ordered world of others. My intention here is not to paint a psychological portrait; it is to show how the work that you wish to honor today has come about. The invented world of my first novel and my first poetry was a non-existent world of romantic longing, an escape. No one has seen that more clearly than Rüdiger Safranski. It is a blessing to meet people who recognize in your work what you did not see yourself when you were writing it. You had already written it, but you did not yet know it. This is, for me, the paradox of my writing. It has happened to me twice, both times in Germany. And that brings me to the next rhyme. There is a kind of line running from that moment when the men fell from the sky to the present day. This too is perhaps a paradox. This line is made up of friends; first the friends from my own country who suffered because of this country, but wanted to share with me their relationship to that past and so brought me here, starting my fascination. They were later joined by other friends, people I met here and who have remained my friends to this day.

After the war, Germany was not my country. It was destroyed, and somber, like my own country. Anyone who wants to know what the Netherlands was like after the war should read the two great novels by my fellow Dutchman Willem Frederik Hermans: *De tranen der acacia's* (*The Tears of the Acacias*) and *De donkere kamer van Damokles* (*The Darkroom of Damocles*), dark masterpieces, magnificent literature, miles away from my own poetic debut, which did not describe the real and bitter world of post-war society, but rather a dreamer's escape to an imaginary paradise, where the light of the south shone, a fantasy world that could not be sustained, but which I will never deny. Since that time, I have constantly lived in two worlds, the world of the north and the world of the south, of the visible reality of my travels

and that other world, interwoven with it, the world of fantasy.
You do not want your dream to fade, but the discrepancies
between the fantasy and the world around you are too strong,
and you reject the course of cynicism, sarcasm or other
forms of self-delusion. Your only solution is to turn and
face the world of chaos, with your imagination as your only
weapon. So you sign up for duty on a ship and sail to the
tropics, that other form of light, where it gets dark at the same
time every day, a darkness in which a cruel chaos can strike.
You attempt to escape from the dilemmas of writing or not
writing by writing a book in which a writer comes to grief on
that very dilemma. And as though it were you yourself who
had committed suicide in that book, *De ridder is gestorven*
(*The Knight Has Died*),* you let fiction remain fiction and
ceaselessly make your way through the epiphany of the world.
What takes place in the hidden layers of your being can be
said only in poems now, poems which, as Anselm Kiefer said
this week in his acceptance speech for the Friedenspreis, are
buoys, buoys that he swims to, from one to the next, because
otherwise he is lost, a feeling I recognize. Poems, then. You
still lack sufficient knowledge of the world for stories, and you
know it, because even imagination requires a foundation and
abhors the anemic vacuum. You have to wait and you do not
know whether that waiting is a lazy lie or the acknowledgment
of a destination. This uncertainty dominates your life for a
long time. You take it with you to America and Australia,
among Muslims and among Buddhists, when you attempt
to describe the things you perceive, until the moment comes
when you can let go of the world of appearances and write

---

* *The Knight Has Died*, translated by Adrienne Dixon (Louisiana State
University Press, 1990).

about all that it has left behind in you, and so create a story according to your own laws, a narrative that was visible only in your own imagination. Later, people will say that this world is "light," and intend this as an accusation or a compliment, and only you will know that the lightness was wrested from a gravitational force originating in the darkness of the chaos that has surrounded you since the beginning, the Dionysian chaos that lies beneath the thin skin of civilization, waiting for us with unflagging desire.

Then, once again, comes a moment of rhyme. The book you waited so long for is translated into German and published by Volk und Welt in Berlin. Together with two friends who were in Natzweiler and Buchenwald, you travel to this city, which knows more about the history of the twentieth century than any other and lives on the sharp dividing line between two mutually hostile systems. Your other, non-fictional self, is going to cover an S.E.D. conference, where Khrushchev will speak. The friends who have brought you with them to the land of their former fate take you to the most German of all restaurants, in an orgy of cathartic nostalgia. And they talk. You write your first notes on Berlin, which you will dedicate to one of these friends, notes that, although you do not realize it, are sketches for the novel that is already stirring deep within you, a novel in which they will play a part. A year later, you are living in Berlin. These are the years just before 1989. You are invited by the D.A.A.D. and it changes your life. You meet other people who become friends: a painter, a philosopher, a poet, all of whom will be woven into your web of appearance and reality without you or them being aware of it. You travel around their country, read their history, are there when another bronze page is turned as a wall falls with a crash that reverberates around the entire world. That was yesterday. The circle is full, or so it seems. In Tübingen, you meet an old man with white hair who once had to flee from Austria, where he studied philosophy and *Germanistik*, and who learned German poetry by heart on a tractor in New Zealand. In Hölderlin's tower, he gathers young people around him and they read poems together.

He invites me to one of these legendary gatherings. When he dies a few years later, I write the poem that I would like to read now, in conclusion. It is called "De dichter van het lezen," the poet of reading, a title that his widow had engraved on his tombstone in his beloved Latin: *Poeta Legendi*. His name was Paul Hoffmann.

De dichter van het lezen
In memoriam Paul Hoffman

Kwam mij tegemoet
in mijn verduisterde onschuld
een lichtspoor,

in een toren
van heilige waanzin,
deze ene,

hoorde wat ik zei
toen ik het niet hoorde,
hoorde mijn ander,

stemde mij,
met het fijnste oor voor verhulde gezangen,
stemde mij toe,

in verbanning had hij,
in een leeg land van anderen,
woorden herhaald en geslepen

tot ze zich werden.
Gewapend kwam hij terug
naar hun eerdere schande,

hun van leugens
geluidloos geworden,
hun bedorven taal

die hij opneemt en koestert,
geneest met gedichten,
teruggeeft aan zichzelf.

Licht groeit uit zijn ziel
sneeuwlaurier om zijn hoofd.
Schitterend ben jij het, de leraar,

de dichter van het lezen.

The Poet of Reading
In memoriam Paul Hoffman

Towards me
in my shuttered innocence,
came a trace of light,

in a tower
of holy madness,
this one man,

heard what I said
when I did not hear it,
heard the other me,

found my chord
with the keenest ear for hidden songs,
gave me his accord,

banished into exile
in an empty land of others,
he had repeated words, polished them

until they became themselves.
Armed, he came back
to their former disgrace,

to their language
silenced by lies,
their corrupted tongue

which he embraced, nourished,
healed with poems,
returned it to itself.

Light grows from his soul,
laurels of snow around his head.
You are dazzling, the teacher,

the poet of reading.

October 2008

It is almost time for my farewell. Yet again, I am leaving Berlin, and like every other time it will not be easy. I go through the enormous pile of newspaper cuttings once more, read about all the things I have not written about, look at a page of designs for the Schloss they are planning to build on the site of the old Volkspalast. In real life too, I visited the Kronprinzenpalais one cold winter's day to look at the models based on those designs. On days like that, arctic winds blow over the wide open spaces and Berlin reminds you that it borders on Russia. The designs were hung on the walls, lots of losers alongside the one winner. There were so many of them. I tried to imagine what Unter den Linden would look like when the winning design was in place, but I could not picture it, perhaps because I did not really believe in it. Nostalgia in stone, an antiquated grammar of construction, a half-hearted attempt to bring something back to life that had disappeared for good: archaeology in reverse.

What does it mean when a city does not wish to make the leap into the modern day, but instead harks back to a vanished past, which is then masked with a little pseudo-modernity? Friends say that, one way or another, Berlin will be "beautiful" in fifty or a hundred years' time, but I have learned to mistrust such predictions, and besides I do not have enough time to wait that long. I see tiny human figures populating the large courtyard of the Schloss in the designs, and I imagine that I am one of them. It is 2089 and the little man who is me has just taken out his notebook to write something about the great day that is being celebrated all around him. But no, I will not be there; it will be other people who are walking around in a festive mood to mark the passing of a hundred years, even though they were not around to see the first of those years, the year when everything changed, when a city and a country began to heal the wounds that had torn it in two.

December 2008. The *Frankfurter Rundschau* has asked me to write a Christmas article for the space where the editorial usually goes, and because I am on a book tour of various German cities, I decide to collect things I encounter on that long journey and hang them on my Christmas tree. The resulting article was published on Christmas Eve, with the title of "Dunkle Tage," Dark Days:

And so it came to pass in those days that a Dutch author went on a reading tour of Germany. He travelled from east to south and from west to north, visiting a different city every day and reading from his book *Roter Regen*, and yet again he realized how large Germany is, how varied the landscapes, and how different the people who live there, who are called Germans by foreigners, but who usually think of themselves as residents of Bavaria, Hessen, or Brandenburg, and who generally eat the food from their own part of the world. Night

Berlin,
Hauptbahnhof,
detail

fell at half past four in the afternoon, but fortunately there was always room for him at the inn, in every town and village he passed through.

I am that Dutch author and my journey took place during what we in the Netherlands call the "dark days" before Christmas. Every one of the newspapers I read on my travels talked about the worst crisis since 1945, as though it had not been preceded by something far worse. The forecasts were gloomy and the weather outside the train windows was attempting to match the melancholy of the stock market and the money. And yet, at the market in Berlin where I buy my vegetables, everyone wished me a happy first day of Advent, a wish that is not common in the Netherlands, but which put me in a gently euphoric mood.

Everywhere I went, there were Christmas markets, with *Glüh-wein* and lots of light, as though everyone wanted to gather as much light as possible for the dark times that would soon be upon us, the Armageddon of the last days, the final catastrophe, which would wash over all five continents in a storm flood, with no lifeboats.

Maybe it was because everyone is so nice to you on reading tours, but I simply could not work myself into a gloomy frame of mind. I once watched a video of the English painter Francis Bacon. He was slightly tipsy, the interview took place in a gay bar in England, and the interviewer was trying hard to discover the life credo of this painter, who is known for the dark, sometimes almost cannibalistic themes of some of his paintings. As an admirer of his work, I too was waiting with bated breath for the magic words that would bring relief—you really want to know what kind of mentality it is that drives someone to produce works that are so extreme and brutal, yet also so fantastically well painted. The moment when, after much insistence, Bacon finally answered the increasingly desperate interviewer was an unforgettable one, or at least it was for me. Theatrically, he tilted back his head so the light caught his face—painters know about such things—and he crowed (there is no other word for it) into the camera, "I believe in nothing! I'm an optimist."

Since then, this paradox has been my motto, one that serves me well in this dark season. Cold fog in Hamburg, the first flurries of snow in Berlin, melancholic forests around Frankfurt, frost on the fields of Idar-Oberstein, drizzle over the straw-colored landscape along the Elbe—I stored all of these images in my inner archive, but it seemed that I was determined to find everything magnificent. The Deutsche Bahn stole through forests and mountains; I read my work and signed books, sat in lonely hotel rooms watching Steinbrück and Merkel and the others who were weaving a huge safety net to catch all of Germany. They were greatly hindered by an impetuous French juggler and an English grocer who had managed the finances of his island kingdom for years and yet had not seen the crisis coming, a crisis that he himself had helped to create with his policies, while a banker from Bavaria, who had just narrowly avoided bankruptcy, thought he was the only one with better schemes for preventing the certain ruin of the entire country.

If you are constantly travelling, you cannot take a Christmas tree along with you. And so I decided to decorate my own virtual Christmas tree with the images I had gathered on my wintery tour, images that had given me cheer during those dark days. Firstly, there was the large black man in Idar-Oberstein, a figure from a book of fairy tales. It was raining in Idar-Oberstein. Writers on reading

Schlossbrücke,
Berlin Mitte

tours may be compared to souls in Purgatory. They are waiting for the rest of eternity to arrive, without knowing quite how to fill their days until that happy moment. By doing penance, of course, but provincial hotels are not really equipped for such purposes. Yesterday's reading in Birkenfeld was over, the audience had been quiet and attentive, I had spoken without a microphone, no one had coughed, and now I was free to walk down the high street of this gemstone town and peruse the window displays of opals and sapphires as though all of these treasures belonged to me. Suddenly I heard loud voices speaking a language I did not recognize; it sounded like singing. I walked over and found that these voices belonged to three black kings who had arrived too early for their appointment, one of them wearing a long robe in the liturgical color of Advent, the superlative form of purple. It cast a blinding glow over the entire rainy street.

Maybe they had just sold a bag of precious stones from their bloody homelands, but they were in high spirits, their voices resounding in the cold winter air, and I decided to hang them on my Christmas tree as a point of light.

The next morning, still in Purgatory, I was walking along the Main in Frankfurt, on my way to the Städel to see the exhibition "*Der Meister von Flémalle und Rogier van der Weyden.*"

There is something peculiarly touching about those paintings. You look back over more than five centuries at people wearing the same bright colors as that man in Idar-Oberstein, telling a story that has occupied the world for some two thousand years. A man with wings and Flemish features, who probably, like all people from Flanders, speaks my language, has suddenly appeared in this small room and is delivering a message to a woman who has sat on the floor in shock or joy. The woman too has a Flemish face, full of radiant beauty. He is bowing reverently and delivering his mysterious message: she will be the mother of God.

We have heard this story so often that, whether we are religious or not, the immensity of what he is saying no longer hits us. The sound of those wings, the sudden physical presence of the bird-man in the snug, bright, Flemish interior. It is no wonder that the woman, confronted by the sight of so much heaven, has sought the proximity of the earth and fallen to the floor in her full, richly colored dress with its fantastically painted folds. I hang that angel and all those other colorful, magical creatures hanging on my Christmas tree.

That evening at the Literaturhaus in Frankfurt there is lots of rowdy coughing—perhaps Birkenfeld is a healthier place to live— but I travel on to Göttingen and read, in a large attic full of serious faces, about my first journeys and the Spanish island where I live in the summer and about my neighbors' donkey. The following morning, I go to an exhibition about the brilliant scholar Albrecht von Haller, who once studied in the Netherlands, in Leiden, and looked more deeply into the human body than anyone before his time. I gaze at the flowers he mounted in his herbarium almost three hundred years ago, flowers that once bloomed in an age without cars, when the world was still quiet. I thank the old botanist, and add his flowers to my tree.

At the end of that week, my German tour is over. I read in Lüneburg, walk down the quayside at night, along the still, mysterious water. Someone comes to pick me up the next morning. Not far from Gorleben, I see motionless human figures standing in the fields and on the roadside. They are deceptively real, as though someone stopped the film when they were working in their fields. They are designed to express the local people's fear of the radioactive waste that is going to be stored in the ground here and is now hanging as a threat over the daily lives of these people.

That same evening, I travel back to the Middle Ages. Some friends of mine live near the castle of the von Bernstorff family, and the count is going to dress up as Santa Claus and address the local children. Everything looks like a painting by Brueghel. Open fires are crackling, and festoons of lights lend luster to the dark night. Candles glow in the windows of the simple pink castle. The children push forward and the count speaks to them first from the balcony, flanked by two angels, figures of light from another world; it would not surprise me if they suddenly flew away over the market stalls and the expectant crowd, who have to step aside for a tractor pulling a trailer bringing another regiment of winged beings. At that moment, the music begins: a group of older men and boys with trombones and trumpets. I can see their faces in the light of the torches, red, with chilled, round cheeks from all that blowing, small puffs of white among the gleaming copper as they draw breath, and I hang that image too on my imaginary Christmas tree, which I now throw over my shoulder before heading off through the other Christmas trees to the stand where two men with faces by Rogier van der Weyden are serving up hot lemon punch with honey liqueur. My reading tour is at an end and, together with my invisible tree, I can disappear into the merry crowd, which, like me, has sought light in this darkness, and found it.

December 19, 2008

PART IV

A Visit to the Chancellor

THE RATE OF CHANGE IS INCONCEIVABLE. *IL TEMPO invecchia in fretta* (Time ages rapidly), the title of Antonio Tabucchi's last book, best expresses what is happening around us, but perhaps that speed can also be measured by the change in the color of the jackets that the Bundes-kanzler wears at summit after summit, among the somber suits of her male colleagues. Carefully camouflaged turbulence is the political watchword, designed to allay the turmoil in markets, minds and parties. If, like me, you have kept clippings from European newspapers over the past year, you can attempt in retrospect to catch up with that velocity and turbulence, but it is sure to make you giddy. "Thinking through the unthinkable," writes the clairvoyant Martin Wolf in the *Financial Times*, who predicted the extent of the current crisis some years ago. "Barroso openly fears end of the euro," says *De Volkskrant* of November 17, 2011. "Mario Monti presents a cabinet of professors." "Merkel and Sarkozy clash over treaty revisions." And then the *Financial Times* again: "The steely headmistress with Europe in her thrall."

According to my dictionary, "thrall" means "bondage, servitude, captivity," and this assessment of Merkel's powers is polite in comparison with what you can sometimes hear in Greece, Spain or Italy. Such opinions are not without a certain malicious and theatrical charm.

The front page of *El País* of November 12, 2011 ("Italy ends the Berlusconi era with revisions dictated by European Union") presents a peculiar photograph: three men dressed in black, including Venizelos, the burly Greek finance minister. The outstretched fingers of their right hands resting between two candles on a table, they are apparently swearing an oath. Another three men stand opposite them, all bearded, attired in gold and wearing strange headgear. On the same front page is a report that one might think was unrelated, but that would be a mistake. It explains that the autonomous Spanish region of La Rioja is refusing to treat any more Basque patients, as the autonomous Spanish "nations" are practically bankrupt and, unable to appeal to the Spanish government for help, every region has to put itself first, even though the Basques are still Spaniards, just like the inhabitants of La Rioja—and they are neighbors to boot. The atmosphere is becoming acrimonious, because the crisis is real, and its presence can be felt all over, not only in those pessimistic predictions, but in all areas of everyday life, some more apparent than others. The misery of some household on the bottom rungs of society happens to be less obvious than the cancellation of French and German at the University of Leiden or the death knell of a library or a chamber choir.

One thing is certain: this crisis has its own iconography, both in photographs and in caricatures. Merkel with a Prussian helmet and an Iron Cross, with a Hitler moustache and other vile symbols that Germany would prefer to forget; Merkel with a huge European bull on her shoulders; Merkel alongside the tricky gentlemen of her difficult coalition, to show that she is fighting not only an external battle, but also an internal one; Merkel with politicians from the other parties standing around Gauck, who was not yet president and looks like the prisoner of Zenda, a foreign body, out of place among this company; Merkel flying through the air with Sarkozy; and then Merkel on her own again, in black, making her apologies to the families of Turkish-German citizens who were murdered by neo-Nazis.

It is astounding how quickly some icons have fallen into disuse: stamps that are no longer good for anything; the erased Berlusconi, the deleted Zapatero, the dissolved Papandreou—three kings who cannot find their way back to the stable, with all the appeal of bit players with no role in the next act. And Merkel appears yet again, almost jabbing her finger into Cameron's stomach, and Sarkozy, borrowing the vocabulary of the angry Right in his attempt to defeat Hollande, and becoming increasingly Gallic and rooster-like in his caricatures, the countertenor of La Grande Nation, crowing on a large, empty stage where an unpleasant draught blows.

More than twenty years ago, when the euro was still in prenatal darkness and we had no inkling that all of this would happen, I said farewell to Berlin and Germany for a while. I had been invited to Los Angeles by the Getty Institute for the Humanities, where I was given a year to work on my book *All Souls' Day,*[*] a novel about people in Berlin who, like me, had lived through the *Wende*, the huge shift that would dramatically tip the balance so painfully imposed upon Europe at Yalta. Far away from those developments, in the bright and distant California, I wrote a book about a harsh Berlin winter in the snow, a book that still exists in Germany but sank like a stone in England. My farewell was a wistful one, and not without rhetoric. I had come to love that country, had made friends

* Translated by Susan Massotty (London: Picador, 2002)

there, and had closely followed the turbulent events, creating my own daily chronicle.

On one of the last days before my departure, I went for a long walk through the somber gardens of Sanssouci in Potsdam, amidst the faded splendor of Frederick the Great, which had now also become the faded glory of the D.D.R., and I had plenty to think about. The Russians were taking their troops home, Europe was facing a new reality and, like me, people in many different capital cities were probably wondering what Germany was going to do when it was reunited. It was a legitimate question, the result of three wars and millions of victims. Yet again in that fateful century, Europeans were forced to reflect upon history, and the role that a large Germany had played in it, and would now be able to play again. At the time, I formulated my thoughts as follows: "But do we know Germany? Does Germany know itself? Does this country know what it wants to be when it is big?"

And now, twenty-two years later? Is there a satisfactory answer to that question? Yes, some Greeks, Italians and Portuguese will say. But what do the Finns think, the Poles and the Czechs?

And do right-wing populist party leaders in Finland and the Netherlands know exactly what this new Germany will mean for them? Will it help or hinder their cause? And more importantly, do the Germans themselves know? If there is one word that has been bandied about lately, it is *Steuerzahler*, Taxpayer, an already mythical figure who surely deserves a capital letter, that hard-pressed citizen who is going to have to foot the bill for everything the politicians have cooked up so far and all the ideas they will concoct in the future. The word echoes around the media; no one knows this Taxpayer, but everyone is scared of him. Does he actually grasp what European unity signifies for Germany? Is he aware that, as far as such a thing is possible, it means a wicked past can now be buried away in a form of forgetfulness? That it also suggests peace? And does the Taxpayer know that if he does not fully appreciate the value of those higher European ideals, he may be undermining his own best interests? In order to drive this message home, doomsday scenarios abound. From one summit to the next, the hour of truth is postponed. When will the financial firewall be high enough? And at what point will the Taxpayer, with the fear of Versailles and humiliating devaluation tucked away deep in his bitter memory, but never entirely forgotten, refuse to contribute to the further construction of that wall? What will happen then? Is this simply a more elevated form of poker, and do Schäuble and Merkel know exactly what they are doing, even if Obama and Lagarde have their own ideas on the subject? Should the masters of Germany, as they impose their financial diktat on the chaotic and undisciplined south, keep looking over their own shoulders to make sure their regiments are still following them? In the *Frankfurter Allgemeine* (March 28, 2012), that south is referred to as "die Europeriferie"; one does not need to be a philologist to sense the contempt in such an expression.

I have spent the past three months in what the French charmingly describe as *l'Allemagne profonde*, on an isolated country estate among woods and meadows in the south of Baden-Württemberg. During my stay in Germany, I have spent a week in Munich and a week in Berlin, and whenever I returned to that silence it struck me how many different countries make up Germany. Different accents, different tempos, different characters. From that place within the silence, I was better able to perceive the distant commotion. For a moment, it seemed as though the European storm had abated, the money was sleeping, spring had arrived on the stock markets, the great predator appeared to have retracted its claws, at least temporarily, and perhaps a solution would be found, will be found, but no one can be certain. At home, within the country's own borders, huge dramas were unfolding, which have at least distracted the Taxpayer for the time being. For a while, the unpredictable world outside Germany, with its towering, ever-expanding debt, a debt that the Taxpayer was supposed to settle, ceased to exist. That large country, where inequality has constantly increased over the past ten years, now focused inward, with the aim of performing a grand ritual of guilt and atonement and demonstrating the meaning of integrity to those corrupt countries beyond its borders. A president who, in his five hundred days, had spoken some unexpected but welcome words ("Islam is part of Germany") was made to disappear for reasons that would at most damage presidents in other countries, but a media witch hunt centerd upon this man, creating the impression that an entire nation had erupted in moral indignation. Apparently some miracle along the lines of an Immaculate Conception was expected, which this president and his young wife were unable to provide. Talk shows, columns, editorials, the entire arsenal of the orchestrated holiness and hypocrisy of All against One was repeated over and over, until finally the man and his wife were driven out of their palace. Just a few days before, together with his Italian counterpart, a former Communist, he had been permitted to review the honor guard in Rome, where Berlusconi had recently been ejected, and for infinitely better reasons.

So, was he innocent? Heaven only knows, but perhaps his actions were not entirely above board. There was a judicial inquiry that had not yet reached its conclusion, but the suspicion alone was sufficient reason to deprive this man without power of his powerless position. This much is clear: when it comes to German presidents, it is not about power, but about something else, something that the new president must be sure to deliver. It is all about the preaching the Word. This is a task that a Lutheran pastor who stood firm under East German dictatorship should be able to handle. However, it remains to be seen whether the same politicians will be as happy with the situation in a year's time.

What does he look like, this Taxpayer who will soon determine the fate of Europe and play a part in providing the answers to the questions I asked back in 1991? It is a mystery; he is invisible. Right now, he is on strike. The union is demanding 6.5 percent and the employers are offering 3.3. There is nothing new about that. If he receives more, he will also contribute more in taxes, but that too is all part of normality; the great secret of peacetime is normality, a state we long for when peace is absent.

When the Wall came down and when the Russian troops withdrew from East Germany a few years later, it looked like History. Nouns always have a capital letter in German, but I feel the need to use one here in other languages too, so as to lend more weight to my next question: why is it that these wage negotiations do not look like History? Does it mean that they are not? Are they not just as important as the "real" historical events?

Will they not have an influence on the coming elections, which may result in a new coalition that will determine the fate of Europe just as Merkel does now? Or perhaps she does not, because everything, done or not done, bears the hallmark of impermanence, as she dances her complicated duet with Christine Lagarde. Is this all part of the game of poker, with the financial collapse of Greece and the ensuing chaos already factored in? Or is it just a waiting game, a form of floating on the stream of "rapidly ageing" time that will later be referred to as history? In the past we had philosophies such as Marxism or Edmund Burke's conservatism to provide answers, but now all we have is politics.

"Europe's reluctant Goliath is hiding its true strength," wrote the *Guardian* on Saturday, 18 March, and that same Saturday the *Neue*

Zürcher Zeitung led with the following headline: "*Zahlmeister in Zugzwang*," paymaster in zugzwang, in a tight spot. The word "*Zahlmeister*" conceals the same verb that gets the *Steuerzahler*, the Taxpayer, so excited: *zahlen*, to pay, because he or she is the one who will have to do just that. How are you supposed to do that when you belong to the large section of the population that has to live on, below or just above the poverty line? And how should impoverished local authorities react when they can no longer make ends meet and cannot go to the State for help either, as the State needs to reserve its money for the firewall?

And yet, according to the *Frankfurter Allgemeine Zeitung* of March 21, 2012, the German citizen is still dedicated to the idea of Europe: 61 percent of Germans believe that Europeans belong together, in spite of all their problems, and 57 percent think that Europe is "our future."

Such figures are unlikely to be found among those who vote for the P.V.V., Geert Wilders' party in the Netherlands, and certainly not in Britain, which is probably why many Europeans feel that country does not actually belong, because Britain has to some extent left the production of *things* to the Germans, living instead on the alchemy that transforms the froth of the markets into gold. In the latest issue of *Lettre*, Marcel Hénaff refers to the conjurers who devote their lives to this pursuit as the "dandies of the apocalypse."

Anyone who has travelled widely throughout the three "big" countries of Europe over the past fifty years cannot help but realize that they do not really know one another. This of course does not apply to the minority that travels, reads foreign newspapers and speaks different languages, but how the locals "tick" in the part of Germany where I am currently living must be a mystery to most British people, and vice versa. For a sense of this, you only have to read what the British popular press has to say about both the French and the Germans: ancient prejudices, traditional insults so eager to be repeated, deliberate or feigned ignorance, and a fundamental aversion to Europe that extends into the highest spheres, based partly on the transparent and imaginary special relationship with an America that is increasingly looking over the Pacific.

What about France? When the trumpet fanfare of La Grande Nation sounds in those election speeches, it is more than just a rhetorical gimmick; beneath it, there is always the same fear, a fear that holds sway not only in France. It is the fear of losing sovereignty, which is in fact the cause of the crisis that is now making its way across Europe. When it really mattered, no one wanted to submit to a foreign power that was aiming to unite Europe's fiscal and financial fate under one roof. Who would those national politicians be if they handed over not only the *appearance* of their power, but also the *actual* control of the national coffers to an entity such as Brussels? This response can even be seen in a small country like the Netherlands; people are certainly keen to discuss the issue, but they do not want to think about it happening. If I were the infinitely patient leader of more than one and a half billion Chinese people, pursuing a policy designed to create hegemony, how would I feel about fragmentation in a Europe that has a large, ageing population and, within the foreseeable future, will no longer be able to support itself? While Europe concentrates on Europe, and the individual countries turn inward and America wears itself out in uncontrollable and distant wars, China is scouring the earth in search of raw materials.

Eighteen months ago, Chancellor Merkel went on a tour of China, followed by Russia and Kazakhstan. I saw her on television with Hu Jintao, and then with Medvedev and the oil-rich leader of Kazakhstan. The day after her return from this exhausting journey, I was invited, along with a number of other, mostly German authors and literary agents, to the Bundeskanzleramt, a building that I had previously seen only as a *fata morgana* in the distance, with one exception, when Chancellor Schröder had invited a number of East European authors and essayists so that he could question us about the attitude to German reunification in the different countries. He knew that I spend part of the year in Spain and he wanted me to tell him how the Spanish were reacting to the sudden shift of Europe's center to the East. But this time it was Merkel, and what struck me was how fresh she looked after her tiring journey, and how different it feels when someone you have only ever seen on the television is suddenly standing only a meter away. The weather was fine and we chatted on the balcony before heading inside to eat. It was clear from the outset that the conversation would not be about politics. She wanted to talk about agents, about fixed book prices, about V.A.T., e-books, foreign rights; in short, everything that writers should be interested in—unless they think they have a chance to cast a curious glance into the center of power from close up. But she had done her homework and was extremely well informed, an academic, almost a literary trade unionist, and she kept on asking questions. I was sitting on her right and I tentatively enquired how things had gone in China, by which I mean that I started by asking her about interpreters, and how it feels when languages are inherently incompatible, so that conversations can never be direct but always have to travel via the interchange of one or more translators. I remember her answer, which of course revealed nothing about the essence of those conversations; she mentioned a "murmuring" in Chinese and then in German going on behind you, often out of sight, a buzz of incomprehensible sounds that suddenly turns into your own language and conveys a political truth, or at least a message. What has stayed with me about Merkel is a kind of calmness, her persistence in keeping to the literary theme, an academic approach that focused on other people's problems; in short, genuine professionalism. But the question remains: do those shifting policies involve calculated moves, or is it simply drifting with the weather system of the political moment?

And now? Yet again, I am leaving Germany. In the twenty years since that first departure, a great deal has changed. This country, whose relative density weighs so heavily on neighbors both near and far, borders on nine other lands. It is rich and powerful, and even now continues to perform its politics with a great caution that is prompted by its troubled and increasingly distant past, but when everyone is trying to guess your next move, how carefully can you wield the power that you find at your disposal?

In the part of Germany where I am now, the people are calm and cautious. Bavaria, Austria and Switzerland are not far away. The regional government is Green, and the peaceful landscape is green and rolling, full of large farms. Along the roadside are crucifixes and chapels dedicated to the Virgin Mary, while in the small country pubs calm men very slowly drain large glasses of beer. I listen in on the conversations they have in their Swabian dialect; the financial crisis rarely comes up. How much does Britain understand about this place? How much do France, Spain and the other European countries know about this land that will play an important part in determining their own fate? Europe's problem is the mutual ignorance of the countries, which is not helped by a lack of language skills.

I wrote this piece on 16 April. Since then, the cards have been reshuffled: Sarkozy is heading for the purgatory of political oblivion, the Greek government has evaporated, the Dutch government is half alive half dead, a new player from France has joined the game, and everyone is calculating the odds. The anti-Europeans are sharpening their knives as Europe waits to see if the Greeks will be able to put the genie back in the bottle or commit suicide in the public agora.

When I first said farewell, now so long ago, I did not know what was going to happen, and still I do not know. On both sides of that firewall, the great poker game continues, sometimes in plain sight, sometimes behind the scenes, and time ages both rapidly and slowly and, along with it, so does history.

April 16, 2012

EPILOGUE

WHOEVER WRITES A BOOK IN A FLUID POLITICAL SITUATION is writing on an icefloe. When the book goes to press the writer is slowly drifting away, aware that elsewhere the frenzy of politicians, rating agencies, protests, populists, austerity programs and macchiavellian manipulations is going on at full speed. Musing on his piece of drifting ice, carried away from actuality by the slow current of memory, he remembers a moment in 1993, when he was asked to read a text on Europe in the Munich Philharmonie, with the Royal Concertgebouw Orchestra under Ricardo Chailly behind him, who would play "Zarathustra" after his reading. He chose the form of three small fables. These were the pre-Euro days, the embryo was already there and called Ecu. Twenty years later they seem to have a rather melancholy, and, who knows, prophetic hue.

On the Spanish island where I live, every village has a festival for its patron saint in the summer. Young men and women, the village priest and the marquis ride on black horses through the village streets. They wear bicorn hats and white trousers and resemble people from a different era. These festivals must have their origins in ancient pagan rituals. They signify a farewell to the summer and herald the arrival of a winter that was often long and hard on these islands. The boat to the mainland used to sail only once a week and took at least fourteen hours to make the crossing. Most of the inhabitants never left the island; a sense of that isolation still remains in the character of the people and the wildness of their celebrations. The horses march to the rhythm of a stirring tune, always the same. The young people of the village perform a daring dance with the horses, which rear up and walk on their hind legs, and the riders have to dodge the human dancers as the horses descend. This pandemonium lasts three days before the festival is concluded with a large fireworks display. People come from all the other villages, and an orgy of glitter and noise explodes into the sky, enough to drive away the evil spirits for another year.

Everyone agreed that the firework display was not as good this time, which they saw as the result of both the economic crisis and the weather, regarding the crisis as a kind of natural phenomenon. The weather remained dry, but there was a strong wind, and so, just as the fireworks were writing the European circle of stars in the night sky, a gust tore the twelve stars apart, scattering them across the heavens, where, as fireworks do, they glowed briefly before merging with the darkness of the night in a rhetorical gesture of climatic coincidence.

"There goes Europe," I heard someone say behind me, and it felt as though that one little sentence and those few stars, now descending in a rain of ash, had intended to say something similar, to express something about the disappointment, the fear, the bitterness, the impotence, the indifference, the aversion that have come to accompany the sacred word "Europe," whether we like it or not.

Where has Europe gone? Where has it disappeared to? Who has stolen it away?

Let me tell you three little fables. They do not entirely hold water—fables never do—but their simplicity is more suitable for communicating what I wish to say than political lectures *ex cathedra*, which are neither my style nor my domain.

In a large club, which is elegant but somewhat dilapidated, the kind of place one might see in London, all the European currencies were gathered together. Every day, their temperatures were measured in a side room of the club and the results were posted outside, for the stock markets, banks and speculators to see. It should come as no surprise that, in spite of their names, they were all men. I do not know if you have a mental image of what the Mark or the Guilder might look like, but in comparison to the Drachma and the Escudo, or the Dinar, not to mention the Leu or the Zloty, the two of them look prosperously, even outrageously, healthy.

"They're just a couple of show-offs," said the Pound to the French Franc, who had been trying to attract the Mark's attention for some time. The Franc did not reply, but stood up because he could see the Rouble heading towards him.

"I always said it would come to nothing," mumbled the Pound, but the Guilder, who had heard him, replied, "You've done your best to make sure of that!"

The Peseta was not too happy either. "First they said we could join in," he said to the Lira, "and then suddenly we weren't good enough. You try so hard for all those years and you believe every word they say, and then suddenly they tell you that you haven't saved enough and that maybe, if you behave yourself, you can come back in a few years' time."

"It's all a question of priorities," muttered the Lira, who was rather preoccupied with trying to fend off the Albanian Lek while also coming up with something intelligent to say to the Mark.

Just then, the door flew open and a young man in a tracksuit came running in.

"Oh, God, that's all we need," sighed the Pound to the Swiss Franc. "The thought of having to slum it with that newcomer, that upstart!"

The Ecu—because that is who it was—appeared not to have heard this remark, because he gave the Pound a resounding slap on the shoulder and shouted, "So, old chap, how it's going? A bit better? And Mrs. Thatcher, how's she doing?" before running straight on to the Mark and the Guilder, who seemed to be expecting him.

"Could I have a word with the two of you?" said the Ecu. "I just met the Dollar and the Yen at McDonald's and they said . . ."

The others did not hear the rest, because at that moment the Forint summoned up all of his courage and went over and tapped the Ecu on the shoulder. "Do you have a moment?" he asked. The Ecu looked at the Mark, then at his watch and said, "Sorry, mate, not right now. Leave a message with my secretary."

At around the same time, at Vienna's Arsenal, where the Museum of Military History is located, the old European battles were holding their annual reunion. Everyone was there, from the Battle of Thermopylae to Lepanto, the Relief of Leiden and the Battle of the Somme, Stalingrad and the Battle of the Bulge. The atmosphere was pleasant. The gentlemen—battles are also men—were poring over a map of the former Yugoslavia and busily moving flags of different colors around.

"I told you," said Monte Cassino to Austerlitz, "Europe is still Europe, and if that lot are left to their own devices, it will remain Europe for a long time to come."

"The crazy thing is," said Waterloo to Arnhem, "that it's Sarajevo *again*. You didn't see that coming either, did you? Just take a look at the map they're concocting. Balfour and Palestine have nothing on it!"

"No, one really needs the British for such things," said Trafalgar proudly.

"Don't forget the Germans," said Verdun. "If they hadn't recognized Croatia so quickly, it would never have become such a heap of rubble!"

"They thought they were ready," said Troy to Hastings. "It's the same mistake every time: not taking the human element into account."

"Exactly," agreed Poitiers and Saguntum. "What is lacking is historical awareness. If people try to live without memories, they're sure to end up with us. Now, would anyone care for another port?"

Around fifty years ago, there was a young composer living in France. One night he dreamed that he had been asked to write the anthem for the new Europe. The happiness he felt was the kind that exists only in dreams, just as it is only in dreams that we can fly. And so he flew, soaring above the snowy plains of Finland, the lofty peaks of the Tatra Mountains, along the fjords of Norway and across the flat country of Holland. He gazed out over the charms of Umbria and the lagoon of Venice and swooped over the Forum Romanum and the Acropolis, along the red walls of the Kremlin, and followed the banks of the Tagus through Spain and Portugal. As he flew, he heard the sound of his song, which he sang without words, and with the clarity of dreams he knew his composition would resolve all differences, and that the melody would lose nothing of the greatness of the past, yet also nothing of the bitterness, encompassing the inventions and the battles, the words of Socrates and the poems of Ovid, the writings of Rousseau and the songs of Mahler, the painter of *The Night Watch* and the organist from Leipzig, the library of Erasmus and the memory of Goethe. The abbeys and cathedrals would appear in his anthem, along with the hammer blows of Wittenberg, the synagogue of Amsterdam and the pilgrimage to Santiago, the burning of the heretics and the braying of the dictator, the whispers of Romeo and the wit of Sancho Panza, the psalms of Cluny and the guitar of Seville, the hell and the heaven of a past that would seem endless, its underlying theme formed by the millions of conversations that had ever taken place in this continent, the singsong of the languages of the four corners of the world, the scattered words, forever forgotten and forever remembered, the lamentations of the camps, the euphoria of liberation, the whiplash of judgment, and the song of the lonely vagabond on the country lane. As he heard those individual sounds, he sang in his dream the song that they would all combine to form and he wrote the notes for the instruments; there would be thirty-one of them, one for every country in his continent, because he had no time for the twelve-tone scale of politics.

The day came when his song was to be played for the first time. Slowly, silently, he walked to his music stand, looked at the members of the orchestra, and raised his baton. Then he gave the signal for the first note. What happened next must have made him scream out loud in his dream. It was a miserable cacophony that ended in stunned silence after just a few bars . . . With the implacable logic of dreams, he knew what had happened. The musicians had not played the new song, but had all embarked upon their own national anthems: *Deutschland über Alles* mixing with *La Marseillaise, God Save the Queen* rubbing shoulders with the *La Brabançonne*—and all of this was multiplied by thirty-one.

As I said, fables are simple; they do not express a truth, but a feeling. Where is the Europe we dreamed about for so long? Where has it gone? Who has stolen it away? Was it the Serbians? Was it the speculators? Was it the Danes with their "no" vote? Was it the French farmers? The Polish steelworkers? The Spanish fishermen? The powerless politicians with their empty words? The dead of Sarajevo? The minorities? The neo-fascists? The East German unemployed? The Bundesbank? The British Eurosceptics?

Where is Europe now? Is it in Brussels or is it in London? Is it in Athens or is it in Kosovo? If it still exists somewhere, we would like to have it back, not the Europe of the market and the walls, but the Europe that belongs to the countries of Europe, to *all* of the European countries.

A German philosopher, Helmuth Plessner, once wrote a book called *Die verspätete Nation* (The Belated Nation). That was in the 1930s, and nobody listened to him at the time. Europe really must be returned to us before "belated" becomes "never."

GLOSSARY

INCLUDING BIOGRAPHICAL AND OTHER EXPLANATORY NOTES

Adenauer, Konrad (1876–1967)—First chancellor of the Federal Republic of Germany, or West Germany. Adenauer had excellent democratic credentials, having been mayor of Cologne from 1917 until 1933, when the Nazis removed him from that post. Chairman of the center-right Christian Democratic Union party (C.D.U.), Adenauer remained as chancellor for fourteen years, until he was eighty-seven.

Adorno, Theodor (1903–69)—A leading figure of the Frankfurt School of critical theory, which also included Walter Benjamin.

Baader, Andreas (1943–77)—A leading member of the Rote Armee Fraktion (Red Army Faction, R.A.F., commonly known as the Baader-Meinhof gang), a militant left-wing organization chiefly active in the 1970s in West Germany and responsible for a number of high-profile bombings and assassinations. Baader was arrested in 1972 and found dead in his cell five years later, the official conclusion being that he had shot himself.

Bahr, Egon (1922–)—A West German S.P.D. politician and, under Chancellor Willy Brandt, one of the architects of *Ostpolitik*, the policy which aimed to normalize relations between the Federal Republic and Eastern bloc states, especially the Soviet Union and East Germany.

Barschel, Uwe (1944–87)—A West German C.D.U. politician and Minister President of the *Land* of Schleswig-Holstein, Barschel resigned in the wake of an internal political scandal. A few weeks later he was found dead in a bathtub in Geneva. Subsequent inquiries were unable to prove or disprove suicide.

Benn, Gottfried (1886–1956)—German poet who initially supported National Socialism, but soon abandoned these sympathies.

Bismarck, Otto von (1815–98)—Nineteenth-century Prussian statesman and first chancellor of the German Empire, remembered principally for his leading contribution to German unification in 1870–71 following victory in the Franco-Prussian War.

Böhme, Ibrahim (1944–99)—Co-founded the East German Social Democratic Party in October 1989 and became its chairman. Böhme resigned from his post after only a few months when allegations surfaced about his past role as an informer for the Stasi.

Boutens, Pieter Cornelis (1870–1943)—Dutch poet and classicist.

Brandt, Willy (1913–92)—West German S.P.D. politician, mayor of Berlin, and chancellor from 1969 to 1974, Brandt sought to improve relations with East Germany and other states of the Eastern bloc (*Ostpolitik*). In 1972, Brandt's efforts led to the Basic Treaty, by which the two Germanies first recognized each other as sovereign states.

Braun, Volker (1939–)—Writer who advocated an independent "third way" for his native East Germany following the fall of the Wall.

Brugsma, W. L. (1922–1997)—Dutch journalist and author of *Europa, Europa*; member of the resistance during the Second World War and concentration camp survivor. Later he became a war correspondent, reporting from the Congo and Algeria.

de Bruyn, Günter (1926–)—Writer who rejected the East German prize for literature in 1989, criticizing the D.D.R. government for its "rigidity, intolerance and rejection of political debate."

Claus, Hugo (1929–2008)—Leading Flemish poet, novelist, author of more than forty plays, film director, artist, and the translator of much of Shakespeare into Dutch. His best-known novels are *De verwondering* (*The Astonishment*) and *Het verdriet van België* (*The Sorrow of Belgium*).

Clausewitz, Carl von (1780–1831)—Prussian soldier and leading military theorist.

Ebert, Friedrich (1871–1925)—S.P.D. politician, one of the founding fathers of the Weimar Republic and first president of Germany.

Erhard, Ludwig (1897–1977)—West German C.D.U. politician, minister of Economics (1949–63) under Konrad Adenauer, and chancellor from 1963 to 1966. Erhard is credited with playing an important role in West Germany's post-war economic recovery, commonly known as the "Economic Miracle."

Fichte, Johann Gottlieb (1762–1814)—Philosopher and, alongside Hegel (see below), one of the leading figures of German Idealism.

de Gaulle, Charles (1890–1970)—De Gaulle's good relationship with Konrad Adenauer helped develop a rapprochement between France and (West) Germany, culminating in the Élysée Treaty between the two countries in 1963.

Genscher, Hans-Dietrich (1927–)—West German F.D.P. (Liberal) politician, foreign minister and deputy chancellor from 1974 to 1992, Genscher is best remembered for his efforts to end the Cold War and bring about reunification between the two German states.

Globke, Hans (1898–1973)—A national security advisor to Chancellor Adenauer, Globke has remained a controversial figure because of his Nazi activity before the Second World War.

Gombrowicz, Witold (1904–69)—One of the most important Polish writers of the twentieth century.

Gorbachev, Mikhail (1931–)—The Soviet statesman's reformist policies were instrumental in the eventual dissolution of communism in central and eastern Europe. When the East German regime failed to stem the revolutionary momentum of its citizens in October and November 1989, Gorbachev rejected any Soviet intervention, later insisting that reunification was a matter between the two Germanies. He had a tense relationship with the East German leader, Erich Honecker (see below), whom he found inflexible.

Grotewohl, Otto (1894–64)—Prime minister of East Germany from 1949 until his death, Grotewohl had also been active politically with the S.P.D. in the interwar period.

Gysi, Gregor (1948–)—German lawyer and politician who played a prominent role in the end of communist rule in East Germany, overseeing the transition of the S.E.D. into the P.D.S. Now a key politician in the left-wing party Die Linke.

Habermas, Jürgen (1929–)—World-renowned philosopher and critical theorist, and a leading voice of the left in Germany.

Hamann, Johann Georg (1730–88)—German writer and philosopher, a representative of the *Sturm und Drang* movement.

Hegel, Georg Wilhelm Friedrich (1770–1831)—Major philosopher and the leading representative of German Idealism.

Heidegger, Martin (1889–1976)—German philosopher whose main interest was ontology, or the study of existence, but who made important contributions to a variety of fields in philosophy. Heidegger is a controversial figure because of his early sympathies with Nazism.

Hein, Christoph (1944–)—German writer and translator who was also a leading commentator on the events of 1989 and the subsequent process of reunification.

Herder, Johann Gottfried (1744–1803)—German writer and philosopher, one of the key thinkers of the Enlightenment.

Hermans, Willem Frederik (1921–1995)—Dutch writer; author of *De donkere kamer van Damokles* (*The Darkroom of Damocles*) and *Nooit meer slapen* (*Beyond Sleep*).

Heym, Stefan (1913–2001)—German-Jewish writer who left Nazi Germany in 1933 and returned to the D.D.R. in 1953, where he came into conflict with the authorities on a number of occasions.

Hildesheimer, Wolfgang (1916–91)—German writer known principally for his dramatic works.

Hirsch, Ralf (1960–)—Civil rights campaigner in the D.D.R. who was arrested and expelled from East Germany in 1988.

Honecker, Erich (1912–94)—Honecker was the East German premier from 1971 to 1989, when he was removed from office by his S.E.D. party. Under his rule, the material lives of East Germany's citizens improved, but there was no tolerance of political dissent: about 125 people were killed during these years while attempting to flee to the West. Honecker rejected Gorbachev's reformism, but his rigid political outlook left him powerless in the face of the growing protest movement in his own country. Seriously ill, he escaped prosecution for abuses of power and was allowed to emigrate to Chile, where he died.

Hoornik, Eddy (1910–1970)—Dutch poet and journalist; concentration camp survivor.

Janka, Walter (1919–94)—East German publisher sentenced to five years' imprisonment for his alleged involvement in a counter-revolutionary plot. In the face of international protest he was released after three and a half years and later rehabilitated.

Jaruzelski, Wojciech (1923–)—Polish general and last communist leader of Poland (1981–89).

Jünger, Ernst (1895–1998)—German writer perhaps best known for his work *Storm of Steel*, which documented his experiences of the First World War.

Kiefer, Anselm (1945–)—Painter and sculptor; one of the most successful and renowned German artists since the Second World War.

Kirsch, Sarah (1935–)—German writer who moved from East to West Germany in 1977 after being expelled from the S.E.D. for protesting against the expatriation of a fellow writer.

Kohl, Helmut (1930–)—A C.D.U. politician from the Rhineland, Kohl was chancellor of West Germany and, later, united Germany from 1982 to 1998. In November 1989 he presented a ten-point plan for German reunification which envisaged a gradual political fusion of the two states. In the event, the process of reunification took place far more quickly than expected. Kohl was also a key player in the creation of the European Union.

Königsdorf, Helga (1938–)—Writer and mathematician who started her career in the former D.D.R. She documented the end of the East German state in her book *Adieu D.D.R.*

Khrushchev, Nikita (1894–1971)—The struggle for power in the Soviet Union which followed Stalin's death in 1953 led to Khrushchev becoming party leader. It took him a few years to consolidate his position and he remained in power until 1964. Even though Khrushchev had taken part in Stalin's purges of the 1930s, he denounced the former leader and introduced a reformist policy of "de-Stalinisation." He was unsuccessful in his attempts to reach an agreement with the Western Allies over the status of Berlin.

Krenz, Egon (1937–)—The last communist leader of East Germany, Egon Krenz replaced Erich Honecker, whose deputy he had been since 1984. He lasted in office less than three months, and later served almost four years in prison for the manslaughter of four East Germans who had tried to escape over the Wall.

Kunert, Günter (1929–)—Writer who, like Sarah Kirsch, left East Germany in 1979 after his protest against the expatriation of Wolf Bierman resulted in his expulsion from the S.E.D.

Lafontaine, Oskar (1943–)—S.P.D. politician and finance minister (1998–99).

Leopold, Jan Hendrik (1865–1925)—Dutch poet and classicist.

Liebknecht, Karl (1871–1919)—Revolutionary and co-founder of the German Communist Party (K.P.D.) He was killed by right-wing *Freikorps* troops in the aftermath of the Spartacist Uprising of January 1919.

Luxemburg, Rosa (1871–1919)—Co-founded the German Communist Party with Karl Liebknecht. Like him, she was killed following the Spartacist uprising.

Mann, Golo (1909–94)—German writer and historian, and son of novelist Thomas Mann. A supporter of Willy Brandt's rapprochement with East Germany, he was nonetheless equivocal about German reunification.

Mann, Klaus (1906–49)—German writer and son of Thomas Mann. He left Germany when Hitler came to power and became a vociferous critic of the Nazi regime.

Maron, Monika (1941–)—Writer who moved to East Germany with her politician stepfather in 1951.

Meinhof, Ulrike (1934–76)—Along with Andreas Baader (see above) a leading member of the Red Army Faction (R.A.F.). Arrested in 1972 on a number of charges, including murder, she was found hanged in her prison cell in 1976.

Mielke, Erich (1907–2000)—East German politician and head of the Stasi from 1957 to 1989. After reunification he was tried for the 1931 murders of two police officials in Berlin. Mielke served less than two years in prison.

Mittag, Günther (1926–94)—East German politician and politburo member, Mittag was a key figure in managing the D.D.R.'s planned economy.

Modrow, Hans (1928–)—The de facto leader of East Germany after Egon Krenz's brief tenure in 1989, Modrow remained in power until the elections of March 1990.

Moltke, Helmuth von (1800–91)—Chief of staff of the Prussian army for more than thirty years, Moltke planned the campaigns for, and led the troops in, the successful wars against Austria (1866) and France (1870), which paved the way for German unification.

Molotov, Vyacheslav (1890–1986)—Soviet politician and diplomat, Molotov signed the non-aggression pact with Nazi Germany in 1939, which is also known as the Molotov–Ribbentrop pact.

Mulisch, Harry (1927–2010)—Major Dutch author, perhaps best known for his novels *De ontdekking van de hemel* (*The Discovery of Heaven*) and *De Aanslag* (*The Assault*).

Müller, Gerhard (1928–)—East German politician; member of the S.E.D.'s central committee.

Müller, Heiner (1929–95)—East German writer and dramatist.

Noske, Gustav (1868–1946)—S.P.D. politician and minister of defence 1919–20, Noske is best known for quashing the revolutionary uprisings in Germany in the immediate post-war period.

Ohnesorg, Benno (1940–67)—Student killed by a policeman during a demonstration in West Berlin, protesting against a visit by the Shah of Iran. His death was one of the events that served to radicalise the left in West Germany.

Pieck, Wilhelm (1876–1960)—Pieck was the first president of the German Democratic Republic (East Germany), a position which was abolished upon his death.

von Ribbentrop, Joachim (1893–1946)—Champagne salesman turned Nazi politician, Ribbentrop became Foreign Minister in 1938 and was a co-signatory of the Nazi–Soviet non-aggression pact a year later. He was tried and hanged at Nuremberg after the war.

Salazar, António de Oliveira (1889–1970)—Prime minister of Portugal from 1932 to 1968, Salazar presided over a right-wing, authoritarian regime with an interventionist economic policy.

Schalk-Golodkowski (1932–)—East German politician who founded the department in the foreign trade ministry which was chiefly responsible for procuring foreign currency.

Scheidemann, Philipp (1865–1939)—S.P.D. politician and second chancellor of the Weimar Republic.

Schinkel, Karl Friedrich (1781–1841)—A Prussian architect who principally worked in the neo-Classical style, his most famous buildings are to be found in and around Berlin.

Schmidt, Helmut (1918–)—Chancellor of West Germany (1974–82), Schmidt became a well-respected international statesman.

Schnur, Wolfgang (1944–)—German lawyer who defended many dissidents in the D.D.R. He became a politician during the revolutionary period 1989–90.

Scholl, Hans (1918–43) and Sophie (1921–43)—Brother and sister who co-founded *die Weisse Rose*, a non-violent, anti-Nazi resistance movement. Caught while distributing leaflets, they were guillotined in February 1943.

Steinbrück, Peer (1947–)—German Social Democrat politician who was Minister for Finance under Angela Merkel (2005–09).

Stoph, Willi (1914–99)—Leading East German politician who served both as head of state and prime minister. Arrested for corruption in December 1989, his poor health spared him imprisonment.

Toller, Ernst (1893–1939)—Left-wing playwright and leading figure in the Bavarian Soviet Republic, which lasted for less than a month in spring 1919. Suffering from depression, Toller took his own life in 1939.

Ulbricht, Walter (1893–1973)—A prominent figure in the German Communist Party (K.P.D.) in the interwar years, Ulbricht was a Stalinist who rose to become party leader in East Germany after the war. He held this position until 1971.

Vestdijk, Simon (1898–1971)—Dutch novelist and essayist, author of *Aktaion onder de Sterren* (Aktaion under the stars) and *De verminkte Apollo* (The maimed Apollo).

Weizsäcker, Richard von (1920–)—C.D.U. President of West Germany (1984–90) and of Germany (1990–94).

Wilhelm I (1797–1888)—King of Prussia, Wilhelm helped bring about the unification of Germany together with his chancellor, Otto von Bismarck. He was German Emperor between 1871 and 1888.

Wilhelm II (1859–1941)—Grandson of Queen Victoria and German emperor (1888–1918), Wilhelm was forced to abdicate at the end of the First World War.

Wolf, Christa (1929–2011)—German writer who lived in the D.D.R. and was known in her country as a "loyal dissident." After the fall of the Berlin Wall she opposed moves towards reunification, a stance which attracted much criticism.

Wolf, Markus (1923–2006)—Co-founder and head of East Germany's foreign intelligence service.

C.D.U. / CHRISTLICH DEMOKRATISCHE UNION—CHRISTIAN DEMOCRATS / DEMOCRATIC UNION
The C.D.U. was founded in 1945 as a conservative political party guided by the principles of Christian democracy. It was the leading coalition partner and provided the chancellor for the first two decades of West Germany's existence. The C.D.U. returned to power in 1982 under Helmut Kohl, and is currently in government with the F.D.P. (Liberals).

F.D.J. / FREIE DEUTSCHE JUGEND—FREE GERMAN YOUTH

The official youth movement in East Germany, which promoted communist ideology and organized leisure activities and holidays for young people.

P.D.S. / PARTEI DES DEMOKRATISCHEN SOZIALISMUS—PARTY OF DEMOCRATIC SOCIALISM

Successor party to the S.E.D., it merged in 2007 with a western German party to form Die Linke (The Left).

REPUBLIKANER

The Republikaner, or Republicans, are a right-wing party, founded in Munich in 1983. Their platform is eurosceptic and anti-immigration. They have never been represented in the German parliament, although in 1989 they won seven seats to the European Parliament. The party's support has been in steady decline since that electoral high point.

S.E.D. / SOZIALISTISCHE EINHEITSPARTEI DEUTSCHLANDS—SOCIALIST UNITY PARTY OF GERMANY

The governing party in East Germany, the S.E.D. was the result of a forced merger in 1946 between the Communist Party and Social Democratic Party in the Soviet occupation zone. In the aftermath of the 1989 revolution, the S.E.D. lost its leading role and restyled itself as the Party of Democratic Socialists (P.D.S.).

S.P.D. / SOZIALDEMOKRATISCHE PARTEI DEUTSCHLANDS—SOCIAL DEMOCRATIC PARTY

Already active in the last quarter of the nineteenth century, the S.P.D. participated in government for short periods during the Weimar years. Banned by Hitler in 1933, the party went underground, resurfacing after the Second World War. In West Germany, it was a coalition partner from 1966 to 1982, and later governed with the Greens from 1998 to 2005 under Gerhard Schröder.

B.R.D. / BUNDESREPUBLIK DEUTSCHLAND

The Federal Republic of Germany or, informally, West Germany. Created in May 1949 from the British, U.S. and French zones of occupation. Its administrative capital was Bonn. Officially, the Federal Republic still exists, as reunification involved the dissolution of the East German state and the absorption of its constituent elements (the *Länder*, or states) by the West in October 1990.

D.D.R. / DEUTSCHE DEMOKRATISCHE REPUBLIK

The German Democratic Republic or, informally, East Germany. Created in October 1949 from the Soviet zone of occupation, after the British, U.S. and French zones had amalgamated to form West Germany in May 1949. Its administrative capital was East Berlin. The state was liquidated upon reunification in October 1990.

AFTERWORD TO PART I

From the beginning of 1989 until June 1990, with the exception of my usual summer months in Spain, I stayed in Berlin, at the invitation of the D.A.A.D., the German Academic Exchange Service. Articles about that period, which was so calm at first, but later so eventful, appeared in *Elsevier* (chapters I to IX) and *De Volkskrant* (chapters X to XV).

I left Berlin at the end of May 1990, so my book stops at that rather arbitrary moment. Since then, I have maintained a constant watch on what happens in Germany and Berlin, but from a distance. As I write this, it is the end of August 1990. Perhaps, in retrospect, I should have said some things differently, but I do not think I should intervene in the account I wrote back then. Besides, I am still largely in agreement with myself, and any inaccuracies are all part of the book. The dates following the pieces correspond to the dates of publication.

First and foremost, I would like to express my thanks to Barbara Richter and Dr. Joachim Sartorius of the D.A.A.D., and to the organization's other staff who helped me during my stay in Berlin. Also to W. L. Brugsma, thanks still for that first time, back then, once upon a time; and to Armando and Tony, for their friendship and for revealing Berlin's secrets of time and place; to Rüdiger Safranski, Roland Wiegenstein and Arno Widmann, for their answers to impossible questions; to Egbert Jacobs, our last ambassador in the

D.D.R.; to Rosemarie Still, who, often under great pressure, translated these pieces from Dutch into German faster than I could write them; and finally to Simone Sassen, with whom I shared this adventure. Without her photographs, this would be a different book; without her company, it would have been a different year.

C. N.
Es Consell, Sant Lluís,
September 28, 1999

NOTES ON THIS EDITION

PART I OF THIS BOOK WAS FIRST PUBLISHED AS *Berlijnse notities* in 1990 by Uitgeverij De Arbeiderspers, Amsterdam. The prologue "Grensoverschrijding" (Crossing the Border) has been added, and was previously published in *Waar je gevallen bent, blijf je* (Uitgeverij De Arbeiderspers, Amsterdam, 1983), and the intermezzos "Vestigia pedis" and "Oeroude tijden" (Ancient Times), previously published in *De wereld een reiziger* (Uitgeverij De Arbeiderspers, Amsterdam, 1989), were then added to a later Dutch edition.

Part II includes three pieces from *De filosoof zonder ogen* (Uitgeverij De Arbeiderspers, Amsterdam, 1997): "Berlijnse suite" (Berlin Suite), "Dode vliegtuigen en overal adelaars" (Dead Aeroplanes and Eagles Everywhere, previous title: "Hamburg") and "Dorp binnen de Muur" (Village within the Wall, previous title: "De verdwenen muur").

"Rheinsberg, een intermezzo" (Rheinsberg, an intermezzo) was published in *de Volkskrant* on January 1, 1997. "Terugkeer naar Berlijn" (Return to Berlin) is a speech given by Cees Nooteboom on December 7, 1997, in Berlin at the invitation of Bertelsmann AG ("Berliner Lektionen"). It has previously been published in book form by Uitgeverij Atlas, Amsterdam, 1998.

Part III was published in Dutch for the first time in 2009, with the exception of a few pieces: the opening speech for the exhibition at the COBRA Museum appeared in *Vrij Nederland* on 18 October 2008; the acceptance speech for the award of the honorary doctorate from the Freie Universität Berlin was previously published in *Vrij Nederland* (January 31, 2009), "Dunkle Tage" (Dark Days)appeared in the *Frankfurter Rundschau* (December 24, 2008) and the "Orgel Feldberg" (Feldberg's Organ) piece was in *Preludium* (May 2009).

These texts are published for the first time here in English, and Part IV (p.315–325) was written for this edition.

The fables that make up the Epilogue were first published in N.R.C. Handelsblad, Amsterdam, in 1993, and were read by the author at the Munich Philharmonie on September 16, 1993, on the occasion of a performance by the Royal Concertgebouw Orchestra of Richard Strauss' "Also sprach Zarathustra."

INDEX

Page numbers in *italics* denote illustrations